With the introduction of this excellent work, Mr. Remer, who is a software developer and publisher in addition to his own legal practice, has created the first comprehensive guide to protecting your work.

This volume should be on every software developer's desk . . . If you are involved in the development of software in any form or fashion, then I strongly urge you to make an investment in Mr. Remer's work. It could be the best purchase you have made since the day you bought your first computer!

Micro Moonlighter, Issue #20

An outstanding job. Any developer of microcomputer software who reads it will undoubtedly benefit.

Gerry Elman, J.D., Editor-in-Chief, Biotechnology Law Report

An excellent primer . . . which should be read by anyone who intends to market software as a writer or distributor.

Computer Age, January 1983

Legal Care
FOR YOUR Software

A Step-by-Step Guide for Computer Software Writers

DANIEL REMER, ATTORNEY

A NOLO PRESS BOOK
950 Parker St., Berkeley, CA 94710

Library of Congress Cataloging in Publication Data

Remer, Daniel.
  Legal care for your software.

  Includes index.
    1. Computer programs—Specifications—United States.
  2. Copyright—Computer programs—United States.
  I. Title.
  KF390.5.C6R35   001.64'2'024344   82-1822
  ISBN 0-917316-58-4   AACR2

contents

acknowledgments

I'd like to thank the following lawyers who have contributed many valuable suggestions and criticisms:

Theodore J. Bielen, Jr., Patents, Trademarks and Copyrights, Oakland, California

Brad Bunnin, Copyrights and Entertainment Law, San Francisco, California

Charles E. C. Harris, Computer Law, San Francisco, California

Anthony Mancuso, Attorney and author

Franklin Remer, Attorney.

Special thanks to Ralph Warner, Editor and Publisher of the Nolo Press who worked with me throughout the book. I'd also like to thank Bill Baker, Information Unlimited Software and Larry Weiss, both of whom have been essential to my education as a computer lawyer.

This book is dedicated to Janet Remer

Legal Care for Your Software was written using EasyWriter Professional Wordprocessing System on a 48k Apple II Computer and on a North Star Horizon using North Word. The index was typed on an IBM PC.

introduction

Here is a legal guide designed for software program developers and software publishers. It clearly and simply sets forth the legal rules relating to the development, protection, and marketing of computer software. This book covers hiring programmers, understanding trade secrets, establishing a trademark for your program name, copyrighting your work, protecting yourself from irate customers, negotiating and writing contracts, and much more. The legal areas that are important to the software industry are fully explained in easily understood language. Moreover, the emphasis is placed on showing you how to do most of the work yourself.

THE SOFTWARE DEVELOPER

You spent the last ten months working on a program. It's fast, professional, and, with good marketing, stands a chance of making lots of money. You put in fourteen-hour days and forgot what a weekend was. Perhaps you hired a couple of assistants to write some of the code. Now, as part of the final debugging, you are about to distribute a few copies to friends and get their feedback. But wait! Have you taken the essential steps to protect yourself legally? What happens if one of the test copies falls into the wrong hands? What if your so-called friend doesn't realize how much work your program represents and lends a copy to a business associate, who mails a copy to a relative who owns the biggest computer store in Aurora, Illinois? Without your knowledge and without proper legal precautions your program could enter the public domain. Despite all your efforts you could wind up with a great deal of fame and not much fortune.

What can you do to protect yourself from this and the many other legal pitfalls that await the unwary? A big dog may guarantee you privacy while you are programming, but no security measures can stop a pirate from buying your program at the local computer store and then copying it. Happily, you needn't ensconce yourself within a fortress to achieve a sensible degree of legal self-protection. What's more, providing legal care for your software isn't that difficult—it's certainly easier than programming. All it normally takes is a knowledge of what the legal problems are, what to do about them, and when to do it. This book provides you with these necessary tools. Even more important, our emphasis is on how to prevent these problems from occurring in the first place. The best legal care for your software is preventive care.

1

THE SOFTWARE PUBLISHER

You have just been approached by a software developer who has a dynamite program. With your marketing abilities you should have no trouble selling ten thousand programs—and that's in the first quarter. Besides writing fine code, the programmer has taken steps necessary to protect his work. You needn't worry about its having fallen into the public domain or about the source codes having been so carelessly distributed as to invite piracy.

But before you start scheduling four-color ads and printing gold-embossed product sheets, you must first arrive at an agreement with the program developer. What royalty percentage will be acceptable? How long will your license to publish last? Who will fix any program bugs? Will the program be modified in the future to run on other kinds of hardware? If so, who pays for the modification?

These are just a few of the questions that must be addressed and included in a contract before you spend money promoting the program. This book clearly explains the process of drafting a contract from the initial meeting to signing on the dotted line. It includes a cookbook of sample contract clauses that are fair to both publisher and programmer. There are suggestions throughout the book on ways to structure your contractual relationships so that you leave maximum breathing room for both parties. In the appendix to this book you will find many sample contracts— ready to tear out and use—governing everything from trade secrecy to your agreement with your distributors. In addition, the publisher and the developer are given sound legal advice on such potential problems as negotiating techniques, insurance, employee-employer relationships, and using a contract to creatively allocate responsibilities.

WHAT ABOUT LAWYERS?

This book is neither designed nor intended to replace lawyers. In many complicated situations, especially when you have already acted unwisely, a lawyer knowledgeable in the software field can be invaluable. With the sound legal information presented here, however, there is a good deal that well-informed publishers and pro-grammers can do for themselves. Indeed, lawyers familiar with the software field well know that many legal protection measures necessarily involve self-help. For example, most programmers and publishers simply can't afford, nor do they want, a lawyer standing by every time they file a registration form with the Copyright Office, or have an employee sign a nondisclosure agreement, or place an advertisement in a computer magazine. Even those who have readily accessible legal advice must understand the day-to-day legal realities affecting their business lives. In sum, if you want full legal protection for your software, you are going to have to do much of the work yourself.

chapter 1

an overview

Let's begin with an overview of software law. Perhaps the first thing to realize is that "software law" is a misleading term. Software law is actually a combination of several well-established fields of law, all of which affect the software industry. The second thing to remember is that although these legal fields have old and venerable roots, computer programs, particularly those for the mass market, are very new. As always, when old laws meet new needs, problems and ambiguities crop up. Eventually these problems are solved, but in the meantime there are some areas where the law is not so hard and firm as it might be.

Copyright law is a case in point. For many years a copyright could be used to protect only the written word. Then came the player piano. As the popularity of this instrument increased, so did the competition between those who printed sheet music and those who made piano rolls. Finally, the Apollo Company was accused by the Smith-White Music Publishing Company of stealing one of its copyrighted songs and making it into a piano roll.[1] The U.S. Supreme Court decided the case, and for ninety years its legal decision stood for the principle that if the human eye could not read it, the Copyright Office would not copyright it. For a time it seemed as though the Apollo ruling would be applied to software as well. After all, a perforated piano roll is not much different from a computer punch card. But then Apollo was overruled by new laws including the Copyright Act of 1976 (17 USC) and the Computer Software Copyright Act of 1980, both of which specifically provide that software may be copyrighted.

The Copyright Acts are important links in the chain of software protection, but they are not the ultimate solution to software piracy. We will discuss copyrights and other techniques of legal protection in detail later. The point to keep in mind now is that computer software is probably the fastest moving technology in the history of the world, and as technology advances, the law tries to keep pace (but, of course, is left from months to centuries behind). Since the technology will continue to advance far faster than the law, we will have to borrow legal principles from many different legal fields in order to protect software adequately.

There are a number of legal theories on how best to protect software. Some writers on law advocate trade secret, others copyright, and still others patent law. The almost religious zeal with which some legal commentators air their views reminds me of several programmers who, at a cocktail party I attended recently, were loudly arguing about which programming language was best. Sometimes programmers and lawyers denigrate all approaches to a problem except one—the one they know best. There is, of course, in law as in programming, no single best approach. The various legal protection doctrines are nothing more than tools to be used when the situation calls for them. The best strategy is to familiarize yourself with all the available tools, determine the result you want, and then select the appropriate tool for the job. Just as a good programmer may choose to code part of a program in BASIC and part in assembly language, so a person familiar with software law may choose to protect a program by applying a combination of legal doctrines. Solid results are obtainable in both fields when flexibility prevails over dogmatism.

There are several legal approaches to protecting software, and they should in many situations be combined for maximum results. What exactly is the best legal protection strategy for your particular software? Your program will dictate the method. If you are selling only your object code, copyright protection may be the best legal device. If you need to protect your source code, a combination strategy of trade secret and contract law in addition to copyright law may be most suitable.

What about software under development? How do you protect your tender and still unfinished work at this vulnerable stage? One way is to trust no one and do your programming locked in your closet. Fortunately, there are legal ways of protecting your program while you and your employees write it. To aid you in hiring programmers with the confidence that you are legally protected, I will discuss how to set up employee relationships using nondisclosure and work-for-hire agreements in Chapters 2 and 6.

Let's assume you have adequately protected your program in the development stage and have chosen a sensible combination of legal devices with which to safeguard your rights in the finished product. Though you may think you're now done with law, you've really just begun. Your next step is seeing that the program is marketed well. Unless you plan to publish your product yourself, you will need to enter into a contract with a publisher. A good contract will settle all important issues equitably. How, for instance, is the developer ensured of getting a royalty that's fair and on time? How does the publisher obligate the developer to maintain the software and fix bugs? When, where, how, and to whom will the program be marketed? Readily usable and easily modified contracts that answer these questions are presented throughout this book.

Finally, once your software is on the market, how do you protect yourself from unhappy customers who have relied on your programs and, for one reason or another, are dissatisfied? I will explain how advertising or packaging may unintentionally create a warranty. The legal steps necessary to limit or disclaim warranties and liability insurance will also be discussed.

Now let's briefly define the legal doctrines and devices that are the heart of the rest of the book.

AN OVERVIEW OF LEGAL PROTECTION METHODS

Trade Secret

Trade secret has long been the favorite protection tool of the software industry. It is simple, practical, and yields immediate results. Most software is protected at least to some extent by trade secret.

Protection by trade secret involves little more than keeping your program secret. Not surprisingly, the legal devices for implementing this principle, such as nondisclosure agreements, are a bit more complicated than the principle itself. The nondisclosure agreement is a contract that obligates the person signing it to keep your secret. You should keep a supply on hand for people to sign before you give them access to your secrets. (There are several ready-to-use nondisclosure agreements in the tear-out section at the end of this book.) Trade secret is a prime example of your having to rely on yourself if you want solid legal protection. Even if you have the best lawyers in the world, they can't keep your program secret. It's up to you!

The trade secret doctrine can protect many business assets besides software. Items that can be protected by trade secret range from customer lists to prized recipes to source codes. But like all forms of legal protection, trade secret has its weaknesses. These will be discussed in detail in Chapter 2 as will the strong legal remedies that trade secret law provides when a secret is stolen. In the meantime, let me suggest a word of advice. If you have developed something innovative, a program or a piece of hardware perhaps, don't show it to anyone until you have read the chapter on trade secrets. As easily obtained as protection by trade secret is, it is much more easily lost if the proper precautions are ignored.

Copyright Protection

What does a copyright do for you? Basically, a copyright protects the expression of an idea, *not* the idea itself. Philosophical though this may seem, it in no way means that it's difficult to get copyright protection. In fact every original program is born with a copyright. To keep your copyright intact and your protection secure all you need do is to follow the simple instructions given in Chapter 3. Follow these and you will have fairly solid recourse in the courts if someone should try to steal your program.

Here is the concept of copyright in a nutshell. Suppose you wrote a short story about a trip down the Colorado River. Because your story was born with a copyright, which you automatically own, no one can copy your story without permission. A would-be plagiarist who changes the names of the characters is still legally prohibited from copying it. Even if the dates and the name of the river were changed, it is still illegal to use your story. But now suppose, on a raft twenty feet behind you, a person sits writing a story about the trip. Even if this story is nearly identical to yours, there has been no infringement of your copyright. Why? Because you can legally protect only the expression of your ideas, not the ideas themselves. If your story was not copied, there has been no plagiarism.

Since copyright is one of the most widely misunderstood forms of protection—even among lawyers—let's clear up a few of the common misconceptions right now.

1. Forget everything you've heard about sending yourself copies of your program in sealed envelopes. While it's always nice to receive mail, sending yourself programs will not provide copyright protection.

2. A pirate can't circumvent your copyright by changing a few lines of your program.

3. Don't put the following symbols on your program unless you know what they mean: ®, TM, Pat., Patented. They have nothing to do with copyright. How and when to use these symbols will be discussed in Chapters 9 and 10.

4. If you forgot to put a copyright notice on a piece of software that's already on the market, don't despair. All is not lost. Thanks to the new copyright law there is a good chance that prompt action will recover most, and in some cases all, of your copyright.

5. Names of companies, names of programs, and book titles *cannot* be copyrighted. They very likely can be protected in other ways, which will also be discussed.

Patent Protection

In theory, patenting your software would seem as though it were an ideal way of protecting it. While a copyright protects only the expression of an idea, a patent protects the idea itself. What more could you ask for?

Unfortunately, patents have serious drawbacks—so serious that for most programs I recommend they not be used. Assuming your software is patentable in the first place (despite new case law dealing with this, most is not) the two biggest drawbacks are time and money—obtaining a patent takes lots of both. The registration process alone can last two or more years. And if that isn't a sufficient deterrent, you should also realize that the process is complicated and technical. What's more, to maximize protection a patent lawyer is usually required to handle the paperwork and the vital task of defining the scope of the product.

Historically, the Patent Office has taken the position of granting patents "unwillingly," which simply means that you must prove your case in order to get your patent. The merit of this tough-minded approach becomes apparent when you realize that a patent is simply another name for a seventeen-year monopoly on your idea. However, since the life expectancy of a program is often shorter than the time it takes just to get the patent, you can see how this approach presents serious problems for programmers. Suppose, for example, you wrote a program for a game that you expect will storm the country and make you a million bucks before it's replaced by the next hot game. It would be silly to try for a patent, since the very process would be longer than the market life of the program. You would do best to rely on a combination of trade secret protection, copyright law, and trademark law because these approaches are cheap, effective, and fast. For all these reasons we will deal only cursorily with patent law in Chapter 10. At this time it is simply inapplicable to 99.8 percent of the software being written.

Trademarks

A trademark protects the name of your software. It doesn't protect the software itself. We include it in this book because names can be important sales tools, and everyone in the business competes to find good ones. VisiCalc, Apple, Magic Pencil, and Easy Writer are only a few of a long list of obvious examples. A great name might not sell horrible software, but it can be invaluable in selling a good product. So if you have a good name, you will want to see that it is protected. Chapter 9 tells how.

Copy Protection

Copy protection is another way of protecting your software. It is not another means of making use of the law but is instead an electronic response to an electronic problem—disk piracy. The technical aspects of copy protection are beyond the scope of this book. I mention it only to emphasize that, even though copy protection makes sense in some situations, it shouldn't be relied on as a subsitute for establishing a solid legal protection scheme.

Should you copy protect your software? Many designers deliberately make their software difficult to copy. This may be done by arranging the program on a disk or in memory so that standard copy programs are baffled. In the words of a programmer friend, "Copy protection helps keep honest people honest by removing the temptation to copy." Given enough time, however, a qualified programmer can crack any copy-protect code. Indeed, the development of inexpensive programs called *nibble copiers*, which are designed to copy supposedly copyproof software, makes it easy to duplicate just about any program. Ironically, since a nibble copier is capable of copying itself, there are now pirated copies of the most popular nibbler. It's named "nibble" because a nibble is two bits, and the nibbler program copies a nibble at a time. Not only does the software industry like good names, but it revels in puns.

There are some good arguments against copy protecting software. End users hate not being able to make backup copies. It is terribly inconvenient and frustrating for a legitimate user to have to wait a week or two while the publisher sends a replacement disk for one that went bad. Also, most accounting and business application software must by its very nature be capable of being copied for backup purposes. If you do copy protect your software, make sure your customer service department is able to promptly send out replacements for clobbered program disks.

Contracts

One of the best means of protecting software is through the use of a contract. A contract is simply a legally enforceable agreement that details the parties' rights and responsibilities. It doesn't always have to be in writing to be legal, but if the software is important, it should be. Included in the appendix are contracts that you can use or modify to suit your needs. Usually a contract will not stop end-user piracy, but it can cover an infinitely wide variety of subjects from employment to worldwide licensing. In short, the informed use of contracts is essential to the successful marketing of software. See Chapter 5 for more about this.

Limiting Liability

Once you have protected your software and entered into a marketing contract, you still need to protect something else—yourself. Unhappy customers can spell trouble, especially since it is becoming increasingly clear that the personal computer is covered by consumer protection laws—even when it's used exclusively for business applications. If you are ignorant of the pitfalls, you may find yourself cursing the very consumer protection law that you happily invoked two weeks ago forcing the local discount store to take back a faulty hair dryer. Chapter 11 explains how to limit your liability to end users by creating an *effective warranty disclaimer*. Matters of insurance and protection from personal liability are also discussed.

OBJECT AND SOURCE CODES

Throughout this book I refer to object and source codes. Programmers will understand these terms, but if you are unsure of the distinction between them, please read this short definition.

Source code is the actual program that a programmer writes. Often source code is written in a high-level computer language like BASIC, FORTRAN, C, Forth, or Pascal. Sometimes source code is written in assembly language. Whatever language is used, the source code is written in such a way that it can be revised or updated by the programmer. Usually remark or comment statements are sprinkled throughout the source code to provide the programmer with reminders about the way various parts of the program work.

Object code is created from the source code. The object code is a series of machine-readable instructions, often represented in binary form (1's and 0's). The object code is made by running the source code through another program called a compiler. In other words, the object code is a compiled version of the source code.

The distinction between object and source code is important because the two versions of the same program are often protected in entirely different ways. I will discuss these different forms of protection in detail in Chapters 2 and 3. Readers who don't understand the distinction should ask a programmer for a more detailed explanation.

LEGAL PROTECTION TECHNIQUES

Here is a chart summarizing the ways legal protection techniques may be applied to software. You may want to glance at it now and refer to it from time to time as you read on. When you become more familiar with legal techniques you may use it as a review.

Legal Protection Methods

Activity	Copyright	Trade Secret	Contract	Disclaimers	Trade Mark
Idea		*			
Flowchart	*	*			
Hiring Programmers		*	*		
Writing Code	*	*	*		
Alpha Testing	*	*	*		
Beta Testing	*	*	*	*	
Negotiating w/Publisher	*	*	*		
Publishing	*	*	*	*	*
Selling to Retailer	*	*	*	*	*
Selling to End-user	*		*	*	*
Manuals	*		*	*	*
Program Name					*

Type of Program

Type of Program	Copyright	Trade Secret	Contract	Disclaimers	Trade Mark
Source Code	*	*	*		
Mass-Marketed					
Object Code	*			*	*
Limited Distribution					
End-user Programs	*	*	*	*	*
Operating System					
or similar	*	*	*	*	*
Compilers	*	*	*	*	*

chapter 2
trade secrets

INTRODUCTION

Trade secret law may be used to protect object codes as well as source codes. It may also be used to protect other proprietary items valuable to your business such as mailing lists, customer lists, and special tools or processes that you wish to keep secret. In short, trade secret law may be applied to almost any secret used in your business that gives you an edge over the competition. The doctrine of trade secret, unlike copyright, is not a federal law. Each state has its own version. Legal remedies vary only slightly from state to state.

The most important thing to remember about trade-secret law is that in order to take advantage of it, you have to be able to keep a secret. Unlike patent or copyright law, there is no government-sanctioned process that establishes trade-secret protection. Trade secret is like acetone. Let it out of the bottle and (poof!) it evaporates. Consider the following unpleasant episode.

Example

Tom wrote a mailing-list program that he named JunkMail. JunkMail contains some innovative sort routines and is a very good program. The source code was written in Forth, which was compiled into object code. When a customer buys JunkMail, he gets a copy of the object code on a floppy disk.

Tom, justifiably proud of his program, agrees to give a computer-show seminar on his innovative sort routines. As part of his presentation he passes out mimeographed copies of his source code. Unfortunately, Pirate John is in the audience and slinks off with a copy of the source code. John believes that with a few changes, including the name, the program will be a best-seller. The changes John makes are trivial. Within a month a look-alike program appears on the market under the name Speed-O-Mail. Tom immediately recognizes the pirated program as his own and trundles off to see what his lawyer can do. Unfortunately, when Tom thoughtlessly blew his trade secret protection, he also severely limited his legal options. As far as trade secret goes, there is nothing to be done. One option that may still be available, if Tom has done what's necessary, is copyright protection. (See Chapter 3.)

Again, the most important step you can take is not to reveal your source code in the first place. If you want trade secret protection, you must treat your program as a secret.

11

Example

Now let's change the situation a bit. Assume that Tom treated the JunkMail source code as a trade secret and didn't pass it out. Pirate John, however, not easily discouraged, managed to get it by bribing one of Tom's employees who knew the combination to the safe where the source code was stored.

It is at this point that trade secret protection comes in. If Tom took the proper measures to keep the source code secret and John wrongfully obtained it, the law protects Tom. In fact, Tom can go to court and invoke some or all of the remedies discussed later in this chapter.

HOW TO ESTABLISH TRADE-SECRET PROTECTION

Now that you understand the importance of keeping a trade secret, what next? There must be more to trade secret than keeping a zipped lip. Right you are, and here is what you need to do.

Step 1

Select a secure place to store working copies of your source code. A safe is best, but a heavy-duty filing cabinet with a lock will also work. Backup copies of any particularly valuable source code should be stored in a safe-deposit box.

Step 2

When you're done working on the code, lock it up.

Step 3

Buy a rubber stamp that reads "CONFIDENTIAL" and stamp all copies of the source code (including disks and disk jackets).

Step 4

Include a notice like the one below at the beginning and end of and sprinkled throughout your source code. (A copy is included in the appendix.) The idea is to have the notice print on hard copy or appear on the screen when the program is listed.

NOTICE
THIS PROGRAM BELONGS TO (insert your name or company). IT IS CONSIDERED A TRADE SECRET AND IS NOT TO BE DIVULGED OR USED BY PARTIES WHO HAVE NOT RECEIVED WRITTEN AUTHORIZATION FROM THE OWNER.

Step 5

If you must show the source code to others—a coworker, program tester, or software publisher, for instance—have them sign a trade secret nondisclosure form. If these persons are likely to have access to the source code for a long time, periodic letters should be sent reminding them of the trade secret status of the source code. The form letter shown below includes an acknowledgment line at the bottom that should be signed by the recipient. If employees who have seen your trade secret(s) have resigned or been fired, be sure they receive copies of the form letter. (A blank copy is included in the appendix).

Dear _____ :

This letter is to remind you of (company name) position regarding the trade secret status of the following items:

(list trade secrets that employee has had access to)

(Company name) owns all rights, including trade secret rights, in the above-listed item(s). This means that you may not legally divulge or discuss the item(s) with third parties without our written permission. This obligation to keep the items confidential will continue to exist even if you are no longer connected with (Company).

Please don't hesitate to ask any questions you might have regarding trade secrets, ownership rights, or anything else related to this subject. If you have no questions, please sign the acknowledgment at the bottom of this letter and return it to me, keeping the copy for your own records.

Thank you for your cooperation.

Sincerely,

Chief Executive Officer

ACKNOWLEDGMENT
I have read and agree with the statements in the above letter.

(signed)	*(date)*

Step 6

Establish a project log and have everyone sign in and out each time they use the source code. This lets people know that they are accountable for the code when it is in their possession. A good project log can be made from a bound, page-numbered book such as can be found in any stationery store. The bound book makes it difficult to remove or add pages without detection. You log should look like this:

DATE	NAME	TIME IN	TIME OUT	COMMENTS

Each program or project should have its own log. Programmers should be encouraged to note in the comments section anything unusual, such as "Copy of source code left out on table." This kind of information will help locate any potential leaks as well as remind programmers that the project is secret.

Step 7

Keep a master roster of all trade secret information, and advise your employees as to which information belongs to you and is considered secret. They needn't know the details—just that you consider the information to be yours and yours only. But don't go overboard. Just because you say it's secret doesn't mean the information qualifies as a trade secret. To obtain the protection of the law the trade secret must not be generally known in the industry; it must be kept secret. Therefore don't take a blunderbuss approach. Claiming things as trade secrets when they are not could cast a shadow over the validity of your true trade secrets. Claim only information that really belongs to you and is a genuine trade secret.

Step 8

In addition to taking the steps necessary to establish a trade secret, make sure the trade secret is truly yours. "Of course it is mine—who else could it belong to?" you say. If your relationship to your partners and employees is not clearly defined, the trade secret might belong, at least in part, to them.[1] If you have key employees, they should sign, along with the trade secret nondisclosure agreement, an employment agreement. This agreement should contain a section prohibiting employees from working for competitors or starting their own company with your information. Unfortunately, we cannot provide a universally valid sample because the validity of restrictive employee agreements varies from state to state and from employer to employer. Have your lawyer draw one up for you. It won't be costly, and if it ever has to be invoked the expense will seem minor compared with the benefits. Keep in mind that courts of law generally dislike interfering with a person's ability to earn a living. Therefore your restrictions are going to have to be fairly mild if you want them to be enforceable in court. You can't, for example, stop an experienced programmer from *ever* writing code for another company or from *ever* starting a new company. You may, however, require a former employee not to use programs developed while working for you, and you can require that a programmer not use very special knowledge that could only have been obtained from your company.

As a final thought let me suggest that you spread a programming project over as many employees as possible so only a few have the complete picture. This lessens the likelihood of one person's departing with the whole bag of beans.

These steps offer a sensible measure of protection. In many cases, especially if the programmer is working in a crowded area, tighter security precautions should be taken. The point to remember is that following these steps is not a ritual but a line of conduct designed to keep a program secret and to hold those with access to it accountable should the secret be divulged. I have found that maintaining a trade secret works best when the people involved understand the legal as well as the practical need for secrecy. Once the need is explained, the paperwork and other minor inconveniences seem less burdensome and can even lend a project an aura of importance or glamour that might previously have been absent.

NONDISCLOSURE AGREEMENTS

As I mentioned above, nondisclosure agreements are the cornerstone of trade-secret protection. They provide you with the flexibility to hire and fire programmers and to retain consultants while still maintaining your legal right to trade secret protection.

Before you give people access to your program, have them fill out a nondisclosure agreement, which you will find in the tear-out appendix at the end of this book. Keep blank copies of the form handy in case you suddenly decide to show the code to someone. Let me emphasize that all those with access or potential access to the code should sign a nondisclosure agreement *before* being given access to the trade secret. This means everyone from your secretary to your partner.

The nondisclosure agreement is valuable for several reasons. First, it stresses that you take your trade secret seriously and insists that anyone with access to it do the same. Second, it legally binds the signer from disclosing the secret. Anyone who blabs would be legally liable for the harm caused. Third, if the signer should disclose the secret to Pirate John, John cannot legally make use of it without facing the possibility of monetary damages, court injunctions, and so forth. Obviously, even with a signed nondisclosure agreement, you're not likely to show the source code to someone you don't trust or who has no legitimate need to know. No agreement or legal device will transform thieves into honest people.

We encourage our employees to enjoy the glamour associated with secrecy.

I mentioned earlier that your partner should sign a nondisclosure agreement. I suggest this not because I believe you shouldn't trust your partner but because it may become important for you to prove to a potential customer or investor that you actually have a trade secret. The law doesn't recognize a trade secret if there are people who have seen it without obligating themselves not to divulge it. In theory, at least, it's an all-or-nothing proposition. So have everyone sign.

Example

Firstware, a large software publishing house, approaches you because they want to buy a program you wrote. To be sure of their prospective investment, Firstware checks to see if you have kept the source code under wraps. They are pleased to see that your secretary and your assistants have all signed nondisclosure agreements, but they are disturbed to find that your partner has not. Their initial apprehension is confirmed when they discover that your partner used to work for Firstware's main competitor, Secondware. Their fears might be allayed if they could see a nondisclosure agreement signed by your partner.

GENERAL NONDISCLOSURE AGREEMENT

The first sample nondisclosure agreement is a general-purpose agreement designed for all employees, whether or not they know your trade secrets. It alerts the employee that trade secrets exist in your business, gives a general idea of what constitutes a trade secret, and obligates the employee not to disclose any.

(T-1)   NONDISCLOSURE AGREEMENT

I. Introduction

This is an agreement between _____ (Employee) and _____ (Company) in which the employee agrees not to disclose trade secrets or other confidential information belonging to Company.

II. Agreement

In consideration of Employee's employment by Company, Employee agrees to keep all trade secrets and/or proprietary information of Company in strict confidence.

III. Trade Secrets

A trade secret is any information, process, or idea that is not generally known in the industry, that Company considers confidential, and that gives Company a competitive advantage. Example of trade secrets include:

Computer program listings, source code, and object code.

All information relating to programs now existing or currently under development.

Customer lists and records.

_____

(Additional examples of trade secrets)

Employee understands that the above list is intended to be illustrative and that other trade secrets, which shall also be held confidential, may currently exist or arise in the future. In the event that Employee is not sure whether certain information is a trade secret, Employee shall treat that information as confidential unless Employee is informed by Company to the contrary.

Employee agrees to surrender to Company all notes, records, and documentation that was used, created, or controlled by Employee during employment upon termination of that employment.

IV. Attorney Fees

If any legal action arises relating to this agreement, the prevailing party shall be entitled to recover all costs, expenses, and reasonable attorney's fees incurred because of the legal action.

V. Duration

This agreement is considered by both parties to be a binding contract and shall remain in effect indefinitely, even if Employee's employment with Company terminates.

VI. Execution

This agreement is executed on _____ (date) and covers all Company trade secrets currently known to Employee as well as all trade secrets that shall become known during Employee's tenure at Company.

_____ Employee _____ Company
(signed)   (signed)

SPECIFIC NONDISCLOSURE AGREEMENT

The following nondisclosure agreement is for use with specific projects. It should be signed in addition to, not as a substitute for, the agreement shown above.

(T-2)   NONDISCLOSURE AGREEMENT

I. Introduction

This is an agreement between _____ (Employee) and _____ (Company) in which Employee agrees not to disclose certain confidential information and/or trade secrets belonging to Company.

II. Agreement

In consideration of Employee's employment by Company, Employee agrees to hold the following information belonging to Company in strict confidence.

(1) All information relating to the program development of _____ (insert program name).

(2) All algorithms and interal workings of all Company programs, especially _____ .

(3) _____

(insert other information if necessary).

III. Trade Secret

In fulfilling Employee's obligations under this agreement, Employee promises not to divulge Company trade secrets unless authorized in writing by Company. This agreement shall remain in force even after employment at Company has been terminated.

Employee agrees to surrender to Company upon termination of employment all notes, records, and documentation that was used, created, or controlled by Employee during employment.

IV. Attorney Fees

If any legal action arises relating to this agreement, the prevailing party shall be entitled to recover all costs, expenses, and reasonable attorney's fees incurred because of legal action.

V. Execution

This agreement is executed on _____ (date) and covers all Company trade secrets and proprietary information currently known to Employee as well as all trade secrets that will become known during Employee's tenure at Company.

_____ Employee _____ Company

(signed)   *(signed)*

Contract T-2 is for programmers and project managers. It should be used with specific software development projects. The reason programmers and managers should sign both agreements is that nondisclosure agreements are most effective when they are as specific as possible. Since you might not know when a secretary or shipping clerk will have access (fortuitously or for good reason) to trade secrets, you have them sign T-1, which is a general nondisclosure agreement. But when you have a program that you want kept secret, it is best that those with access to the program sign a nondisclosure agreement specifically for that program.

NONDISCLOSURE AGREEMENTS FOR OUTSIDERS

Sometimes it is necessary for someone who is not on your company's payroll to have access to trade secrets. Potential investors, potential buyers or licensees of the program, independent auditors, bankers, and lawyers all may need to know something about your trade-secret programs. In addition to protecting your secrets, having potential investors, bankers, and others sign a nondisclosure agreement impresses them with your operation. It shows you take your business seriously, and tells them you own something of value.

(T-3) NONDISCLOSURE AGREEMENT FOR OUTSIDERS

I. Introduction

This is an agreement between _____ and _____ (Company) in which _____ agrees not to disclose trade secrets belonging to Company.

II. Agreement

In consideration of being made privy to trade secret information belonging to Company, _____ hereby agrees not to disclose this information to third parties and to treat this information as a trade secret belonging to Company.

III. Trade Secret

The information to be treated as a trade secret is all confidential information relating to

_____

IV. Attorney Fees

If any legal action arises relating to this agreement, the prevailing party shall be entitled to recover its court costs, expenses, and reasonable attorney's fees.

V. Execution

This agreement is executed on _____ and shall remain in effect until the information included herein is no longer a trade secret or until Company sends _____ written notice releasing him/her from the obligations of this agreement, whichever event occurs first.

_____   _____ *Company*
(signed)   *(signed)*

NONDISCLOSURE AGREEMENTS FOR END USERS

Sometimes it is appropriate for an end user to sign a nondisclosure agreement. With mass-marketed programs an end user nondisclosure agreement would be a sham, but if the program is marketed to only a few end users it might be wise to have them sign the following agreement. The question arises, how many programs must be sold before a program is "mass" marketed? Naturally the answer depends on the facts of the case. Courts have upheld the validity of a trade secret in cases where as many as five hundred parties had signed nondisclosure agreements. Whether the nondisclosure agreement is considered a sham depends less on the number of sales than on the relationship between the seller and the buyer. If there is a true face-to-face relationship, then the agreement will more likely be upheld than if the buyer simply picks a piece of software off a store shelf and signs a scrap of paper called a nondisclosure agreement. Therefore if you plan to sell a relatively small number of programs and if you actually have each buyer sign a nondisclosure agreement, you will have the beginnings of trade secret protection. But you still must maintain your protection as discussed elsewhere in this chapter.

(T-4)   NONDISCLOSURE AGREEMENT FOR END USERS

I. This is an agreement in which _____ (User) acknowledges receipt of certain trade secrets of _____ (Company) and agrees to hold these trade secrets confidential.

II. Agreement

In consideration of being made privy to secret information belonging to Company, User hereby acknowledges receipt of the information listed in Section III of this agreement. User also agrees not to disclose this information to third parties and to treat this information as a trade secret belonging to Company.

III. Trade Secret

The information to be treated as a trade secret is all confidential information relating to

_____

IV. Attorney Fees

If any legal action arises relating to this agreement, the prevailing party shall be entitled to recover its court costs and reasonable attorney's fees.

_____ *User* _____ *Company*
(signed)   *(signed)*

_____   _____
(dated)   *(dated)*

REVIEW OF NONDISCLOSURE AGREEMENT INFORMATION

Because having a nondisclosure agreement is so important, especially to people without regular access to a lawyer, let's review the situations in which you will want to have one signed.

- If you are a program developer, use trade secret protection when you hire an employee or begin to work with an independent contractor. Have the employee sign a nondisclosure agreement and, if you wish, a noncompetition agreement. When the employee starts work on a specific project make certain another nondisclosure agreement (T-2), which covers that particular project, is signed.
- If you have already developed software and are in the testing stage, have the people who are testing the software sign nondisclosure agreements if they have access to the source code or if you want the existence of the program kept secret for the time being. I have included a nondisclosure agreement as part of the Beta Test Site Agreement, which is explained in Chapter 7. You will find a copy of this agreement in the appendix.
- Software developers who approach software publishers should try to get a non-disclosure agreement signed. A publisher, however, might refuse to sign. The reasons for this is not necessarily sinister. Publishers are approached with a lot of programs, some of which are similar to others. If a publisher signs your non-disclosure agreement and looks at your software but then decides to use some-one else's similar program, he could find himself in an uncomfortable position. We'll go over this problem in more detail later in this chapter.

Of course once you have a signed nondisclosure agreement, you should file it carefully so you can easily retrieve it.

WHEN AND HOW TO USE TRADE-SECRET PROTECTION

Now that you know how to create and maintain a trade secret, as well as when to have a nondisclosure agreement signed, let's look at some examples that illustrate which software can and should be protected by trade secret.

Trade secret can be used to protect both source codes and object codes. Nevertheless, it is practicable in most situations to protect the source code by trade secret and the object code by copyright law. If the object code were protected only by trade secret, it would have to remain a secret, which, with mass-marketed software, is not easily accomplished. Even the most elaborate read-protection schemes are being broken by eleven-year-old programmers. So if you decide to treat your object code as a trade secret because it is not designed for the mass market, it's wise to provide yourself with a second line of protection—copyright. (I discuss copyrights in Chapter 3.)

Example

With JunkMail, a program designed to be sold to a large number of microcomputer users, Tom could, theoretically, require each purchaser to sign a nondisclosure agreement. This, however, is not only inconvenient but unnecessary. As long as Tom keeps the source code secret, he has to worry only about the object code, which is all the public sees.

Can the object code be protected by trade secret and copyright law concurrently? While a minority of lawyers disagree, I believe that the two forms of legal protection can coexist under the proper circumstances. (I discuss this further in Chapter 3.)

Example

Now imagine a situation where a program isn't designed for the mass market. Instead of selling 25,000 copies of JunkMail for $50 per copy, let's assume that Tina developed a program called FastMail, which was designed especially for a small market comprising the fifty or so largest national mailing-list brokers. It is a very specialized and valuable program that took more time to develop than did Tom's JunkMail. At best, Tina can sell only a few copies of FastMail, which she consequently prices at $75,000 per copy. Because there are only a few users, it is feasible that each customer sign a nondisclosure agreement for the source code (if Tina gives program buyers access to it) as well as for the object code. She will, in addition, wish to use copyright protection. In this situation, however, a nondisclosure agreement is a good primary means of protecting the program. Tina should use the nondisclosure agreement for end users (T-4).

PROBLEMS WITH TRADE-SECRET PROTECTION

By now you realize that trade secret protection is a easily lost as it is obtained. All you have to do is accidentally make it possible for someone to legally get hold of your secret. Forgetting the code at a bus stop or excitedly showing it to someone who hasn't signed a nondisclosure agreement are among the infinite ways of forfeiting your trade-secret protection. Once the secret is out, your trade secret rights are gone forever. So be careful and follow the rules.

Even if you follow all the rules and keep your code locked up in a place the equal of Fort Knox, there is one other way of losing trade secret protection. This is called *independent discovery*. If someone independently develops a program identical or similar to yours, there is nothing you can do about it from a legal point of view. If that person chooses to keep the program secret, both of you may, for the time being, share the same trade secret. Once either of you spills the beans, the trade secret is lost to both of you. Of course, the odds are against someone's writing exactly the program you wrote. Occasionally, however, the saying "Great minds think alike" proves true. That you were first is irrelevant in the eyes of the law.

Another way to lose trade-secret protection is through reverse engineering, which for legal purposes is the same as independent discovery. If reverse engineering is successful, the trade secret has been legally discovered. In most situations it is easier to write a new program from scratch than to reconstruct a maintainable source code from an object code. Incidentally, hardware companies typically seal their integrated circuits in epoxy to inhibit reverse engineering. They hope the chip will be ruined when a reverse engineer tries to remove the epoxy. Of course, there are procedures for disassembling object code and for examining chips. There always will be technological keys designed to open technological padlocks. The question becomes one of practicality. A person with the skills to reverse engineer a complicated compiled program will generally find it more profitable to spend time writing new programs rather than stealing old ones. The industry moves too fast to be satisfied with old ideas.

POTENTIAL PROBLEMS WITH SOFTWARE PUBLISHERS

I mentioned that software publishers are reluctant to sign nondisclosure agreements because they fear the conflicts that might arise if they were to publish similar programs submitted by different programmers. Another reason publishers refuse to review software protected by trade secret is that they are afraid (and rightfully so) that any employee who works with trade secret software will become "contaminated", in other words, that the employee will have to be monitored to make sure the trade secret is being kept. From the publisher's point of view keeping tabs on employees who have been contaminated by all sorts of trade secret programs could become impossibly burdensome, and, from the employee's perspective, career advancement and mobility could be adversely affected.

To avoid contaminating their employees, most publishers agree to take reasonable steps to ensure that the software submitted to them is kept confidential, but most refuse to sign nondisclosure agreements. What does this mean to programmers who want their work maintained as a trade secret? The best approach is to allow the publisher access only to your copyrighted object code. Keep your source code secret until you have signed a contract with the publisher. Perhaps the publisher will never need access to the source code. (See Chapter 8—License Agreements.)

Very few publishers would steal a program. They wouldn't remain in the business long if they did. Since they themselves are so vulnerable to piracy, publishers who would think nothing of photocopying a copyrighted magazine article are usually very sensitive to a programmer's copyright.

Accidental release, not piracy, is the major cause for worry in dealing with publishers. A copy of your program, for example, might be left where unauthorized people would have access to it. From there it's a small step before your secret is all over the grapevine. So try not to give the publisher a copy of your source code until negotiations have proceeded beyond auditioning the program and your confidence in the publisher is well established.

TRADE SECRET—YOUR LEGAL RIGHTS AND REMEDIES

Now let's take a look at exactly what kind of legal protection you may expect from treating your program as a trade secret. Suppose, for instance, that you have a program called CALCULATE which will accept large amounts of data and, according to your instructions, extend that data. You have decided to protect the source code of CALCULATE by treating it as a trade secret and adopting all the safeguards discussed in this chapter. Despite your best efforts, however, someone gains access to your source code and steals it. Two months later your program appears in the classified ads of *Gulp* magazine under the name MANIPULATOR. Proving that MANIPULATOR is the same as CALCULATE would have been difficult if you hadn't had the foresight to embed in your program some identifiable nonfunctioning code, which the thieves neglected to kill. What's more, the pirated program still contains a bug that you fixed after the source code was stolen. In short, you can prove the theft, so what can you expect in the way of judicial relief?

1. You can recover any profits made by the pirate as a result of sales of your pirated program.

2. The court will issue an injunction prohibiting the pirate from marketing or divulging the program. A person who ignores an injunction may be found in contempt of court and fined, jailed, or both.

3. You can recover damages, which include your loss of income owing to decreased sales. Also, if you lowered the price of your program in order to compete with the pirate, you can recover the difference between the original and lowered prices.

4. In most states you can collect attorney's fees and court costs if the person who stole the program had previously signed a nondisclosure agreement that provided for the award of these fees.

5. In many states the person may be jailed for piracy (California Penal Code, section 499c).

Remember that these recompenses are the best you can expect from a court action. Exactly what the court awards will depend on many factors. For example, it is likely you will be awarded more by a court if the pirate is a former employee who had signed a valid nondisclosure agreement. If your employee signed a very specific nondisclosure agreement and you had repeatedly reminded him of the trade secret status of the work, you stand a better chance of recovering than if the employee signed a general nondisclosure agreement at the beginning of his employment and the subject of trade secret was never mentioned again. If the pirate is another company that bribed one of your employees, you have a strong case for punitive damages.

The lengths to which the pirate went to discover your secret and the extent of your protective measures can also be critical factors. One case held that aerial surveillance was particularly onerous. Here the plaintiff accused the defendant of flying a small airplane over the plaintiff's factory in order to inspect the physical plant. The defendant was able to garner information to duplicate chemical processes that were trade secrets belonging to the plaintiff.

In short, the facts of each situation are important and will have a lot to do with whether you can prove your case and be awarded a satisfactory judgment. You should also know that the court has a good deal of latitude and will try to be fair to both parties in making its decision.

Let me warn you, however, that enforcing your trade-secret rights in court is no picnic. We'll discuss this in more detail in chapter 12, but it's well to remember that lawyers are expensive, trials take a long time, and judgments may be difficult or impossible to collect. Therefore, while it is important to know your rights if you should find yourself the victim of piracy, it is far more valuable to know how to avoid victimization in the first place. Never enter into a business or personal relationship if you feel there is a good chance that you'll end up relying on the court to straighten out the mess.

HOW PUBLISHERS SHOULD USE TRADE SECRET

If you are a publisher and a programmer approaches you with a new program, you might be tempted to pass out a few copies to friends and associates to get their reactions. This is especially likely if the program deals with an area unfamiliar to you. One publisher I know asked Janet, my wife, who has a degree in statistics, to review a statistics program. She was given the object code, which in this case was not a trade secret. But what if the publisher had wanted her to review the source code? The publisher should then have obtained written permission from the program developer and required that Janet sign a nondisclosure agreement (T-2 or T-3).

FOOTNOTES

1 Problems can also develop with partners if you don't have a written partnership agreement. For more information see *The Partnership Book,* Addison-Wesley.

2 E. I. du Pont de Nemours & Co. *v.* Christopher 431 F2d 1012.

chapter 3
copyright protection

_____**INTRODUCTION**

In the previous chapter I discussed how, by controlling access to your source code, you can invoke a powerful legal protection device—trade secret. Perhaps the need to maintain such strict secrecy made you feel a bit paranoid. If so, this chapter should be a relief. The point of copyright protection is not to limit but to allow access to your programs. You want everyone in the world to have your copyrighted program—so long as they pay for it. But doesn't this contradict what I just said about the need for secrecy? Not really, because when I discussed trade secret protection, I was talking primarily about how to protect your source code. Copyright protection is most often used to protect your object code (the program that's bought by the end user), not your source code, which is maintained as a trade secret.

A copyright, theoretically, is automatically born the instant the program is transferred from your mind to paper or floppy disk or other fixed form. But, as you will learn, there is more to be done in order to have a legally enforceable copyright. And while the U.S. Copyright Law now allows you a grace period of five years in which to perfect your copyright, you gain more complete legal protection by promptly registering your copyright within three months of publication.

If you follow the correct steps, including filing with the Copyright Office and placing a proper copyright notice (called by copyright lawyers "the legend") on your program (this chapter tells how to do both), your copyright will offer you a powerful protection tool as a legal remedy and a deterrent to piracy. So long as you can prove who is responsible for pirating your program, copyright law allows you to collect monetary payment by, for instance, recovering the profits the pirates made from your program or any losses you suffered as a result of their copying it. But what if you can't prove, or it is difficult to prove, the amount of your damages? Or what if the damages you suffered weren't primarily monetary? These possibilities are also covered by the copyright law, since it allows statutory damages, which means the court can at its discretion—and even if you can't prove that the pirates made money by their piracy—award from $100 to (if the infringement is willful) as much as $50,000 (17 USC 504 [c]). In addition to monetary damages, you can also request an injunction that would prohibit the pirates from continuing their copying (17 USC 502). The law further provides that you may be awarded court costs and, at the court's discretion, attorney's fees (17 USC 505).[1]

Many countries have reciprocal copyright treaties with the United States. If you follow the U.S. copyright formalities of placing notice, filing, and registering, you will

23

be in a position to enforce your copyright in these other countries as well as in the United States. There is also an effective procedure involving the U.S. customs that can stop, even before you go to court, pirated copies from abroad as they enter this country. I'll discuss this further in Chapter 12.

Copyright law does more than discourage people from copying your programs; it also inhibits the trade in pirated programs. This is because anyone who sells or resells your pirated program is legally considered to be a copyright infringer. Thus (at least in theory) even an innocent buyer must give up any pirated copies of your program.

What is the term of a copyright? Ordinarily, a copyright is good for the rest of the author's life plus fifty years thereafter. If, however, the program is a work for hire or a joint work, the copyright term is seventy-five years from publication or one hundred years from creation, whichever is shorter (17 USC 302). Changes occur so rapidly in the software industry that either of these periods is likely to be far longer than the commercial life of most programs.

In order to comply with the formalities necessary to perfect your copyright you must determine who the copyright holder or owner is. The way a programmer is paid will usually determine this ownership. There are three basic ways of paying a programmer. A royalty (license) agreement almost invariably provides that the program developer is paid a royalty based on how many programs are sold, and the developer remains the copyright owner of the program. Most books are published this way. Turn to the title page of almost any book (this one, for example) and you will find the copyright notice in the author's name. I go into much more detail on royalty (license) agreements in Chapter 8. The point to remember now is that in this type of agreement the programmer is usually the copyright holder (owner).

Another way a programmer can be paid is through a work-for-hire agreement. "Work for hire" is defined under copyright law to include two situations. The first involves programs or manuals that have been created by the employee or free-lancer at the behest of an employer (17 USC 101 [1]). The second situation occurs if an outsider is hired to write an instruction manual *and* if there is a written agreement between the person commissioning the manual and its writer that the work will be regarded as a work for hire (17 USC 101 [2]). In either of these situations the person who commissioned the work is the copyright owner.

The third way a programmer may be paid is under an agreement in which the programmer sells all rights in the program to the publisher. In this situation, the publisher becomes the copyright owner. Such an agreement must be in writing and is called an "assignment of copyright." (See Chapter 6 for more information.)

Now let's look at a few examples of what is and is not work for hire under copyright law.

Example

Tom asked Wendy to write the instruction manual for JunkMail. He gave her a check for $250. Wendy did a fine job. One day she and Tom stopped by the print shop to check on the printer's progress. As the cover came off the press Wendy saw that the copyright notice was in Tom's name. She became angry and threw an ink knife into the gears. As the press ground to a halt, she told Tom that she owned the copyright to the manual, that the $250 was a royalty advance, and that she expected future royalties.

Question: Was this manual a work for hire? Tom thought he had paid Wendy for writing the manual and that he would then own it. Wendy thought she had received an author's advance to write the manual and that she would receive royalties from Tom after he had it published.

Answer: The manual was not a work for hire because it was not commissioned by Tom under a written contract (17 USC 101 [2]). Tom and Wendy should resolve their misunderstanding by arriving at a license agreement or assignment.

Example

Rosalind lived in a remote cabin with her two guinea pigs and Apple computer, which she powered with a solar panel. She worked three years on a program designed to regulate the methane conversion of pig manure. By the time she was done, she was so tired of the project that she decided to sell all her rights in the program to Secondware, a software publisher. Secondware paid her $50,000. No royalties were involved.

Question: Is this a work for hire?

Answer: No. Since Rosalind was not an employee of Secondware when she wrote the program, this is not a work for hire. In order to transfer the copyright to Secondware, and before the software publisher can put its name on the copyright notice, Rosalind must sign an assignment of copyright. (See Chapter 6.)

Example

Paul worked for a defense contractor as a computer programmer. He designed a security program for controlling personnel access to a missile launch center. After leaving the contractor's employ, Paul tried to sell to program to Alarm-a-rama, a burglar alarm company.

Question: Can Paul sell his security program?

Answer: No. It was a work for hire and belongs to the employer, who in this case was the defense contractor.

What exactly is copyrightable? Copyright law protects the expression of ideas, not the ideas themselves. By the expression of ideas I mean that the ideas must be in some retrievable form, in handwriting, for instance, or set in type, or recorded on magnetic tape. Ideas in your head don't count as far as copyright protection goes. What's more, the Copyright Office requires that your program be of original authorship and not in the public domain.

The original authorship requirement is easily satisfied. Almost anything you program is considered a work of original authorship so long as you haven't copied it. Even something as mundane as a database of names and addresses has been considered a work of original authorship and eligible for copyright protection.

Here's an example of something that is *not* a work of original authorship:

```
200 N = 1
210 PRINT N
220 N = N + 1
230 IF N ⟨ 10 THEN GOTO 210
```

This program, copied from The Applesoft Tutorial, is a demonstration of the "IF" statement from Applesoft Basic™. It is not copyrightable because it is not a work of original authorship. There is no originality whatsoever in the *expression* of the program. Remember that we are not protecting ideas with copyrights, just the expression of them.

Here's a piece of code that *is* a work of original authorship:

```
4280 REM (C) Copyright 1981 Janet Remer
4290 REM Subroutine to determine C$ for printing during prompt
4310 I = D5(W-1)\J = I + 2\X$ = STR$(D)
4380 IF D ⟨ = 9 THEN D$ = "0" + X$(2,2) ELSE D$ = X$(2,3)
4390 C$ = D5$(I,J) + G$ + M$ + "/" + D$ + "/" + Y$
```

This piece of code is used in a billing program to determine what date will be printed on an invoice. While the underlying logic behind this code is not original, this particular way of expressing the routine is, at least as far as copyright law is concerned. As you can see, the Copyright Office is not looking for excitement; it is looking for just enough originality so some "authorship" can be said to be involved. Bare equations or algorithms such as those in the first listing are not works of original authorship, but just about anything else is, as long as it is original in the copyright sense of the word and was not copied from another source.

For a work to be in the public domain and therefore not copyrightable, it must be published in such a way that it loses its copyright protection. Suppose, for example, that Tom published an object code listing (in hex, assembly language, or binary) of JunkMail in *Gulp* magazine along with the suggestion that anyone wishing to use it could do so. By doing this Tom has put JunkMail in the public domain. Another way of allowing a work to fall into the public domain is to publish it without a copyright notice and neglect to rectify this during the next five years. If you do rectify an omission of notice you will be able to enforce your copyright against infringers, but you might not be able to collect damages from pirates who began the piracy before you registered.

What about programs containing original as well as unoriginal material or material in the public domain? These programs are copyrightable, but only the original parts are protected by the law. The parts that are unoriginal or in the public domain are fair game for anyone to copy.

ESTABLISHING YOUR COPYRIGHT

It's one thing to have a copyright and quite another to enforce it. True, your copyright is automatically born as soon as you express your program in a fixed form. But unless you place proper notice on your program and register it within three months of publication, your copyright's potency will be impaired. Here is what must be done:

Step 1

Place your notice on the program.

(C) Copyright 1982 Jane Adams
All Rights Reserved

The purpose of the notice is to inform the world that you claim a copyright in the program—that it is *not* in the public domain. If someone copies a program that has your notice on it, they are going to have a hard time explaining to a judge that the piracy was an innocent mistake. In order for your copyright notice to serve its legal and practical purposes it must be conspicuous. If it cannot be readily seen, it is insufficient notice.

Programs on floppy disks or cassette tapes should have a notice label on the disk or cassette. In addition, the notice should be in the program itself so that it appears on the video screen (CRT) when the program is loaded or a listing is printed. When in doubt about whether you should put the notice in a certain place, do put it there; duplication never hurts. Some lawyers recommend that you sprinkle your notice throughout the program so that if someone should make a printout, your notice will appear in many places. I think this is a good idea, but make sure your notice is the same throughout the program. Some programs take years to develop, so you want to guard against inadvertently allowing different years or names to appear in your program. This can create needless confusion and in some circumstances even impair your copyright protection.

Example

Tom began programming JunkMail in 1980. At that time he put the following notice at the beginning of his program: Copyright (C) 1980 Tom Tompson—All Rights Reserved. He stopped work on JunkMail in 1981 and took a trip around the world. At the end of 1981, weary of travel and broke, he resumed programming. In 1982, when he finished JunkMail, he added the following notice at the end of the program: Copyright (C) 1982 Tom Tompson—All Rights Reserved. In 1983 he released the program to his distributors for sale to the public. What is the correct notice date? In this case the correct notice should read: Copyright (C) 1983 Tom Tompson—All Rights Reserved. This is correct because 1983 is the year of publication. As I will soon discuss in detail, that is the key year as far as the copyright notice is concerned. Tom should go through the program and change all prior dates to 1983, the date of publication.

Since copyright notice is very important, here are some more details:

The internationally recognized copyright symbol, ©, should always be the first part of the notice. Since CRT screens and most dot matrix printers don't have a ©, you can substitute a (C). The second part of the notice is the word "Copyright." Technically this is unnecessary as long as you have a ©, but use it anyhow. It can't hurt, and it makes the notice absolutely unambiguous. (You may substitute the abbreviation "Copr." for "Copyright" if you want.) Next comes the year. The year is important. Don't leave it out. If you omit the year, copyright law regards it as an omission of the entire notice!

The United States and most of the rest of the world require only the notice, © 1982 Tom Tompson. However, many of the South American countries also require All Rights Reserved. Therefore if your program has any South American sales potential, your notice should look like this: © 1982 Tom Tompson—All Rights Reserved.

The next question is what year to use. The answer is simple. Use the year in which the program was first published. This year of publication will stay the same for all copies of the program sold. The word *publish* in copyright law does not mean manufacture or create; it means make available to the public or to distributors. You can have ten thousand copies of your program sitting in a warehouse, but if you haven't yet made the program available to the public or to distributors, you have not published it. The year in which you release the first copy is the year of publication as far as copyright law is concerned. This is the year that appears on the notice.

Example

You are about to market a game called *Killer Kite,* in which two kites fly around the screen trying to down each other. The game was written and copies were produced in December 1982. You have decided to release the game in March 1983, however, because you know that more kites are sold in March than in any other month. The year in the copyright notice should be 1983, because this is when the program will be released to distributors and thereby published. This is so even though you had copies of the game in your storeroom in 1982.

After the year comes the copyright owner's name. Except in work-for-hire situations or outright assignments, the name will be that of the program developer. As far as copyright protection goes, the name can be either the individual's or the company's. Tax-wise it could make a difference, especially if you are incorporated. (Tax law is beyond the scope of this book, so talk to your accountant. You may be able to save some money.)

Occasionally publishers will want to have copyrights in their company's name even though the program was not a work for hire. For this to be legal the programmer must assign the copyright to the publisher in writing. This is not a common practice in the software field and, from the programmer's point of view, is usually inadvisable. If there were a dispute between the programmer and the publisher, or if the publisher were to go bankrupt, the programmer would most likely find having notice in his or her own name to be a strategic and legal advantage.

If you own a corporation and want to publish your own program, you might consider the following example.

Example

Tom Tompson decided to publish Goony Goblins under the auspices of his solely owned corporation, Wary Ware Inc. He copyrighted the program under the name Wary Ware Inc., rather than under his own name. A few months later he sold half his company to Jane. By copyrighting the program under the name of his corporation, Tom has in effect sold Jane half of the copyright ownership in Goony Goblins since the copyright was the corporation's asset and not Tom's. If Tom had not desired this result, he should have kept the copyright in his own name and merely licensed Wary Ware to publish Goony Goblins. (See Chapter 8 for details on how to license software.)

Step 2

Fill out Copyright Office Form TX

Now that all copies of your object code have your copyright notice on them, the next step is to file a registration certificate with the Copyright Office. You must use Copyright Office Form TX, which may be obtained at no charge by writing:

U.S. Copyright Office
Library of Congress
Washington, D.C. 20559

Let's examine Form TX. It comes with fairly complete instructions, most of which have little to do with registering software. It's a threefold form, so start by tearing off the two instruction sheets. Fill in the blanks by printing in ink or using a typewriter. At the very top of the first page you will see a box headed "Registration number." This number will be assigned by the Copyright Office when they receive your form.

FILL OUT SECTION ONE

The first information you must supply is the name of your program. Write down the exact name you are using (or plan to use) in marketing it. To the right of the name box is an area in which to write previous or alternative titles. This should be used if you are updating a prior registration and have changed the program's name since the last time you filed. If you have merely changed the name of your program during development (who hasn't) but never registered the old name, you need not list the old name here. Ignore the line below the program title line unless your program was published in a magazine or is sold on a floppy disk with other programs. If the latter is the case, you should write the name of the anthology of programs here.

1

TITLE OF THIS WORK ▼

JunkMail

PREVIOUS OR ALTERNATIVE TITLES ▼

PUBLICATION AS A CONTRIBUTION   If this work was published as a contribution to a periodical, serial, or collection, give information about the collective work in which the contribution appeared.   **Title of Collective Work ▼**

If published in a periodical or serial give: **Volume ▼**	**Number ▼**	**Issue Date ▼**	**On Pages ▼**

FILL OUT SECTION TWO

This section calls for information about the author(s). There is room for three authors. If there is just one author, however, only the first three lines should be completed, and the rest of section two should be left blank. If the program has several authors, information about all of them should be entered. If you run out of room, use the continuation sheet that you tore off the main form.

Who is a program author? Normally it is the person(s) who wrote the program. But if the program is a work for hire, the author, for copyright purposes, is the person or the company that hired the writer or programmer.

Example

John Wright writes a program called CHECKWRIGHTER. He worked independently and is now trying to sell the program. Since he is the author, he should write his name in the space for author.

Example

Bank of Combray has Janette Guermantes, one of its in-house programmers, write a program called CHEQUERITER. This is a work for hire, and Bank of

Combray is the author. The words "Bank of Combray" should appear in the space for author.

Example

Jonathan Avalon, a Bank of Prague teller, develops a program called CZECH-WRITER at home on his Apple computer. During the development Jonathan tells his manager about the program, and the manager encourages his efforts. Bank of Prague would like to offer the program to its customers who own computers. This is not a work for hire. In this situation, since Jonathan was not a Bank of Prague programmer and since he did the work at home without pay, his name should appear in section two of Form TX. If the Bank of Prague wants to use or sell the program, they will have to come to terms with Jonathan. There are two possible ways of doing this. The bank could enter into a license agreement with Jonathan and pay him royalties for CZECHWRITER. If this happens, Jonathan's name should appear as the author. Or the bank can buy the program outright and have Jonathan assign the copyright to them in writing. If the bank buys all rights to the program, Jonathan will still appear as the author, though the bank is entitled to use its name in the copyright notice.

To the right of the author's name is a space for dates of birth and death. This is left blank if the work is for hire (even if an individual did the hiring). Obviously, the death date is left blank if the author is still living.

Below the name of the author is a space for the citizenship or domicile of the author. If the author is a U.S. business or citizen, write United States. Otherwise give the country of the author's citizenship or the country in which the author lives. I recommend that noncitizens living in the United States mention this country because people interested in the program (for good or evil) should know that the author is living in the United States and can be conveniently reached, whether it be for licensing proposals or to vigorously pursue infringers.

To the right of the nationality box is a question that asks whether the work is anonymous or pseudonymous. Usually the answer to both these questions will be "No," though if you program under a pseudonym, check "Yes."

2

NOTE

Under the law, the "author" of a "work made for hire" is generally the employer, not the employee (see instructions. For any part of this work that was "made for hire" check "Yes" in the space provided, give the employer (or other person for whom the work was prepared) as "Author" of that part, and leave the space for dates of birth and death blank.

a NAME OF AUTHOR ▼ Tom Doe

DATES OF BIRTH AND DEATH
Year Born ▼ 1950   Year Died ▼ --

Was this contribution to the work a "work made for hire"?
☐ Yes   ☒ No

AUTHOR'S NATIONALITY OR DOMICILE
Name of Country
OR { Citizen of ▶ United States
{ Domiciled in ▶ _____

WAS THIS AUTHOR'S CONTRIBUTION TO THE WORK
Anonymous? ☐ Yes ☒ No
Pseudonymous? ☐ Yes ☒ No
If the answer to either of these questions is "Yes," see detailed instructions.

NATURE OF AUTHORSHIP Briefly describe nature of the material created by this author in which copyright is claimed. ▼
JunkMail, a computer program for Apple][Computers

b NAME OF AUTHOR ▼

DATES OF BIRTH AND DEATH
Year Born ▼   Year Died ▼

Was this contribution to the work a "work made for hire"?
☐ Yes   ☐ No

AUTHOR'S NATIONALITY OR DOMICILE
Name of country
OR { Citizen of ▶ _____
{ Domiciled in ▶ _____

WAS THIS AUTHOR'S CONTRIBUTION TO THE WORK
Anonymous? ☐ Yes ☐ No
Pseudonymous? ☐ Yes ☐ No
If the answer to either of these questions is "Yes," see detailed instructions.

NATURE OF AUTHORSHIP Briefly describe nature of the material created by this author in which copyright is claimed. ▼

c NAME OF AUTHOR ▼

DATES OF BIRTH AND DEATH
Year Born ▼   Year Died ▼

Was this contribution to the work a "work made for hire"?
☐ Yes   ☐ No

AUTHOR'S NATIONALITY OR DOMICILE
Name of Country
OR { Citizen of ▶ _____
{ Domiciled in ▶ _____

WAS THIS AUTHOR'S CONTRIBUTION TO THE WORK
Anonymous? ☐ Yes ☐ No
Pseudonymous? ☐ Yes ☐ No
If the answer to either of these questions is "Yes," see detailed instructions.

NATURE OF AUTHORSHIP Briefly describe nature of the material created by this author in which copyright is claimed. ▼

FILL OUT SECTION THREE

Section three calls for the year that the program was completed. This is not the publication date but the year that all the work on the program was finished. To the right of this space is a question that asks for the date and nation of first publication. This is the publication date mentioned in my discussion of copyright notice earlier in this chapter. The publication date should always be the same as the date you listed in the copyright notice that appears on the program.

YEAR IN WHICH CREATION OF THIS WORK WAS COMPLETED	This information must be given in all cases.	DATE AND NATION OF FIRST PUBLICATION OF THIS PARTICULAR WORK
1981 ◀ Year		Complete this information ONLY if this work has been published. Month ▶ May Day ▶ 15 Year ▶ 1982 United States of America ◀ Nation

FILL OUT SECTION FOUR

Section four asks for the name and address of the copyright claimant(s). The claimant is the person who, as far as the Copyright Office is concerned, owns the program. Usually it will be the author, though when the author assigns the program outright, this will not be true. In every case the name listed on the copyright notice should be the name that appears on the screen when the program is booted and on printouts of the program. If the name of the claimant in section four is different from the author in section two, fill out the box headed "Transfer." For example if a publisher is the claimant because he bought the copyright from an author, he would write, "Author sold publisher copyright in above work per written agreement on (insert date)."

Let's pause for a moment to examine the implications of copyright ownership a bit further. I said that as far as the Copyright Office is concerned, the person whose name appears in section four is the owner of the program. What does it mean to own the program? And what do I mean by "as far as the Copyright Office is concerned"?

4

See instructions before completing this space.

COPYRIGHT CLAIMANT(S) Name and address must be given even if the claimant is the same as the author given in space 2.▼

Tom Doe
1545 East West Court
Palatine, Washington   *ABBEY Lisbon Dr.*

TRANSFER If the claimant(s) named here in space 4 are different from the author(s) named in space 2, give a brief statement of how the claimant(s) obtained ownership of the copyright.▼

Sole Proprietorship of Author

DO NOT WRITE HERE OFFICE USE ONLY

APPLICATION RECEIVED

ONE DEPOSIT RECEIVED

TWO DEPOSITS RECEIVED

REMITTANCE NUMBER AND DATE

When a program (or other work) is put into fixed form, the programmer, unless it is a work for hire, is the owner of the copyright. A copyright is a form of property that can be given away, sold, leased, licensed, depreciated for tax purposes, and even left in a will. The copyright can be transferred, in part or in full, to an individual, a partnership, or a corporation. A common example of an author selling part of a copyright occurs when a novelist sells the publication rights in a copyrighted manuscript to a publisher and the movie rights to a film company. The movie rights are actually part of the copyright. In this case the book publisher has bought the right to publish the book, and the movie producer has bought the right to make a movie based on the book. It is important that any agreement to divide a copyright be in writing. Later in this chapter I will deal with how to write contracts that allow you to divide your copyright.

Example

Tom wrote JunkMail to run on a Apple computer. He copyrighted it. JunkMail won't work on any other computer without substantial modifications. Tom, under a royalty agreement, sold the exclusive right to market JunkMail to Firstware, a well-known Apple software publisher. However, Tom specifically reserved the right to modify and separately sell a version of JunkMail that will run under CP/M and thus work on many other computers besides Apple. In this situation Tom has sold part of his copyright to Firstware, but has kept the rest of the copyright for himself. Tom can sell his remaining interest in the copyright as a unit or he can further divide it.

How does all of this relate to section four of Form TX? Tom's name appears in section two, since he is the author. It also appears in section four, since he is the claimant. As far as the Copyright Office is concerned, Tom seems to own the entire copyright for JunkMail. However, as a result of the written agreement that divided the ownership of the copyright, Firstware, in reality, owns the part of the copyright relating to the software's use on Apple computers. The point is that unless Firstware notifies the Copyright Office of this, they, or anyone else who looks at the records, will have no way of knowing that Firstware owns a copyright interest in JunkMail.

Example

Suppose, in violation of his agreement with Firstware, Tom decides to license the Apple version of JunkMail to Secondware. What can Firstware do to protect its exclusive rights to the Apple version of JunkMail? Firstware can get an injunction against Secondware, which will stop them from selling JunkMail for Apples. But can Firstware be awarded damages from Secondware? The answer is no, because Secondware thought Tom was the sole copyright owner of JunkMail and wasn't aware that Firstware's contract with Tom prohibits this sale. Secondware innocently distributed JunkMail in violation of Firstware's rights.[2] Before Firstware could even qualify to take legal action against either Secondware or Tom it would have to file a copy of its contract with Tom at the Copyright Office (17 USC 205 [d]). Even after doing so, however, Firstware's legal recourse is much more limited than it would have been if the contract had been filed promptly, because Secondware innocently relied on Tom's being listed on the copyright notice and on Form TX as the claimant and apparently sole owner of JunkMail (see section four of Form TX). Firstware cannot get damages from Secondware nor invalidate any of Secondware's existing sales. It might, however, be able to stop Secondware from selling in the future.

What about Tom? Is he off the hook? No. Firstware could sue Tom for breach of contract and recover damages. It could also sue Tom for copyright infringement. These remedies would be worthwhile only if Tom had assets. If he were broke or going out of business, Firstware would be out of luck. But here's a point to remember: just because someone has no money and no other tangible assets doesn't mean he has nothing. Before Firstware decides that trying to get anything out of Tom is going to be a legal exercise in futility, it should investigate whether he owns any copyrights (he does own JunkMail for CP/M) or copyright licenses. These can be valuable pieces of property and, like other kinds of property, can sometimes be attached or appropriated.

The way to keep this depressing scenario from happening to you is by promptly filing a copy of all copyright assignments with the Copyright Office. I show you how later in this chapter.

FILL OUT SECTION FIVE OF FORM TX

Now back to Form TX. Turn it over. Section five concerns the registration history of your program. The first question asks whether the program has already been registered with the Copyright Office. If it hasn't, check "No" and go on to section seven. Otherwise check "Yes" and fill out the rest of section five. There are three questions in section five to be answered if you check "Yes."

Question one asks whether this application form is the first filing or whether there was an earlier filing made before the program's publication. If there was an earlier filing, check the first box. Incidentally, I don't generally recommend filing with the Copyright Office for unpublished software because I believe it can best be protected through trade secret rather than through copyright law.

Question two asks whether this is the first application by this author as copyright claimant for the already registered program. This could happen only if there was an earlier registration in another's name—if, for instance, the programmer had previously allowed his work to be registered in the publisher's name.

Question three in section five asks whether this is a changed version of an already registered program. This is the box you should check if you have made significant updates to the program or have adapted it to run on different machines. Also, you will want to fill out a new Form TX and check this box whenever the changes alone are important enough to merit protection. This isn't necessary for small changes or modifications that simply fix bugs. If you update your registration by filing Form TX for derivative works, you still must keep the original date of publication on your copyright notice.

5

If you answered "Yes" in section five, write down the prior registration number and year of registration in the spaces provided. Also fill out section six, which asks for a brief description of the existing work and the new material.

FILL OUT SECTION SIX (ONLY IF YOU CHECKED THE THIRD BOX IN SECTION FIVE)

The first part of section six requires a brief general description of the program before it was changed. The second part requires a brief description of the changes you are now copyrighting.

Here is how section six might look:

6

Sometimes an adaptation project that lets a program designed for one machine run on another results in the program's being rewritten to such an extent that it is less a changed version of the original program than a new program altogether. If this happens you should register the program as a new program and not as a derivative work. In this situation your copyright notice would contain the date on which the new program was first published.

Example

Janet wrote a program called Billing-I in North Star BASIC for use on a North Star computer. She registered Billing-I with the Copyright Office, and her diskettes contain the following notice: © 1982 Janet Jacobsen—All Rights Reserved. A year later Janet totally rewrote Billing-I to run on Apple computers. The new billing program is written in Forth, but it performs exactly the same functions as the North Star version. It was published in 1983 under the same name she had used for the North Star version (Billing-I). When Janet registered the new program with the Copyright Office, the program contained the notice: (C) 1983 Janet Jacobsen. Since a copyright protects the expression of a program and not its logic or what it actually does, both programs can and should be copyrighted individually. This is so despite both programs' having identical names and performing identical tasks. The reason for this is that the programs are totally different forms of expression: one was written in BASIC and one in Forth.

SECTION SEVEN (FOR DOCUMENTATION/INSTRUCTION MANUALS)

Skip section seven unless you are registering the user manual or documentation to your program. If you are, provide the name and address of the company that set the type as well as the name and address of the printer.

SECTION EIGHT (SKIP)

Section eight doesn't apply to software. Leave it blank.

FILL OUT SECTION NINE

Section nine asks about deposit accounts and where to send correspondence. Ignore the question about deposit accounts, but give the address where you want the Copyright Office to send correspondence.

DEPOSIT ACCOUNT If the registration fee is to be charged to a Deposit Account established in the Copyright Office, give name and number of Account.
Name ▼   **Account Number ▼**

9

CORRESPONDENCE Give name and address to which correspondence about this application should be sent. Name/Address/Apt/City/State/Zip ▼

Tom Doe
1545 East West Court
Palatine, Washington 9x234

Be sure to give your daytime phone ◄ number

Area Code & Telephone Number ▶515/124-4567

FILL OUT SECTION TEN

Section ten calls for your signature, printed name, and date.
First check the appropriate box above the signature line:
Check "Author" if you're the author.
Check "Other copyright claimant" if you are the publisher or someone else who does not have exclusive rights to the software.
Check "Owner of exclusive rights" if you have acquired exclusive rights by a written contract.
Check "Authorized agent" if you are the lawyer or another person who has been authorized to fill out the form. In this situation write, on the dotted line next to the box, the name of the person who authorized you. Now sign on the line, and print your name and the date below the signature.

CERTIFICATION* I, the undersigned, hereby certify that I am the

Check one ▶

☒ author
☐ other copyright claimant
☐ owner of exclusive right(s)
☐ authorized agent of _____

10

of the work identified in this application and that the statements made by me in this application are correct to the best of my knowledge.

Name of author or other copyright claimant, or owner of exclusive right(s) ▲

Typed or printed name and date ▼ If this is a published work, this date must be the same as or later than the date of publication given in space 3.

Tom Doe   date ▶ May 17, 1982

Handwritten signature (X) ▼

FILL OUT SECTION ELEVEN

Section eleven requests the address where the Copyright Office should mail your registration certificate. You may give any safe address, such as your lawyer's office or your own post office box. Print clearly since the certificate will be mailed in a window envelope with your writing showing.
That's all there is to filling out Form TX

MAIL CERTIFI-CATE TO

Certificate will be mailed in window envelope

Name ▼
Tom Doe
Number/Street/Apartment Number ▼
1545 East West Court
City/State/ZIP ▼
Palatine, Washington 9x234

Have you:
• Completed all necessary spaces?
• Signed your application in space 10?
• Enclosed check or money order for $10 payable to *Register of Copyrights?*
• Enclosed your deposit material with the application and fee?

MAIL TO: Register of Copyrights, Library of Congress, Washington, D.C. 20559

11

FILING FORM PA

Form TX should be filed for all programs. In addition, some people will want to file Form PA. This form, obtainable from the Copyright Office, registers your copyright in the actual screens of a program. Not every program's screens are eligible for copyright protection. Generally, original games, software stories, and software art are appropriate programs for Form PA. Word processing screens, spread sheets, business graph generators, and database screens are not copyrightable. Remember, I am now talking only about the visual aspects of the screens, not the program itself, which would be copyrightable using Form TX. If you have some doubt about whether you can use Form PA to protect the layout of your screens, go ahead and file. The worst that can happen will be that the Copyright Office refuses registration. Just because the office accepts registration, however, does not guarantee that you have a copyrighted screen. It is possible that the Copyright Office might accept registration and that a court would hold the copyright invalid.

Form PA is filled out the same way as Form TX. Instead of filing the first and last twenty-five pages of object code (see Step 3, below), however, you should instead file a videotape or movie of the screens you want to protect. The quality should be good enough to make the screens easily identifiable. Be sure you send a ten-dollar filing fee with Form PA—and don't forget to file FORM TX as well.[3]

Step 3

File form TX with the Copyright Office. Once you've completed Form TX (and PA if applicable), send it/them along with:
A. A check for ten dollars made out to Register of Copyrights at the above address.
B. A copy of your object code. This should be a printout or listing of your object code or your source code if you have decided not to treat it as a trade secret. It may be in binary, hexadecimal, or source. The Copyright Office requests only the first twenty-five pages and the last twenty-five pages of the program. This requirement is somewhat strange. Most compiled programs for microcomputers will be fewer than fifty pages long. Additionally, a program might contain some useless code or comment for its first twenty-five pages. Some observers have even suggested that by adding essentially meaningless code or statements to a program there is no need to file much, or indeed any, important code. The rationale behind filing a copy of part of the program is that the Copyright Office would like some way of identifying the program that was registered. If a copyright problem should ever get to court, the theory is that the filed material (the first twenty-five pages and the last twenty-five pages) would help identify the program as the one originally registered. Because some programs are very large, the Copyright Office decided, as a matter of storage convenience, that it would request only these first and last identifying pages of the program.

A final note: if your program is like many and really doesn't contain trade secrets, you should consider filing the first and last twenty-five pages of source code. If, however, you do wish to file object code, you should know that the Copyright Office will accept your registration under what is ominously referred to as the "rule of doubt". This means that the office will accept your object code listing but that it can't really examine it to determine whether it is copyrightable. Therefore, if you do deposit your object code, you must also submit a cover letter stating that the material submitted is a work of copyrightable authorship. Also, it is important that you arrange that on the first page of the submitted object code your copyright notice prints out so that the Office can read it.[4]

Technically it is possible to file Form TX first and send the listing of the object code later. I don't advise this. If you forget to send the code you may, theoretically, be liable for a fine. While the fine has rarely (if ever) been imposed, why look for trouble? It's best to send the ten-dollar check, the first twenty-five pages and the last twenty-five pages of the program, and Form TX in one envelope.

That's all there is to it. If you follow the steps shown, you will have a valid copyright.

COPYRIGHT ASSIGNMENTS

Any time there is a transfer of all or part of a copyright, make sure this transfer is recorded with the Copyright Office (17 USC 205). You can do this by sending ten dollars to the Copyright Office along with a copy of the contract between the person selling the rights to the program and the buyer of those rights (17 USC 708 [a][4]).

However, because this contract is usually long and confidential, the Copyright Office will accept a form contract, which I call an Assignment of Copyright, in lieu of the contract itself (see Chapter 6). This should be sent to the Copyright Office as soon as possible after any transfer of any parts of a copyright. You will find a tear-out form ready to use at the end of this book. When the Copyright Office receives the assignment and your money, it will file a copy of the assignment and will return the original along with a Certificate of Recordation (17 USC [b]).

ASSIGNMENT OF COPYRIGHT

In return for certain valuable consideration, receipt of which is hereby acknowledged, the undersigned hereby transfers to Firstware Inc. the following copyright:

The exclusive right to sell JunkMail, a computer program (Copyright Office Registration No. 1009008790) on Apple computers. The undersigned specifically reserves the right to sell JunkMail for use on all computers other than Apple.

This assignment is subject to the terms, conditions, and restrictions of an agreement dated January 24, 198x, between Tom Tompson and Firstware Inc.

_____   _____

(signed)   *(signed)*

Tom Tompson   *Firstware Inc.*

January 28, 198x   *January 28, 198x*
                              2555 Virginia St.
                              29 Palms, CA

Be sure that you describe exactly which rights are granted and include the program's Copyright Office Registration number. Before purchasing a copyright you are advised and expected to check with the Copyright Office to make sure that what you intend to buy hasn't already been sold to someone else. You may check on this in person or you may have the Copyright Office or a private firm check for you. The Copyright Office charges ten dollars per hour, and it takes a long time (17 USC 708 [10]). A private firm charges about thirty-five dollars per search and is a good deal faster.[5] All material filed at the Copyright Office is arranged by serial number, title and author's name.

Example

You are a software publisher. A programer, who has developed a blackjack program for the TRS-80 offers you a chance to buy the rights to market the program on Commodore machines. You think the terms are right, but before buying you check with the Copyright Office to see who is the registered owner and to be certain there are no transfers of ownership on file. You find out that the programmer's name is indeed listed as claimant on Form TX but that she executed an assignment of her rights in the program to a person named Diamond Jack. Upon checking with Jack you find that the programmer lost all rights to the program during a poker game in Nevada.

COMMON COPYRIGHT MISTAKES

Now that you know how to establish a valid copyright, let's see what happens if it's not done correctly. We include this material for those who have already proceeded with some aspects of the copyright process and would like to know what, if anything, they have accomplished and how they might fix any mistakes.

The Copyright Act of 1909 was intimidatingly formal. One small slip and you lost your copyright. The current copyright law (the Copyright Act of 1976) is much more forgiving. However, there are still valuable incentives for following the rules. Suppose, for example, you published a program but forgot to put a valid copyright notice on it. Under the old law publication without proper notice resulted in loss of copyright. The current law allows you five years to rectify notice problems (17 USC 405 [a] [2]).

Here are some common defects in copyright notices and how the new copyright law treats them:

1. Not including the date in your notice: © Jake Adams. This is a fairly common mistake. The law treats it as though the whole copyright notice had been omitted. This means that innocent people can copy the program without facing damages until Jake tells them to stop. He must also register if he has not already done so (17 USC 406 [c] and 17 USC 405).

2. Postdating your notice: Jake publishes a program in 1982, but the notice reads, "© Copyright 1985 Jake Adams." The law once again treats this as though the copyright notice had been omitted entirely. The law, however, forgives a notice postdated by one year and treats it as completely valid (17 USC 406 [b]).

3. Predating your notice: Now assume a program was published in 1982 and the notice reads, "© Copyright 1980 Jake Adams." The copyright law treats the term of the copyright as though it began in 1980. This chops two years off the length of Jake's protection. For authors this would have no practical effect, unless the author is already dead, since the term of protection is fifty years from the author's death. For companies that have registered copyrights it would mean subtracting two years from their seventy-five-year protection period. Aside from decreasing the term of protection, there is no other penalty for predating notices. And since copyright protection lasts a long time—far longer than the life of most, if not all, software—having a few years subtracted isn't much to worry about (17 USC 406 [b]).

4. Omitting your name: If Jake were to leave his name off the notice, the law would treat it as though the entire notice had been omitted. This too is a fairly common mistake. It happens on occasion when two parties who have a joint interest in a program aren't sure who owns it. They compromise by leaving off the name. Don't do this; it's as bad as omitting the notice altogether (17 USC 406 [c]). While it is legal to list two or more names in the notice, only one of the copyright owners needs to include his name for the notice to be legally valid.

5. Misspelling your name or inserting the wrong name: In either case the law treats the notice as valid. In the unlikely event that people are misled by the mistake and innocently infringe the copyright, they will not be liable for damages if they can prove their innocence. They may be prevented from further infringement, however. If, for instance, Jake Adams' secretary absent-mindedly puts her own name on the notice, the notice should be corrected to read Jake's name. Regardless of whose name is on the notice, however, it will still be valid (17 USC 406 [a]). If for some reason people misled by the wrong name's being on the notice copied the program, they could be prevented from copying or selling the program in the future, but Jake could not receive damages.

6. Putting the parts of a notice in the wrong order: This will not affect the validity of the copyright so long as all the parts of the notice are present and correct. It is, however, best to use the order given previously.

7. Omitting the symbol "©," and/or the word "Copyright": Assume that the notice simply reads "1981 Jake Adams." The law would treat this as though the notice had been omitted altogether. If, however, you have a notice that reads "© 1981 Jake Adams," it is valid. Similarly valid is "Copyright 1981 Jake Adams," even though the © is missing. In some foreign countries you will have trouble enforcing your copyright if the © does not appear (17 USC 401). Again, if you want protection in South America, be sure to include the words "All Rights Reserved."

Now that we've discussed some common mistakes made in establishing a copyright, let's look at how they can be corrected. The general rule is that as long as you take steps to rectify defects within five years of the program's publication, you can cure a defect so far as future (but not always past) infringers are concerned.

In the situations where the copyright law treats defects in the notice as though you had omitted the notice altogether, the following steps may be taken:

1. First make sure that all copies of the program in stock or in production now have the correct notice. This may involve putting correct labels over mislabeled diskettes and correcting the notice as it appears on the screen and within the program.

2. Make reasonable efforts to correct the defective notice on all released copies. This could mean recalling copies of the program from your dealer or sending the dealer labels to put on his inventory of your disks. With mass-marketed programs it doesn't necessarily mean tracking down every copy of your program; in many cases this would not be reasonable. However, if you provide owner-registration cards for people to fill out when they buy your software, it would be reasonable to send each user a label with the corrected notice on it. (Incidentally, I highly recommend the use of registration cards. They form the basis of a customer mailing list that will have a wide range of uses such as customer demographics, fixing copyright problems, and recalling programs.)

Example

Problem—Sandyware, a software publisher, forgot to put a copyright notice label on five hundred floppy disks that it distributed to dealers. The software itself has a proper copyright notice, which appears on the screen when the program is booted. What should be done?

Solution—Sandyware should send a supply of labels to the dealers along with a cover letter explaining that, although its software is copyrighted, Sandyware would appreciate the dealers' taking the time to label the disks so the public would be fully aware that the software must not be copied. Sandyware may want to offer to pay shipping or do something similar on the next order to make up for the inconvenience. Sandyware should also be sure to register its copyright immediately if it has not done so.

Example

Problem—This time Sandyware has inadvertently released five hundred pieces of software without notice anywhere on the software, jacket, or documentation. In this case the Copyright Office would act as though notice had been omitted entirely.

Solution—When the defect is such that the Copyright Office would treat the program as though it had been published without notice at all, I recommend measures more stringent than those mentioned in the preceding example. If it is feasible, I think Sandyware should attempt to recall all copies of the software that are in the distribution chain. This would mean recalling copies from distributors and retailers. A recall is mandated especially if the disk is not covered by some sort of copy-protection scheme. The most efficient way of organizing a recall is to telephone dealers and ask them not to sell the software. Ask them to ship, at your expense, the software lacking notice back to you. Follow up the call with a letter. Then immediately send the dealers enough software with the proper notice to tide them over. Fix the notice on the returned software so it appears on a label attached to the diskette and so it appears on the CRT screen.

As you can see, the solution in this example is time-consuming and expensive. You may decide a recall is impractical and not worth the trouble; there is certainly plenty of software in this marginal category. If you feel this is the case, then at least send the dealers labels with the correct notice printed on them. Ask the dealers to put the labels on the diskettes. As in the first example, send any registered users a label as well as a letter explaining that the software is copyrighted.

Example

Problem—Now, suppose Sandyware is not in the mass market but is a consulting firm that sells fairly high-priced software directly to people or companies. A production manager neglected to include the copyright notice on an important piece of software.

Solution—In this situation Sandyware should contact each customer individually to explain that the work is copyrighted. The customer should be asked to affix on the software a copyright-notice label, which will be supplied by Sandyware. If the customer seems unwilling to cooperate and if problems arise, Sandyware should send the customer a registered letter identifying the software and explaining that Sandyware is the registered copyright holder. (Sandyware should register with the Copyright Office if it has not already done so.) The letter should cite the registration certificate number, if available, and enclose a gummed label with the notice typed on it. Sandyware should specifically request that the customer affix the label on the software and/or documentation. In this way the customer has effectively been put on notice. If the matter should ever wind up in court, the customer could not claim to be an innocent infringer.

If you have concluded that the law is reasonably relaxed and forgiving about copyright notice, you are right. But don't be lured into a false sense of security. There are some strong incentives for setting your notice right the first time. Programs without notice (or programs whose notice is so defective that the law regards it as being omitted) can be copied by "innocent" people until you fix the copyright notice and inform the infringers they are violating your copyright. This doesn't mean that you lose your copyright protection. It just means that people can copy your program until you tell them to stop—assuming that you also take reasonable steps to correct the notice defect within the allowable five years. It also means that you can't collect damages from these innocent copiers. Once an innocent user is told to stop, however, all innocence is lost. You can collect damages from that time on if the user continues to infringe.

Copyright is a relative form of protection; there are degrees to it. Unlike trade-secret protection, where you have it or you don't, with copyright you can have some parts of the protection and not others. The way to have complete protection is to follow the rules discussed in this chapter. But if you neglect some rules, you lose some protection.

FAILURE TO REGISTER YOUR COPYRIGHT

We've examined the consequences of defective copyright notice. Now we'll look at what happens if you make the most common error of all—failing to register with the Copyright Office. Before taking an infringer to court you must first register; the practical and legal implications of having failed to register are no statutory damages, no court costs or attorney's fees (17 USC 505), and no criminal penalties or fines for any infringement before registration.

Now assume you have registered your program properly, but either you neglected to include your notice or it was so defective that the Copyright Office regards it as having been omitted entirely. Normally the situation is the same as we've just discussed: until you cure the defect you can't sue successfully.

Some lawyers advise their clients not to register until and unless they are about to sue someone. Other lawyers believe this advice to be a form of malpractice. I believe the advice is good *if and only if* your program is worth less than the ten-dollar filing fee. People who suggest your waiting to register are probably unaware that the copyright owner loses his right to claim statutory damages and the possibility of attorney's fees and costs if registration does not occur within three months of publication. These are the very benefits that may make the difference between being able to afford to take a pirate to court and having to grin and bear it. Therefore, subject to my discussion later in this chapter regarding registering source-code programs, I feel that promptly registering your copyright makes sense.

Thus far we've discussed copyrighting software. However, in many instances it will be at least as important to copyright the program's documentation. In the following discussion documentation refers to instruction manuals and to the programmer's notes on how a program was constructed. If your program is accompanied by a detailed set of instructions, by all means copyright those instructions if you believe they're valuable. After all, it is often a good instruction manual that sells a program. What's more, it is often easier to prove a copyright infringement of the manual than of the program itself (see Chapter 12—Remedies).

Since the instruction manual is so valuable, it should be routinely copyrighted, filed, and registered. In some cases, however, you may feel that registering a particular manual or piece of documentation is scarcely worth the trouble of filling out the form and sending in the ten-dollar filing fee. But even if you don't register the documentation, at least put your copyright notice on it. This is a bit of free protection that might deter someone from copying it. Then if someone does copy the manual, you can, if necessary, file Form TX and sue them. Use the same notice you used on your program except that the date should be that on which your documentation was first published. This may or may not be the same as the date that appears on the program's copyright notice. I also recommend that you include a copy of the program's notice on the documentation. Place your notice on the title page of your documentation. Here's a sample:

Plant Invaders Documentation:
© Copyright 1982 Daniel Deronda
All Rights Reserved

Plant Invaders Software:
© Copyright 1982 Daniel Deronda
All Rights Reserved

Besides copyrighting manuals and program notes, you may also copyright advertisements (Form TX), product sheets (Form TX), and other printed materials. Training films (Form TA), records (Form SR), or video tapes (Form TA) can also be copyrighted. Request the appropriate forms, all of which are similar to Form TX, from the Copyright Office.

COPYRIGHTING PUBLISHED SOURCE CODES

Until now I have assumed that your program will have a source code and an object code. Most programmers realize that there are some exceptions to this generalization. BASIC is the main exception. Sometimes programs in BASIC are sold uncompiled as source code. Since I have advocated that source codes be treated as trade secrets and object codes be copyrighted, what, you may wonder, should be done to legally protect a program that for one reason or another is to be sold in an uncompiled form?

First, if your program lends itself to copy protection, you should make it difficult to obtain a listing of the program and to copy it. (Unfortunately, it is not within the scope of this book to tell you how to implement copy-protection schemes.)

After you do your best to protect your software from being read and copied, the best approach for mass marketed programs, I believe, is to copyright the source code. This isn't ideal because you do have to register the first twenty-five pages and the last twenty-five pages with the Copyright Office (in many cases, this could be the entire program!). If your program has certain routines that absolutely have to be kept secret, you can make sure they don't print on these first or last pages. You might also want to design certain routines so they don't print sequentially. As a matter of course you should also add nonfunctioning code that will not be automatically altered if a pirate makes changes in the functioning code. You should sprinkle the program liberally with copyright notices. And of course you should strip all comment statements from your program that might help a pirate, and consider inserting others that would be misleading. At least one attorney has even suggested that you deliberately misspell certain words in the comment statements so that the typo will be repeated in any copied programs.

Now take a deep breath and file the required pages of the source code with the Copyright Office.

While some people recommend not filing source codes that are being mass marketed unless and until you get to court, I disagree. In most situations, being reimbursed for attorney's fees and damages because you filed when you were supposed to far outweighs the scant chance of someone's manually copying the code of your entire program as it sits snugly in the files of the Copyright Office.[6] Anyone that dedicated to piracy will probably find a way to copy the program right off your disk. If after reading this chapter you have questions about which approach is right for you, see an experienced copyright lawyer.

One situation where you might prefer relying on trade-secret law to filing with the Copyright Office as your primary means of protection involves software that is not for the mass market. Although you should still place your copyright notice on the program in this instance, you should not file with the Copyright Office. This is because, if you are dealing with only a few customers, you can gain solid protection using some of the techniques of trade secret. You therefore don't need to run the risk, however small, that someone will be able to steal your code by inspecting a copy of it at the Copyright Office. If you lose your trade-secret protection, however, you should immediately file Form TX with the Copyright Office, and if no more than five years have passed since the publication of your code, you will still obtain many of the advantages of copyright protection.

There is some disagreement among lawyers as to whether trade secret and copyright can coexist in the same work. There are two main arguments on the subject, both of which I feel are invalid. The premise of the first argument is that by filing with the Copyright Office you have compromised your program's trade-secret status. However, as I have already pointed out, if you are careful you can avoid disclosing important things in your program listing, especially if it is in binary. The second argument deals with the constitutional question of federal preemption or, put another way, does copyright law, since it is federal law, override trade-secret law, which is state law?

I believe that both forms of protection can coexist. The issue is currently a subject for debate, and many legal articles support my opinion. However, since this is a developing field of law, and until the matter is decided in court or addressed by Congress, one can only make educated guesses about the outcome.

Here are a couple of examples outlining what I would do to protect BASIC or other programs in source code.

Example

Jeff writes a horoscope program in BASIC designed for the mass market. He deletes all helpful comment statements. He does his best to protect it from being copied, including a routine that causes the computer to lock up so that the program has to be rebooted if anyone attempts to list it. He sprinkles copyright notices throughout the program and inserts some nonfunctioning code that may be used as an identification marker if a pirate were to alter the functioning code. He makes a printout of the first twenty-five pages and last twenty-five pages, and ensures that he hasn't given anything important away. Then Jeff fills out Form TX and files it with the copyright office.

Example

Joy writes a specialized program in BASIC that calculates ground-water movement. She intends to license four or five companies that do research for the government to use it. She places a copyright notice on the program and on the manual but does not register because doing so could possibly jeopardize her trade-secret protection, which she views as her first line of defense against piracy. She has her customers sign nondisclosure agreements and otherwise treats her program as a trade secret.

Example

Bob writes a program that allows one type of computer to communicate with another. The whole program is fewer than fifty pages long. It lends itself to copy protection, and Bob is confident that his copy-protection scheme will thwart even the most precocious youngster (for a while). He decides to place copyright notices on the program but not to register it. Bob's decision is based on the following reasons: the likelihood of a large number of pirated copies competing with his authorized copies is small because his copy-protection scheme is so good; the price of the program is so modest that most potential users would rather buy an official copy than a bootlegged disk; he feels that filing the program will result in giving away its secrets. Considering all these factors, Bob decides not to file and to risk the disadvantages he will face if he ever has to go to court.

I feel that Jeff and Joy made good decisions. Joy might have decided to register the manual and not the program. That way, if the manual was copied at the same time the program was pirated she would be able to proceed against the pirate immediately under the copyright law. Bob's decision is more of a toss-up. He faced a situation in which he had to make a business judgment based on an analysis of possible risks and benefits. Bob understood the pros and cons and didn't make his decision blindly. Most probably it was the right decision for him.

SHOULD UNPUBLISHED SOURCE CODES BE COPYRIGHTED?

I emphasized in Chapter 2 that most source codes are best protected by trade secret rather than by copyright protection. This is especially true if the source code is not distributed to the purchaser of the program. While I believe source codes should be protected primarily through trade-secret law, I also think *all* source codes (published or not) should contain a proper copyright notice. Since original programs that are not in the public domain are born with a copyright, why not put a copyright notice on the source code?

I've mentioned that some lawyers believe that copyrighting a program is contradictory to protecting a program by trade secret. Another argument they use is that the mere placement of copyright notice on a work is, in a sense, an admission that the work has been published. The notice, after all, contains a publication date. And, as you will remember, the basic tenet of trade-secret law is that the program must be kept secret. So how do we reconcile a program's being supposedly published with its being protected by trade secret? The answer lies in semantics. Publication for copyright purposes simply means making a program available to end users. But as long as these end users sign trade-secret nondisclosure agreements there is no disclosure or publication in the sense of trade secret. In other words, there can be a limited publication under nondisclosure agreements that will not jeopardize your trade-secret protection. This is admittedly an ambiguous area of the law, and I cannot go into all the arguments on both sides of the issue. All things considered, however, I feel that putting copyright notice on a program does not, by itself, constitute invalidation of trade-secret protection.

Exactly what notice should appear on source codes? If the source code has been published, the notice will be the regular notice discussed earlier in this chapter. If the source code is unpublished it is not legally mandatory to include a notice, but I recommend the following: THIS PROGRAM IS AN UNPUBLISHED WORK FULLY PROTECTED BY THE UNITED STATES COPYRIGHT LAWS AND IS CONSIDERED A TRADE SECRET BELONGING TO THE COPYRIGHT HOLDER. Leave off the date since there was no publication.

In short, I recommend the following treatment for all source codes that are not published:

- Place the following warning at the beginning and end of the program: THIS PROGRAM IS AN UNPUBLISHED WORK FULLY PROTECTED BY THE UNITED STATES COPYRIGHT LAWS AND IS CONSIDERED A TRADE SECRET BELONGING TO THE COPYRIGHT HOLDER.

- Do not file a Form TX at this time. Instead wait until you feel that someone has infringed your source code. If someone infringes your object code, which you should have copyrighted and registered, you will be able to sue the infringer based on that registration, and your source code may never become an issue. If it does, you may register it at the appropriate time. (It is legally possible to file unpublished works, but I don't recommend doing this.)

PROBLEMS WITH COPYRIGHT PROTECTION OR, PIRATES WILL BE PIRATES

By now you know there is no perfect legal scheme to protect all of your software all of the time. While copyright law will be of considerable help in discouraging and prosecuting infringers, it offers no guarantee that your work will not be pirated. There are problems with copyright that it would be foolish to ignore. The most important of these are practical. The others relate to the development of the law itself and have not yet become practical problems.

Let us first discuss the practical problems. Assuming you did everything right— the copyright notice, the registration form, the filing—you have, in theory, adequate legal protection. But this, of course, does not mean that no one will copy your program. Thieves will be thieves. Pirates are of two main types: the hobbyist and the professional.

Profile of a Pirate as a Hobbyist

Just turned fourteen and not subject to adult criminal penalties, this pirate-hobbyist has been playing with computers for years and learned BASIC before English. The part-time pirate takes pride in being able to defeat copy-protection schemes and has friends with similar tastes. Our hobbyist, who might grow up to be a great programmer, is now happily copying your software and probably giving it away or trading it as though it were baseball cards. I suspect that many of the people reading this book went through a stage like this and are now wondering how to keep the next generation from doing the same. There are those who argue that one reason the computer revolution has been, and continues to be, so fast and so big is the widespread cross-pollination (theft) of software. Nevertheless there is no question that hobbyists' thievery accounts for a significant loss in sales. If, for example, a program that retails for one-hundred dollars is copied by one hobbyist, who gives a copy to a friend, who passes it along to two more friends, who give it to two more, you have a problem in a hurry.

Using a hypothetical retail price of $100, in eight juvenile transaction levels there is a potential sales loss of 255 copies or $25,500. Realistically the sales loss must be significantly lower because many, if not most, of the people who are given the program would not necessarily have bought it if they didn't get it free. Even so, there is a lot of money being lost through the hobby grapevine. Some publishers estimate that certain programs such as the games and word processors are realizing a thirty to fifty percent sales loss due to ripoffs. A *Wall Street Journal* article estimated yearly losses due to ripoffs at between $12 million and $36 million annually.[7] Others in the industry believe that the ratio of legitimate disks to pirated copies is one to three.

Unfortunately, the copyright law is fairly ineffective in a situation like this. The theft is so decentralized and each individual case so small that you would never find it economical to pursue all the pirates. Remember also that we are talking about juveniles, with whom the criminal law is generally lenient. In addition to copy-protecting your software, about all you can do is place your copyright notice conspicuously and include the following warning in boldfaced type:

WARNING

THIS SOFTWARE AND MANUAL ARE BOTH PROTECTED BY U.S. COPYRIGHT LAW (TITLE 17 UNITED STATES CODE). UNAUTHORIZED REPRODUCTION AND/OR SALES MAY RESULT IN IMPRISONMENT OF UP TO ONE YEAR AND FINES OF UP TO $10,000 (17 USC 506). COPYRIGHT INFRINGERS MAY ALSO BE SUBJECT TO CIVIL LIABILITY.

This should stop some piracy by hobbyists. Pirates or would-be pirates do not truly believe they are being dishonest. If the illegality of their actions were forcefully brought to their attention, a certain number of these hobbyists would no longer commit such piracy. It's a little like swatting flies. Even if just a few people are deterred by such a warning, you have the satisfaction of knowing that there are fewer pirates out there and that these particular pirates are not now breeding still others. There is some solace in this even though you know that, as there will always be flies, there will always be pirates. At the very least your conspicuous copyright notice and warning will educate the public and put all classes of pirates on actual notice. No pirate will ever be able to say, "I didn't realize the program was copyrighted."

Profile of a Pirate as a Professional

This group ranges from former employees to fly-by-night mail-order houses to crooked software distributors or jobbers to dishonest computer-store owners who give away pirated software in order to sell hardware. If you were to pursue and catch the hobbyist, who is elusive and probably not worth catching, you could likely prove your case without much difficulty because the hobbyist usually won't go to much trouble to disguise a pirated program. The professional pirate, on the other hand, who is profiting from your software and worth pursuing legally, will, unfortunately, be harder to catch. In the hope of escaping detection, the pro pirate is likely to spend some time making your program look different; alternatively, he might even try to forge your program so that it and the supporting literature look exactly like the real thing. The professional may take your program and make it work on hardware you haven't even seen yet, or may change it cosmetically and beat you to the market. How can you ever keep on top of this? It's hard. You won't succeed in identifying all or even most pirates. But when you do succeed in identifying a pirate, your legal position should be sound and your case well worth litigating if you have followed the instructions in this chapter.

Until now, my emphasis has been on practical matters. Now that you know the procedures to follow that will ensure that your program is copyrighted, let's take a brief look at the law behind these procedures. As I mentioned in the introduction, the Copyright Law is a federal law and is therefore uniformly applicable throughout the United States. The current copyright law was enacted in 1976 and is referred to or cited as Title 17, USC, Copyrights. This means that the actual law can be found in Title 17 of the U.S. Code. A copy of this code is not hard to find; all law libraries will have one. Before 1976 the governing law was the Copyright Act of 1909. This old law, which was superseded by the Copyright Act of 1976, should not be of concern to readers of this book *unless* you have a program that was published prior to January 1, 1978. In this event I recommend your seeing a copyright lawyer.

The 1976 act dealt only cursorily with software. It wasn't until December 12, 1980, that software was more specifically incorporated into copyright law. Prior to that, the Copyright Office accepted registrations of software, and the legislative history behind the 1976 act indicated that software was included, but the law itself was silent on the subject of software. The 1980 change came in the form of the Computer Software Copyright Act of 1980. This was in effect a revision of Section 117 of the 1976 act. First it provided a definition of "computer program" (17 USC 101): "A computer program is a set of statements or instructions to be used directly or indirectly in a computer to bring about a certain result." This definition is hardly startling or revolutionary; it is, however, the first definition of software in a U.S. copyright law.

The second part of the 1980 act is a revision of section 117 of the 1976 act. The new section 117 provides some interesting specifics relating to copying programs. It gives the lawful owner of a copy of a program the right to copy or adapt a copyrighted program as long as the copying is essential to using the program (17 USC 117):

"Notwithstanding the provisions of section 106, it is not an infringement for the owner of a copy of a computer program to make, or authorize the making of, another copy or adaptation of that computer program provided (1) that the new copy or adaptation is created as an essential step in the utilization of the computer program in conjunction with a machine and that it is used in no other manner, or (2) that the new copy or adaptation is for archival purposes only and that all archival copies are destroyed in the event that continued possession of the computer program ceases to be rightful.

"Any exact copies prepared in accordance with the provisions of this section may be leased, sold, or otherwise transferred, along with the copy from which the copies were prepared, only as part of the lease, sale or other transfer of all rights in the program. Adaptations so prepared may be transferred only with the authorization of the copyright holder."

Section 117 allows copying of a copyrighted program for archival purposes provided that the archival copies are destroyed if possession of the original program becomes wrongful. All this means is that you are allowed to keep backup copies of the program as long as you are allowed to keep the original. In most cases there is only one occasion when you must no longer keep a program. That's when you sell it to someone else. Thus when a program is sold by one end user to another, all backup copies must be destroyed.

Somehow I can't imagine a ten-year-old game collector destroying his backup copy of Space Invaders when he trades the original for a copy of Pac-Man. Still, the law does provide a general framework of protection for owners of copyrighted software.[8]

FOOTNOTES

[1] These are civil penalties which are found in the Copyright Act of 1976. The copyright law also contains criminal penalties including stiff fines and up to a year's imprisonment (17 USC 506).

[2] The word "innocent" as used in connection with infringement does not mean a sweet, unsuspicious state of mind. It simply means that when the "innocent" person copied the program, he did so under the impression that the copying was not an infringement of someone's copyright. Being ignorant is not the same as being innocent. For the copier to get off the hook, there must be a serious enough defect in

either the copyright notice or the registration to serve as a reasonable excuse. (17 USC 405[b], 406 [a].)

[3] If your program is a game and you wish to file form PA, videotape the game in both its demonstration (attract) mode and with someone actually playing it. Be sure to include a close-up shot of your copyright notice as it appears on the screen. When you are done, make a note of how many minutes your tape runs. Then send the videotape, the completed form PA, a check for ten dollars, and the following cover letter to the Copyright Office. This cover letter asks the Copyright Office for special relief because you are submitting a videotape of your game.

> Chief of Examining Division
> U.S. Copyright Office
> Washington, D.C. 20559
>
> Re: Request for Special Relief
>
> January 1, 1983
>
> Dear Chief Examiner:
>
> Enclosed please find:
> 1. Copyright registration (form PA) for the audiovisual work entitled _____.
>
> 2. A videotape of the work including its demonstration and play mode. The video tape includes a view of the copyright notice as it appears on the audiovisual work. It will play for _____ minutes.
>
> A brief synopsis of the work is as follows: [Include here a short description of the game, for instance: A maze appears on the screen. A small diamond-shaped object runs through the maze, controlled by the player. The object is to get through the maze without running into the walls.]
>
> Please treat the enclosed identifying material in the form of the videotape and above synopsis as fulfilling the deposit requirements associated with this copyright registration.
>
> Sincerely,

Special relief will be granted routinely in connection with registering video games. Remember that the law is changing in this area. If you file and there is something amiss with the application, the Copyright Office will write back to you letting you know.

[4] I mentioned that if you file your object code the Copyright Office requests that you include a cover letter stating that the deposited material is a work of copyrightable authorship. Here is a sample letter:

> Chief of Examining Division
> U.S. Copyright Office
> Washington, D.C. 20559
>
> January 1, 1983
>
> Dear Chief Examiner:
>
> Enclosed please find:
> 1. A completed registration form TX for the computer program entitled _____ .
>
> 2. The first and last twenty-five pages of the program in the form of a computer listing of its object code.
>
> I hereby certify that the above named program and the accompanying deposit are works of authorship meeting the requirements of 17 USC 102 (a).
>
> Sincerely,

The Copyright Office will accept your registration (assuming everything else is in order) but will attach a memo to a separate file, known as your correspondence file, stating that the registration is accepted under the Copyright Office Rule of Doubt. This means that the Office has not examined the deposit to determine whether it is an act of copyrightable authorship. They will still issue you a certificate of registration and the matter will probably never arise again. If, however, there is any litigation over the validity of your copyright, and if the person who is questioning its validity thinks of checking the file folder containing your correspondence they may find the Copyright Office memo. What impact will this have? Probably none. You may have to prove that the program is an act of copyrightable authorship. This won't be a problem in most cases. See the previous discussion on what is copyrightable. In the event of litigation you will likely have to prove that your program meets the authorship requirements anyway. Therefore, don't let filing under the rule of doubt deter you; it is more of an administrative procedure for the benefit of the Copyright Office than anything else and shouldn't have an impact on the ultimate validity of your copyright.

[5] One such copyright search firm is GOVERNMENT LIAISON SERVICES, INC., Suite 108 Washington Building, P.O. Box 9656, 1011 Arlington Blvd., Arlington, VA 22209. Fees run approximately seventy-five dollars per search.

[6] The Copyright Office allows public access to the material you file, but does not allow photocopying or hand copying of the pages of your program listing. Also, the Copyright Office does not send a copy of your listing to the Library of Congress, as it does with books.

[7] *Wall Street Journal*, May 1, 1981.

[8] There are many nuances to the Copyright Law which might prove interesting to some readers and their lawyers. If you are interested in pursuing this further, I recommend, aside from a close study of Title 17, reading the article, "Protection of Computer Software After the Copyright Act of 1980," by Gordon K. Davidson and Jack Russo, Computer Programs and Data Bases, Law & Business, Inc. (New York: Harcourt Brace Jovanovich, 1981).
I also highly recommend "Software Protection," an informative monthly publication which deals with all facets of legal protection of software. Write to: Software Protection, P.O. Box 4658 T.A., Los Angeles, CA 90051.

chapter 4
introduction to contracts

INTRODUCTION

Before plunging into a detailed discussion of the various clauses that a programmer and publisher will want to include in their contracts, let's slow down for a moment to ask (1) What's the purpose of writing out and signing a contract? and (2) What must be done to make sure your contract is legally binding?

WRITTEN CONTRACTS

The most important thing I can tell you about a contract (even more important than what one is) is to WRITE IT DOWN. Unfortunately many people believe that asking someone (especially a friend) to sign a contract is another way of saying "I don't trust you." And those asked to sign on the dotted line are apt to react, "I gave you my word, if it's not good enough for you, take a flying . . ."

The hesitation to ask a person to enter into a written contract and the defensive refusal to do anything except shake hands on a deal stem from a misconception about the reasons for writing a contract. Many people mistakenly believe that a written contract is sure to insinuate courts and lawyers into their lives. In fact the opposite is more often true. While a written contract can be instrumental in deciding a court case, the real reason for writing down your understanding is to provide an objective record of your memory in the hope of avoiding the misunderstandings that lead to litigation. A well-thought-out contract signed by honest people will usually minimize, not create, expensive legal entanglements. In an oral contract, for example, you may have to remember complex royalty schedules and payment dates, which are precisely the kinds of things that could easily be forgotten by, and that therefore could cause contention between, even the closest friends.

In addition to this most basic reason for writing out contracts, there are a number of important practical reasons. It obviously is not enough for a software publisher, when applying for a loan, to explain to the bank that the software being published has been licensed on the basis of a beer and a handshake. If a brick falls on a programmer's head, the executor of the deceased's estate isn't going to be delighted to learn that that same head alone had recorded and was responsible for all business deals. In short, if you take your business seriously and want others to do the same, make sure your contracts are written down.

47

While oral contracts are a bad idea from a legal and a practical point of view, in many (but not all) instances they are legally valid *if* they can be proved. The problem is the *"if."* Many times it is impossible to prove the existence of an oral contract, and for this reason courts and legislatures have adopted a number of rules restricting their use. Labor contracts, for instance, which cannot by their terms be completed in less than a year, are invalid if they are not in writing. Contracts for the sale of goods that fall under the Uniform Commercial Code (UCC) are voidable, unless they are in writing, if they involve more than five hundred dollars (UCC 2-201).

Example

John verbally agrees to program for Wendy for two years. This is not an enforceable contract. However, if (under a verbal contract) John promised to design JunkMail for Firstware, it would be enforceable, even though the design of JunkMail might take more than one year. The legal distinction here is that the first contract by its terms (the promise to program for two years) could not be performed in one year, but the design of JunkMail could theoretically be accomplished in one year even if this was not in fact likely.

If you have an important contract that is not written, you would be wise to try to get it in writing as soon as possible. If for some reason the other party refuses to have it written down, you should at least write yourself a note detailing all the points of the contract that you can remember. Send a copy of it to the other party along with a letter requesting that you be informed promptly if there is any disagreement with your written recollection of the contract. If the other party does disagree with your recollection of the oral contract, you very likely won't have much difficulty pointing out the need for a written agreement. Be sure to keep copies of all your correspondence.

CONTRACT DEFINED

What is a contract? It's a legally binding agreement. But what kinds of agreements qualify as contracts? Let's look at the few simple elements that are necessary to form a valid contract.

Consideration

We just mentioned that a contract is an agreement. True. But not every agreement is a contract. Consider, for example, the following written agreement.

John agrees to write a program for Firstware that will predict all full and partial lunar eclipses from the year 1980 to the year 3000.

John _____ *January 12, 1982*

(signed)   *(date)*

While this agreement is in writing and is signed, it is not a legally binding contract because John's promise to write the program is a bare promise, that is, there's no indication that he is to receive anything in return for his efforts. In legal terms this contract is said to lack *consideration*, which is the legal term for what one party to a contract gives another, the quid pro quo. The law presumes that no one does something for nothing, so even if you said you would do something gratuitously you can't be forced to.[1] Consideration can be anything that someone gives to someone else. It can be money, labor, property, or even a promise to do something (such as a promise to pay money).

*Tom agrees to pay Jim twenty-five dollars on January 24, 1983, in exchange
for Jim's copy of JunkMail, which is to be delivered on January 27, 1983.*

Jim _____   *Tom* _____

(signed)   (signed)

January 24, 1983 _____

(date)

This is a binding contract. Tom gave as his consideration his promise to pay Jim twenty-five dollars. Jim gave as his consideration his promise to sell JunkMail to Tom for twenty-five dollars. In this example Tom agreed to give his consideration (twenty-five dollars) immediately in exchange for Jim's promise to supply his consideration (the copy of JunkMail) in the very near future. Either present or future consideration can adequately bind a deal.

One last thing about consideration. My former contracts teacher, Professor Coyne, used to thunder, "Past consideration is no consideration!" By that he meant you can't count as consideration something that has already been done. If you voluntarily helped Helen debug her program one day, for example, you can't later enter into a contract that lists the free help you already gave her as consideration. Usually the element of consideration causes no problem. Consideration is very common in business relationships where, when someone does something or gives up something, value is expected in return.

Dates

Written contracts should always contain a time frame. If something is to be delivered, completed, or performed, the contract should specify the date of delivery, completion, or performance. All contracts of a specific duration should state the starting and ending dates. These may or may not have anything to do with the date the contract is signed. If key dates are omitted, you run the risk of a serious misunderstanding later. In some situations omission of important dates may invalidate the entire contract. A court could rule, for instance, that since there was no specific date by which the parties had to perform their obligations, the contract was unenforceable. Besides including the dates when contractors must fulfill their obligations, you should also be sure to include the date the contract is signed, which generally appears next to the signatures and is sometimes referred to as the execution date.

Signatures

A contract must be signed by all parties. It is unnecessary that signatures be notarized, and it is unnecessary that the people signing do so in each other's presence. Typically, one party will sign two copies of the contract before mailing them to the other party for his or her signature. Witnesses are also unnecessary, although they don't hurt.

If you are doing business as a corporation, you should sign as an officer of the corporation, not as an individual, if you want the corporate limited-liability shield to protect you from personal liability. If you do this, the other party, in the event there is a court dispute relating to the contract, will not be able to sue you personally but can sue only the corporation. In a particularly bad circumstance the corporation could go bankrupt in an effort to pay court-awarded damages (or for any other reason), while your personal assets would be safe. Limited liability is one of the main reasons that software programmers and publishers choose to incorporate, though there may be important tax reasons as well. In order to receive this powerful form of protection not only must you form a valid corporation, but you must observe all the formalities and rules associated with operating as a corporation. If you neglect these rules and formalities, you run the risk of having your corporate limited-liability status ignored by the courts. But don't be intimidated. The rules are not difficult to follow. If you are not now incorporated, you might consider becoming so.[2]

Example

Here's how an officer of a corporation should sign to achieve limited liability:

Firstware Corporation, by _____ president. _____

(signed)   (date)

Don't forget to include your title after your signature. If your title doesn't appear, you, the signing officer, could conceivably be found personally liable in a court case.

When dealing with small corporations, the other party to a contract will often request that the officers of the corporation also obligate themselves personally. This means you will be asked to sign not only as the company president but also as an individual. Banks and other lenders are notorious for this approach. If you sign as an individual, the corporate shield will not protect your from personal liability. Sometimes you will be faced with a business deal that will fall through if you don't obligate yourself personally. At that point you will have to decide which is more important— the contract or the corporate shield.

Other Contract Features

Valid consideration, dates, and signatures are the three elements that must be present to create a written contract. For a contract to serve its purpose of recording the agreement between the parties it also should accurately summarize the entire deal. This normally means including the sections that follow:

    I. A short introduction stating the purpose of the contract and identifying the principal parties

    II. Definitions of any ambiguous terms

    III. A detailed outline of the responsibilities of the parties (who does what and how?)

    IV. A description of what exactly is to be delivered (what is the completed work?)

    V. A delivery schedule

    VI. A payment schedule

    VII. An arbitration or other dispute-resolution section

    VIII. Any other clauses specific to your contract

Now let's go over these contract sections to see how they should be used.

Section I—The Contract Introduction

Contract introductions should be short and to the point. They don't accomplish their purpose if they get bogged down with redundant language. Here is a typical introduction to a work-for-hire contract:

I. Introduction

This a contract between Jim McName (Employee) and Firstware, Incorporated (Employer), in which Employee agrees to produce a computer program (Program) as a work for hire for Employer.

This is really all you need for an introduction, though some people also like to briefly describe the program to be written under the contract. The example specifies who the parties are and generally what they are supposed to do. The consideration is that the employee promises to produce a program according to the employer's requirements, and the employer agrees to pay for this program. Identifying the program as a work for hire means that any copyright notice will appear in the employer's name and that the employer will own the entire program (see Chapter 6). This point is sufficiently important to be explained in detail later in the contract. If this were a situation where the publisher had to pay royalties to the program's owner (see Chapter 8), the words *work for hire* would not appear. Notice that the introduction doesn't attempt to deal with the detailed obligations of the contract. These are dealt with later.

Section II—Definitions

If there are terms in your contract that require defining, a definitions section should appear after the introduction. Many contracts will not require definitions. However, if there is even a hint that the parties to the contract do not agree on the meaning of a term, they should work out an agreement and include it in the definitions section. An example of a word that may need to be defined is *documentation*. To a programmer documentation might mean the flowcharts and notes that describe how the program is structured. To a software publisher documentation might mean a user's manual. Thus if the contract calls for the programmer to supply documentation, a definition might be in order. It doesn't matter what definition the parties agree on, so long as they do agree and write down their common understanding.

II. Definitions

Documentation as used in this agreement means information, including flow-charts, that describes the format, organization, and content of the Program on the machine-readable diskettes to be supplied to Publisher by Employee. Documentation shall be detailed enough so that a programmer, unfamiliar with the software but experienced in his work, will have little difficulty learning about the software.

There are, in the definitions section, no specifications on what the documentation should consist of, because they normally are included in a separate contract section devoted solely to that subject. For the sake of convenience I usually include specifications in a separate attachment to the contract entitled "Deliverables." The advantages of this are that the flow of the contract is not interrupted with a lot of technical writing and that the contract is not so exposed since the attachment can be photocopied and given to programmers without their being privy to the rest of the contract. I offer similar advice when it comes to schedules for delivery and payment.

Section III—Duties

The duties section describes what the parties to the contract expect of each other, that is, it allocates responsibilities. Depending on the specifics of a particular contract and the relationship of the parties a duties section can be either simple and general or difficult and detailed. When in doubt about how detailed a duties section should be, I recommend you side with specificity. Again, I prefer to put detailed specifications in an attachment to the contact. Here is an example of some language you might find in the duties section of a hypothetical work-for-hire contract:

III. Duties

Employees shall write a Program that will run on an Apple II computer and that will be used for the organization, maintenance, and output of mailing lists. The Program shall be thoroughly documented. The specifications for the Program and documentation are described in Attachment A, which is specifically made a part of this agreement. Employee shall deliver the Program as per the delivery schedule set forth in Attachment B of this agreement, which is also made a part of this contract.

Employer shall supply Employee with a comfortable work place, all necessary hardware, and, if requested, technical specifications related to the hardware. Employer shall pay Employee as per Attachment C of this agreement, which is incorporated by reference herein.

The duties section of a contract may be much longer, depending on what the contract objectives are. Notice that each time an attachment is mentioned for the first time it is followed either with "which is specifically made a part of this agreement," or with "which is incorporated by reference herein." This is a legal ritual that is used to formally include the attachment in the contract. Use either phrase you wish, but don't forget to use one or the other. Omitting this ritual could result in the attachment not being considered part of the contract. Besides stating that the attachment is incorporated by reference, you must also staple the attachment to the contract. You can incorporate items other than written attachments, such as program manuals, specification sheets, copyright registration certificates, other contracts, or even copies of source code. There are a number of diverse reasons for attaching these items. For instance, a manual is often attached and incorporated by reference to serve as a description of what the program exactly does or should do.

Section IV—Program Description

This section specifies what the program is or, if it has not yet been designed, what it will consist of. Attachments should be used to explain any program that is sufficiently complicated as to warrant detailed elaboration and specifications. Otherwise a description of what is to be delivered can be set down in the body of the contract. An attachment specifying deliverables might read like this:

ATTACHMENT A—DESCRIPTION OF ITEMS TO BE DELIVERED

Employee shall deliver a computer program having the following characteristics to Employer:

1. *The Program shall be a high quality mailing-list program capable of sorting and manipulating numerous records.*
2. *The records shall consist of a number of user-determined keys, which shall be sortable alphabetically and numerically.*
3. *The Program shall include the following functions:*
    a. *Help menu (control H)*
    b. *Print record (control P)*
    c. *Scroll-up screen (control U)*
    d. *Scroll-down screen (control D)*
    e. *Nondestructive back space (control L)*
    f. *Abort print (control K)*

This extract is from a contract containing a program description of several pages. The list of specific features can be as long and detailed as you feel is necessary. Certainly if you even suspect that there may be a disagreement over whether something was supposed to be included in the program, resolve the issue and write the understanding in the contract.

I mentioned earlier that if a complete manual already exists (because the program already exists), it is often convenient to incorporate the manual into the contract as a description of the program. If the program is to have any features not listed in the manual, list these features separately. When the manual is a good description of the program, a clause on deliverables might be expressed like this:

V. Items to be Delivered

Employee shall deliver to Employer a machine-readable diskette containing the object code of the program JunkMail as described in the JunkMail User Manual, which is incorporated by reference herein. The Program shall be capable of performing all functions described in the manual. In addition, the Progam shall be able to sort records by county.

Section V—Delivery Schedule

Every contract must contain a schedule for the work to be completed. Sometimes this is as simple as stating the agreed upon delivery date of a finished program.

If this is the case the date can be included in the main body of the contract in the delivery section.

V. Delivery Schedule

On January 10, 1983, Employee shall deliver to Employer the Program as described in Attachment A of this contract.

Often, however, the details of when various parts of the program are to be delivered or the payments to be made are quite complex. In this case it's a good idea to include your schedule as an attachment to the contract. Here's an example of a schedule that obligates the programmer to deliver specific parts of a mailing-list program on certain dates:

ATTACHMENT B—DELIVERY SCHEDULE

Employee shall deliver the following items required in this contract to Employer on the following dates:

1.	Flowcharts showing programs design	June 10, 1982
2.	Initial working version of program	August 10, 1982
3.	Test cases	September 10, 1982
4.	Final debugged program	January 10, 1983

Section VI—Payments

A payment clause can be very simple or quite complicated. Again, as with the aforementioned sections, complicated payment clauses are best explained in an attachment. Simple payment schedules may be dealt with in the main body of the contract.

VI. Payments

Employer shall pay Employee a total of $25,000 for all rights to the Program. Employer shall copyright the Program in his name and shall be sole owner of the Program. Payment shall be made according to the schedule in Attachment C, which is incorporated by reference herein.

This clause is designed to fit into the main body of a contract. It is used specifically in a work-for-hire setting. Royalty payment clauses are discussed in detail in Chapter 8. Attachment C might look like this:

ATTACHMENT C—PAYMENT SCHEDULE

Employer shall pay Employee $25,000 for all rights to the Program. Payments shall be made as per the following table:

Amount	Task	Payment Due
$5000	completion of Flowcharts	upon delivery
$5000	completion of initial working program	upon delivery
$5000	delivery of tests	upon delivery
$10,000	delivery of final program	upon acceptance

Notice that the final installment is not due until the program is accepted, while the other installments are due upon delivery. A wise programmer might insist on a time limit under which the employer is bound either to accept or to reject the program. Thirty days might be a reasonable time. He might also insist on well-defined standards by which the program would be judged. These could be specified in an attachment on deliverables.

Section VII—Arbitration

I recommend that a binding arbitration clause be included in most contracts that call for the delivery of software. This would include all programming for hire as well as the writing of software on a royalty basis. Programming contracts usually require tight deadlines and invoice a great deal of pressure. People who start out as friends can easily be at each other's throats toward the end of a project. Since many issues can be resolved relatively quickly in an atmosphere less formal than that of a court room, arbitration has the advantage of speed. If the parties are in a deadlock, going to court is seldom the answer, since lawsuits frequently last longer than the anticipated life of the program being argued over. Besides offering speedily resolved disputes, binding arbitration dispels some of the power that the parties have to stalemate a project by saying "I'll sue you unless. . . ." Of course if someone really wants to cause problems, binding arbitration won't perform miracles. If, however, the parties are reasonably sensible and honest, binding arbitration (even if it is never resorted to) could very well help.

XI. Binding Arbitration

If Employee and Employer are unable to resolve any dispute arising out of this agreement, such dispute shall be settled by binding arbitration in Seattle, Washington, in accordance with the Expedited Rules of the American Arbitration Association then in effect. Any judgment upon an award rendered by the arbitrators may be entered in any court having jurisdiction over the matter or the parties.

SUMMARY

In this chapter I have briefly discussed some of the common clauses found in contracts. My bias has been toward simplicity. There are many other sections and clauses that can also be used. You will find many of these in the various sample contracts throughout the book. We'll go over these other clauses as it becomes necessary. It is important to keep in mind that the purpose of a contract is to serve as a reminder of the agreement between the parties involved. At the very least contracts should be written, signed, and dated. A good contract is easily understood and accurately descriptive of each party's obligations.

It is not my goal to explain how to draft complicated contracts. After reading this book you may need more information. If so, a knowledgeable lawyer will be able to help. Besides aiding in drafting contracts, a good lawyer can be of valuable assistance in suggesting creative ways to allocate the risks and responsibilities inherent in every contract. This risk and responsibility allocation is one of the most difficult parts of drafting a contract. I discuss lawyers and how to obtain their services in a cost-effective manner in Chapter 12.

The following chapters contain form contracts that may fit your needs. If so, turn to the appendix, where you will find blank copies. If you have special needs—and many of you will—feel free to use the samples as starting points in drafting your own contracts.

FOOTNOTES

[1] There are a few exceptions to this rule. One is the doctrine of reliance. If someone *justifiably* relies on another's promise, the requirement of consideration will sometimes be waived. If this sounds like your situation you have gone beyond the scope of this book and should see a lawyer.

[2] If you live in California or Texas, see *How To Form Your Own California Corporation*, Nolo Press, or *How to Form Your Own Texas Corporation*, Addison-Wesley.

contracts – nuts and bolts

Now that we've generally outlined what it takes to make a valid contract and what you may expect to find in software contracts, let's take a moment to backtrack and examine the process normally followed in negotiating and finally signing a contract.

It might take a bit of getting used to, but everything in a software contract is negotiable. This includes not only payments but such questions as the length of time a programmer licenses a publisher to sell his or her program under a royalty agreement, who is responsible financially if the program bombs, and who maintains the program. I know that everyone is used to seeing form contracts for everything from buying a car to leaving clothes at a dry cleaners. The contracts we as consumers see every day are not usually negotiated. In fact some are so one-sided and full of fine print that they are not even legally valid.

It is important to understand that your software contract is different from most of the contracts you see on a daily basis. There is, for one thing, no standard form contract in the industry. Indeed, as far as I know, this is the first book containing form contracts designed for people who are not lawyers. As you will see, the form contracts shown here are designed to allow for changes. They provide the skeleton. You provide the muscle. And you do this through negotiation.

There are as many ways to approach contract negotiations as there are people. I like to keep things as low-key and friendly as possible. I can accomplish much more in a cordial and quiet atmosphere than I can in an intense and unfriendly one. Other people have other styles. But whether you like catching flies with flypaper or spraying them with "Raid," there are certain characteristics that all good negotiators share. The best can walk the fine line between looking out for their own interests and making sure the other party feels comfortable with the agreement. I don't believe in getting the best possible agreement at the expense of making the other party detest the deal. Keep in mind that a software contract is usually the beginning of a business relationship.

Now to specifics. Where should contract negotiations take place? This may seem a trivial point, but I've noticed that the location can affect the outcome. I have seen complex negotiations disrupted by unimportant phone calls, by a stockroom clerk asking who stole his packing tape, and by a baby needing a change of diapers. Negotiations require concentration, and they can be exhausting. If your negotiation session is important or involved, you must have a place to meet where you will be absolutely free from distraction. Timing during negotiations can be everything. If you have just conceded something in order to gain something, you may find yourself at a marked disadvantage if this process of give-and-take is interrupted. So whether you use a hotel conference room (not a bad idea if there are a large number of people involved) or your redwood deck, be sure you will not be needlessly disturbed.

Once you have settled on a suitable location, your next concern is trying to put everyone at ease. When one is negotiating with strangers, there frequently is an initial feeling of nervousness. People are often guarded, and sometimes the cliche "He who speaks first loses" seems to hover about the proceedings. To dissipate nervousness and set the stage for productive discussions, I suggest that after general introductions all participants tell a little about themselves and what they want to see accomplished from the negotiations. For example, a software publisher who is negotiating with a programmer might outline some approachable markets, some envisioned ads, and other workable marketing techniques. A discussion of potential markets for a program can be valuable to both sides and will start the negotiations without jumping into the specifics of the contract or, alternatively, wasting a lot of time on the weather. The idea is to dispel the feeling that you are meeting as adversaries by recognizing that if a sensible and equitable contract is signed, everyone will strive to achieve the utmost success for the project.

Be very sure you know who the members of the other side's team are and what roles they play. I remember watching a software developer spend a whole morning trying to impress a very junior executive while the junior's boss was sitting quietly at the other side of the table.

Formal agendas are often unnecessary; indeed, they can be inhibiting because the person who hasn't presented the agenda often feels that the other party is seeking to impose control over the negotiating process. Nevertheless there can come a point in the process when it seems clear that too much is being discussed at once. If this happens, it will make sense for both parties to decide upon an agenda so that the issues can be dealt with one at a time. Be aware, however, that an experienced negotiator will sometimes try to use the device of dividing issues in order to get the other party to make some, apparently, very minor individual concessions. Since each issue is in itself small, each concession may seem equally small. But when you add them all up, you suddenly realize you've been had. So while I recommend your dealing with one topic at a time, I also recommend your being aware of how everything relates to the whole. Generally speaking, try never to concede something without gaining something in return. That which you gain, by the way, need not always be quantifiable. You may want to give in on several points while making it clear that you aren't one to quibble over trifles. Later, when the other party is being adamant on a point crucial to you, it will be time to remind them of your previous generosity.

Now and then people who have worked together before will negotiate a contract by phone. If this is done, it is essential that the substance of the call be put in writing and signed by both parties. This book would be more than twice its length if it included all the tales of woe involving people who jumped into a project on the mere basis of some words said over the phone. In addition to putting in writing any contracts initially discussed over the phone, your standard office procedure should be to send a short note confirming all important phone conversations relating to contracts. Start a file in which all notes and correspondences relating to contracts is kept.

SHOULD YOU NEGOTIATE YOUR OWN CONTRACT?

If you are knowledgeable about how contracts work in theory and in practice, you may want to do your own negotiating. Many people do so successfully. However, there are sound reasons why (if you can afford it) you may want to have someone negotiate for you or at least help you with the process. If you tend to get emotionally involved or if your ego tends to become overidentified with your work product, you should certainly hire someone to aid you. It's a good businessperson who will admit that it is hard to be rational about a project that took a sizable chunk of one's life to complete and that must reach the market quickly and dramatically.

Contract negotiating requires not only a rational frame of mind but also a certain amount of skill and knowledge. Don't, for example, believe the publisher who says, "Don't worry about the contract. We have a standard form that all of our programmers sign." Anyone who has had much involvement with the software business knows there are no standard form contracts in the industry (the ones in this book are no exception). Take a careful look at any proposed contract. It might be fine, but if there is anything you don't like or if there is anything that has been omitted, tell the other side or hire a negotiator to do so. In the book industry an author commonly retains a literary agent. This is not so common in the software field, but it may be soon.

There are some practical reasons for having someone else negotiate your contract. If things get a bit testy, you can call the shots from behind the scenes while letting your negotiator take the heat for being the "bad guy." This way you're less likely to damage your "friendly" relationship with the other party. Moreover, in a deadlocked situation your negotiator has the advantage of being able to say, "I'd love to agree to this point, but I just don't think my boss will go for it. Let me check and get back to you." This gives you time to consider your next move.

A good middle ground between doing all the negotiating yourself and hiring an agent is to hire a consultant, such as a lawyer, to advise you or even to participate in the negotiations on an as-needed basis. Normally consultants are retained at an hourly rate to review the proposed terms of a contract and, if necessary, to write new terms. It is particularly important to review the tax consequences of a proposed contract.

If you are handling your own negotiations and it appears that the process may take more than one session, try not to get bogged down writing out each clause exactly as it will appear in the contract. Instead, summarize what each side agrees on and leave the negotiating session with a memo listing the terms of the contract.. The formal contract can be presented for approval at the next meeting.

Now that you know some of the theory behind contracts and negotiations, exactly what do you do to make sure your contract is "done right"? I recommend that you type your contract (if you are not using a form from this book) on regular 8-½ × 11 inch paper. If you make a typo, correct it neatly. A valid contract could theoretically be written in lipstick on a napkin, but it's not much trouble to take the time to make your contract look as professional as your intentions.

Numbering The Pages

Many lawyers don't number the pages of their contracts. With a software contract, however, particularly a long one with attachments, numbering pages is a good way of keeping track of the contents of your contract, and knowing if a page has been lost or added. A person may remove an attachment for copying and forget to return it. After you have typed a contract that everyone feels is a written expression of your agreement, count the number of pages including the cover page (if any) and all attachments. Then number each page in such a way that the numbering of a five page contract would look like this:

1 of 5, 2 of 5, etc.

Page numbers should be placed at the bottom or upper right-hand corner of the page. They can be hand-written if necessary. (*All* writing should be in ink.)

Check For Typos and Omissions

Now go through the contract and double-check it. If there are any minor changes, make them in ink in the margin or between the lines. Cross out any words that don't apply and check for typos. Be particularly aware of sections where the omission of a work like "not" or "won't" will have a big impact on the meaning. I have found these kinds of errors in contracts from huge companies, so don't be surprised if you find a few of them yourself.

Copy the Contract and Initial All Changes

If everything, including the page numbers, is correct, make a photocopy of the contract. Now you have two copies, both of which (since both will be signed and dated by the parties to the contract) we will consider originals. Starting at the beginning of the contract go through it and every time you find a handwritten change, including any crossed out words or filled-in blanks, initial the change in ink on *both copies*.

Signing

When you get to the part of the contract that calls for a signature, sign and date the contract. Remember to sign as a corporate officer if that's what you are. Have the other side do the same. They should sign both copies but return only one to you. Now that the contract is signed you're done. Congratulations! Keep the contract in a safe place. If you have a lawyer, you might wish to send him a copy. You might also want to keep a copy at home in case the original is lost or destroyed. What happens if a contract is lost or destroyed? Usually it remains valid providing you can prove exactly what the contract said. Sometimes that is difficult—sometimes easy. Since I always write my contracts on my computer, I have an unsigned backup to the paper document on floppy disk.

Modifying the Contract

Most contracts contain a clause under the section headed "General" stating that any changes or modifications in the contract must be in writing and signed by both parties. Whether or not your contract says so, you should do this if there is a change you want to make in the contract. If you were obligated to deliver a program by July 31, 1981, and for various reasons you and the other party agree to change the date to August 15, 1981, the change should be made in writing. Consider the change a miniature contract, that is, state what the change is and that it's being made by mutual agreement, then sign and date it.

Contract Modification

This is a modification to section II of a contract titled "License Agreement" that was signed by the parties to this agreement on July 1, 1981. Section II of the aforementioned contract shall be deleted and superseded by the following section:

Section II

Programmer shall deliver the Program to Publisher by August 15, 1981.

_____   _____
(signed)   *(signed)*

_____   _____
(date)   *(date)*

Make a copy of the modification for each party, and be sure to staple the modification to each copy of the contract.

Despite the contract's stipulation that modifications have to be in writing to be legally enforceable, most modifications are not in fact put in writing. Once a contract has been signed and the real work begun, the contract usually isn't referred to again unless there is trouble. Yet no matter how well a contract is written, often it simply can't predict every contingency. Both parties routinely and without really thinking about it modify a contract by their actions. Whenever possible, especially if there is an important modification, make it in writing. That way there can be no dispute later as to whether the modification was valid. For instance, if the program is going slowly and the developer needs a larger advance on royalties, any commitment to a larger advance should be in writing or the publisher won't be legally liable to increase the advance even if it has been verbally promised. Or if the publisher thinks of a new function to be included in the program and asks the developer to design the new function, the developer won't legally have to do so unless there is a written modification.

If there are modifications that are not in writing, it is questionable whether the modifications are legally binding. They are more likely to be binding if one party has acted in reasonable reliance upon them. For example, if John in return for his receiving an extra $250, was told by his publisher to add a new function to JunkMail that was not in the contract, and if John goes ahead and programs that new function, it's likely that a court would enforce that contract modification. But if John said he would include the new function but ended up not doing so, the publisher probably couldn't force him to do the extra programming unless the modification was in writing. So if something is important to you, put it in writing to be safe.

Sometimes modifications appear to be so trivial it doesn't seem worthwhile taking the time to have both parties sign them. If you run into this, at least consider jotting down a memo of the modification, and send a copy to the other side. This isn't as good as a signed modification, but it's better than nothing.

USING THE TEAR-OUT CONTRACTS

Many of the contracts in the back of the book can be torn out, copied, and filled out using the procedure outlined above. Sometimes a contract will almost, but not quite, fit your needs. If you need to make a small change on a tear-out contract, do so (remember that both parties should initial *all* changes). But if the change is more than minor, retype the entire contract, or if the change is on only one page, simply retype the page. You should take special care to avoid the appearance of a contract that suggests the parties didn't know what they were doing.

work-for-hire agreements and outright assignments

There are three main ways of acquiring programs from programmers who develop new software. The first approach is to give the programmer a royalty payment based on the sales volume of the program. This can be a flat percentage of sales, a fixed amount per sale, or a combination of both. In a royalty agreement a detailed contract between the publisher and the programmer resolves issues such as the royalty amount, what happens if the program doesn't sell well (or what happens if it sells very well), who is responsible if the program bombs, and much more. In this type of agreement, which I usually call a "license agreement", the programmer retains all rights in the program except those granted to the publisher in the form of a license. (See Chapter 8—License Agreements for more details.)

The other two methods of acquiring programs I call "work-for-hire agreements" and "outright assignments." The end-result of both approaches is the same: the person acquiring the program gets all the rights in the software (or manual) for a fixed sum. This leaves the programmer or writer with no interest in the work whatsoever. The new owner of the program, therefore, can do anything at all with the program, while the program developer has no say. The program owner can even toss it in the waste basket if he wants to.

Whether to use a work-for-hire agreement, outright assignment, or license (royalty) agreement is a business decision that must be made by the programmer and employer (publisher). Some programmers won't program under a license agreement because they want to "cash out" of the deal. That way they take no risk that the program will not sell. Other programmers wouldn't dream of working for hire and, despite the risk of making less money, demand a license agreement. Publishers also have their preferences. Usually publishers prefer a license agreement because royalty payments are based on sales. If the program is a dud, the only money the publisher loses is that spent on promotion, since the programmer gets little or nothing. Companies that want programs developed for in-house use often prefer the work-for-hire approach or an outright assignment when dealing with freelance programmers. Whichever approach you choose, the important thing is to negotiate a solid contract.

Since work-for-hire agreements and outright assignments result in the same thing, namely a complete transfer of the programmer's rights to the person acquiring the program, what exactly are the differences between the two types of contract? The main differences have to do with the facts surrounding the creation of the program.

Example

Sam was a Dodgers fan. One day he decided to write a program that would predict the outcome of baseball games. After a year or so of studying past games, he finally developed Oddball, a program that seemed to be able to predict the outcome of any baseball game with a 60% accuracy rate. Naturally several team owners were interested in Oddball. What sort of contract should Sam consider? The choice is between an outright assignment and a license agreement. Since the programming was done before he had an arrangement with any buyer, the program can't be transferred under a work-for-hire agreement. After much thought, Sam decides to sell Oddball outright. He figures that cash in hand now is better than the possibility of future royalties.

When does a work-for-hire agreement come into play? There are a couple of possibilities. The first happens when a person or company commissions a free-lance programmer to write a program. In this case the idea for the program came from the one who commissioned it. The programmer needn't be an employee. All that is necessary is that the program be created at the "behest" of the person who commissioned it and that there be a valid written agreement which makes it clear that the work is a work for hire.

The second situation where a work for hire may be created is when a true employee does the programming for an employer as part of that employee's regular job. In this case the program will automatically be a work for hire, and it is not absolutely necessary—though it is always wise—to draft a written agreement.

Here are some typical work-for-hire situations:

- Company (perhaps a manufacturer or a bank) identifies a need for a program and hires an outside programmer to write it.

- Same situation as above, but the company has a programmer already on staff write the program.

- Company needs a manual for a program and hires a free-lance writer to do the writing under a work-for-hire agreement.

Manuals can be works for hire and follow the same rules as programs. You should realize, however, that it is not uncommon to sell a program under a license agreement (see Chapter 8) while treating the user manual as a work for hire.

If you are a software publisher, a program developer, or a businessperson and want to hire a programmer, a written employment contract is essential. You don't want to invest time and effort in developing a new program only to fight over who owns it.

There are several issues to be resolved in hiring under work-for-hire agreements:

1. What is the programmer expected to accomplish?
2. What is the programmer to be paid, and when are the payments to be made?
3. Who owns the program, manual, or whatever else is created?
4. Is the programmer allowed to use information gained during program development for any other jobs?
5. Is the project a trade secret? (see Chapter 2)
6. Does the employer have to supply the programmer with hardware, facilities, and technical information?
7. When is the program due to be completed?
8. If the programmer is to hire assistants, how is this to be done? Whom do they report to? Must the new programmers be approved by the employer?

Of course other issues may also arise. If they do, you will have to draft your own contract clause to cover them. However, before you do this, read over the sample work-for-hire agreements in this chapter. A clean copy of the contracts without the explanatory material appears in the tear-out section at the back of this book. If you wish to change a sample significantly, you will probably want to retype the entire contract. Details on preparing and signing contracts are covered in Chapter 4.

WORK-FOR-HIRE AGREEMENTS

WORK-FOR-HIRE CONTRACT FOR INDEPENDENT PROGRAMMERS   (WFH-1)

I. Introduction

This is a work-for-hire agreement in which John McName (Programmer) agrees to provide programming services to Firstware Corporation (Company). Company shall pay Programmer according to the payment schedule set forth in Attachment A of this contract, which is incorporated by reference herein.

II. Duties

Programmer shall create a computer source code and complete documentation for Company as per the specifications set forth in Attachment B to this contract, which is incorporated by reference herein.

Company shall supply Programmer all items listed in Attachment B prior to January 5, 1983.

III. Ownership

In consideration for payment as set forth in Attachment A of this contract, Programmer hereby assigns all rights in the Program to Company, including the right to copyright the program in Company's name. Programmer understands that Program is a work made for hire which shall be the exclusive property of the Company.

Consistent with Programmer's recognition of Company's complete ownership rights in the Program described in Attachment B, Programmer agrees not to use the Program created under this contract for the benefit of any party other than Company.

IV. Completion Date

Programmer agrees to complete all work as per the schedule set forth in Attachment C of this contract, which is hereby incorporated by reference herein.

V. Trade Secrets

All types of information relating to the Program, including this contract and its attachments, are to be considered the trade secrets of Company. Programmer shall keep all trade secrets of Company confidential, and shall sign nondisclosure agreements when requested by Company.

VI. Arbitration

Any dispute relating to the interpretation or performance of this agreement shall be resolved at the request of either party through binding arbitration. Arbitration shall be conducted in (city), (state), in accordance with the then-existing rules of the American Arbitration Association. Judgment upon any award by the arbitrators may be entered by the state or federal court having jurisdiction. The parties intend that this agreement to arbitrate be irrevocable.

VII. General Provisions

A. Programmer may neither subcontract nor hire persons to aid in the programming work without the prior written consent of Company.

B. Any modifications to this agreement must be in writing and signed by both parties.

_____   _____
(signed)   (signed)

_____   _____
(date)   (date)

Attachment A—Payment Schedule

The following three payment schedules suggest alternative ways of paying a free-lance programmer. You could pay monthly, weekly, or even daily, regardless of how the work is progressing. Or you could make payment only upon the programmer's having completed certain tasks (see Chapter 4 for an example of this type of payment schedule).

Programmer shall be paid on the first and fifteenth day of each month until the work is completed. Payment shall be $2000 per month.

The above sample is open-ended because it is not tied to the programmer's performance. For this reason many employers will not like it.

Here is an alternative that puts a lid on the amount to be paid:

Programmer shall be paid $500 every Friday beginning on May 1, 198x, and continuing until January 30, 198x. No further payments shall be made after January 30, 198x, until all duties as described in Attachment B are performed to Company's satisfaction, at which time Company shall pay Programmer a final payment of $3,000.

Here is the third payment schedule alternative:

Programmer shall be paid $8000 for completing all work as detailed in Attachment B. Payment of $1000 will be made on the first of each month, starting January 1, 198x, and continuing for eight months thereafter.

Attachment B—Duties

Programmer will be responsible for:

(Here you must insert what the programmer has to produce by describing the program in detail. Besides the actual program, the programmer might be expected to deliver detailed specifications, documentation, a copy-protection scheme, a source diskette from which object diskettes will be made, and so forth. Describe in detail exactly what is expected. For a sample of this kind of attachment refer to the discussion of royalty deliverables in Chapter 8.)

Company will be responsible for:

(List here what the company's responsibilities, other than payment, will be. Is the company expected to provide hardware, technical specifications, a work space? One contract I wrote included the company's having to provide an electronic pager so that the programmer could keep tabs on his assistant programmers.)

Attachment C — Work Schedule

Programmer agrees to complete the programming according to the following schedule:

(Here you include the work schedule, using actual dates. If the work schedule corresponds to the payment schedule, make sure there are no inconsistencies between the two.)

WORK-FOR-HIRE CONTRACT FOR STAFF PROGRAMMERS

Often a work for hire is done by a programmer who is already on the company's payroll. In this situation it is particularly important that the company and programmer clearly understand who will own the completed program. Even though you might think a written contract is superfluous (after all, the programmer is already an employee), if you don't have one it is all too easy for a misunderstanding to arise. This is particularly true if the programmer/employee is aware that the company pays royalties to free-lance programmers. To ensure that no one misunderstands whether a programmer is working for hire or for royalties, write out a contract. The one set out below is designed for use with programmers who are current employees. Of course it is legal, although unusual, to allow an in-house programmer to receive royalties or a percentage of revenues from the sale of programs (see Chapter 8). In some situations an employer may wish to enter into a profit-sharing arrangement with an employee (programmer or not). If this is done, it should be in writing, and a lawyer should review the agreement.

Even without an agreement like the one below, if an in-house programmer has been hired for the purpose of programming (as opposed to, for instance, secretarial work), any program written for the company will normally be considered a work for hire.

WORK-FOR-HIRE CONTRACT FOR STAFF PROGRAMMERS   (WFH-2)

I. Introduction

This is an agreement whereby Madam Lefarge (Programmer) acknowledges that any programming done for Computer Knitware (Company) is the exclusive property of Company.

II. Program Ownership

In consideration of employment by Company, Programmer hereby agrees that any programming done during employment shall be considered a work for hire for the exclusive benefit of the Company. This means that Company shall own all rights to any programs developed, including all copyrights and the right to market (or not to market) the programs. Programmer also agrees not to use the program or any of its parts for the benefit of other employers or for the benefit of anyone other than the Company.

Programmer agrees to sign upon request any documents affirming that any particular program written during employment by Company is in fact a work for hire and belongs exclusively to Company.

III. Payment

Programmer specifically acknowledges that his/her normal salary is full payment for any programming done for Company and understands that this salary is in lieu of any royalties.

My experience has been that if the employer is under a tight deadline and needs a program quickly, a fair bonus tied to a performance schedule is an effective incentive. I've seen bonuses range from $200 to $7500. I recommend a fixed bonus, as opposed to one based on a percentage of sales, because it is easier to administrate.

The following clause is optional and may be used when the employer wishes to provide an additional incentive within the work-for-hire framework. The copy of this agreement at the back of the book does not include the following paragraph. If you want to use it, retype the agreement and insert it at this point.

Notwithstanding that Programmer's regular salary is full payment for all programming done for Company, Company agrees to pay Programmer a bonus payment of $500 if the programming is completed to Company's satisfaction by January 7, 198x.

IV. Trade Secrets

Programmer understands that Company considers all programming to be a trade secret belonging to Company. Programmer, therefore, will neither divulge nor discuss with third parties matters relating to programs on which Programmer is working or any other programs belonging to Company without written permission of Company. In addition Programmer agrees to sign, upon request, nondisclosure agreements relating to any aspect of Company's business.

_____   _____

(signed)   *(signed)*

_____   _____

(date)   *(date)*

HIRING DOCUMENTATION WRITERS

Often the person(s) who write software do not write the instruction manuals that accompany it. There are good reasons for this. By the time the program is done, the programmer is eager to move on to bigger and better things and is usually no longer objective enough to write a good manual for people unfamiliar with the program. In addition, many programmers are simply not qualified to write coherent instruction manuals. While it takes time and money to familiarize a professional technical writer with a program, publishers often find it well worth their while, for a good manual can be essential to selling a program. Sometimes the publisher has the manual written in-house, and sometimes he hires a free-lancer to write it. The following is a sample contract for use when hiring a free-lance manual writer.

WORK-FOR-HIRE CONTRACT FOR FREE LANCE
MANUAL WRITERS   (WFH-3)

I. Introduction

This is an agreement in which Joseph Conrad (Writer) agrees to write a software instruction manual as a work for hire for Firstware, Inc. (Company).

II. Duties

Writer shall write an instruction manual for the Navigator (Program). The manual shall be of professional quality and shall be designed to teach persons unfamiliar with the Program how to operate it. The chapter titles and an outline of the information that must be included in the manual are in Attachment A of this agreement and are incorporated by reference herein. Writer shall submit to

Company chapters of the manual as they are completed according to the schedule set out in Attachment A of this agreement.

Company shall provide Writer all information necessary for writing the manual, including a working copy of the Program and an Apple II computer with monitor, two disk drives, and an 80-column board. All items remain the property of, and shall be returned upon request to, Company.

III. Termination

Company shall review each chapter within one week of receipt. If Company is dissatisfied with the quality of the writing or information presented. Company shall notify Writer and arrange a conference with Writer so that the problems can be corrected. If the problems cannot be corrected to Company's satisfaction, both parties agree that Writer shall stop writing the manual and shall accept as payment in full for his services the money he received up to the date that Company notified Writer in writing of its dissatisfaction. Company may use any parts of Writer's writing as it sees fit.

IV. Payment

Company shall pay Writer as per the payment schedule set out in Attachment A.

V. Ownership

The Program manual is a work for hire. Company shall be considered sole owner of all rights to the manual and has the right to publish and copyright it in its name. Writer's name shall appear on a cover page identifying him as the author.

(The preceding sentence is optional. Delete it if you don't want the author identified.)

Company has the right to change, edit, and add to the manual at any time in any way it sees fit.

VI. Trade Secrets

Writer acknowledges that all information concerning the Program, including information relating to the manual (prior to its being made public), are the trade secrets of the Company. Writer agrees to hold confidential all trade secrets of Company and all matters relating to Program, manual, this contract, and Company's business. Writer agrees to sign nondisclosure agreements relating to the items named in the preceding sentence as required by Company.

VII. General Provisions

A. Modifications to this agreement must be in writing and signed by both parties.

B. Neither party may assign this agreement without the consent of the other. Writer shall not subcontract with other persons in fulfilling this contract without the express permission of Company.

_____   _____
(signed)   (signed)

_____   _____
(date)   (date)

Attachment A—Payment Schedule

Chapter titles	Date due	Payment	Payment due
I. Introduction	9/22/8x	$100.00	10/22/8x
II. Coordinates	10/7/8x	$150.00	11/7/8x
Appendix A	1/4/8x	$200.00	1/24/8x
Index	2/22/8x	$250.00	3/4/8x
Second Draft of entire manual due	3/24/8x		4/5/8x

The Introduction shall describe how to configure the Program, what the hardware requirements are, what the Program does, how to use the manual, and how to boot the Program.

Chapter II shall describe how to find coordinates and generally how to use the Program.

Appendix A of the manual shall contain a list of all longitudes and latitudes of islands in the Indian Ocean.

The Index shall contain the page numbers of all terms used in the manual. A term shall mean a word that either Writer or Company believes should appear in the Index. In addition to writing the above-named chapters, Writer shall also provide:

(Insert items such as table of contents, appendix, and—if the writer is to provide them—photos, drawings, tables, graphs, and so forth.)

A word of caution regarding the hiring of free-lance manual writers: Check any prospective writer's references carefully. A publisher I know was burned by an inexperienced manual writer. This happened because the publisher didn't monitor the writer's progress carefully. When the publisher got around to checking the manuscript against the operation of the actual software, he found that although the program and manual were not completely unrelated, they were at best second cousins. That manual was scrapped altogether and had to be started afresh. Before attempting to write a manual the writer must become acquainted with the software well enough to be capable of explaining how to use it.

SPECIAL PROBLEMS WITH IN-HOUSE PROGRAM AND MANUAL WRITERS

Professional in-house writers usually know that when they work for an employer, the work they create is a work for hire that belongs to the employer. Sometimes, though, the in-house writer is not a professional writer. Some of them, especially manual writers, actually spend most of their time as customer-service representatives or secretaries, and may even be asked to write during their spare time at work or on weekends. In a situation like this, without a specific agreement to the contrary, the writer (secretary or other worker) may legally own the copyright in the manual. This is a gray area of the law. Clearly the issue of copyright ownership is too important to be left to uncertainty. Therefore it is essential that a work-for-hire agreement be signed by employees who have not been hired specifically as writers or programmers but who nevertheless find themselves writing software manuals.

It is, by the way, not necessarily a bad idea from anyone's point of view to allow a writer of a manual (an in-house writer or free-lancer) to hold the copyright ownership of a piece of documentation. As long as the publisher has an acceptable license there should be no problem. (See Chapter 8.)

WORK-FOR-HIRE AGREEMENT FOR IN-HOUSE MANUAL WRITERS   (WFH-4)

I. Introduction

This is an agreement whereby Anthony Trollope (Employee) agrees that all writing done for Finnware (Company) will be a work for hire.

II. Ownership

In consideration of employment by Company, Employee hereby agrees that any writing done for Company during employment, including writing done after business hours, shall be considered a work for hire for the benefit of Company. Company shall own all rights in the Employee's work product, including the copyrights and the right to use or not to use the writing. Company shall have the right to change, alter, or edit the writing as it sees fit. Employee agrees to sign, upon request, any additional documents affirming that any particular writing done during employment is in fact a work for hire and belongs exclusively to Company.

III. Payment

Employee acknowledges that his/her normal salary is full payment for any writing done for Company and understands that this salary is in lieu of any royalties.

(The following paragraph is optional. Retype the agreement if you don't wish to include this clause.)

Notwithstanding the fact that Employee's regular salary is full payment for all writing done for Company, Company agrees to pay Employee a bonus payment of $_____ if the writing is completed to Company's satisfaction by January 1, 198x.

IV. Trade Secrets

Employee agrees that if, in the course of writing, access to trade secrets of Company is given, Employee will hold Company's trade secrets confidential and not discuss them with third parties without the written consent of Company. Employee also agrees to sign nondisclosure agreements relating to Company's business whenever required by Company.

_____   _____
(signed)   *(signed)*

_____   _____
(date)   *(date)*

Once again I recommend using the optional payment paragraph in section III. If you can't afford a large bonus, make it a small one. It's good for morale and probably will help ensure good results.

_____ **OUTRIGHT ASSIGNMENTS**

As I mentioned earlier, the time to use an outright assignment is when you want to transfer complete ownership in a program.

Like the introductions of other contracts in this book, the assignment introduction simply tells who the parties are and, in general, what they want to do.

ASSIGNMENT OF COPYRIGHT

I. Introduction

Scott Cellar (Seller) owns all copyrights and other rights to a computer program (Program) and wishes to assign those rights to Brian Briar (Buyer).

Section II contains definitions that are important to the contract. Be sure you include any definitions you think are necessary. See Chapter 8 for a more complete discussion of how to use definitions.

II. Definitions

A. *"Program" shall mean the computer program described in Attachment A to this contract, which is hereby incorporated by reference.*

B. *(Include other relevant definitions)*

Section III specifies what items the seller is providing the buyer.

III. Items Provided by Seller

A. *Seller shall deliver to Buyer the following items:*

1. *One printout of the Program source code.*

2. *Two machine-readable floppy diskettes containing the source code.*

3. *Two machine-readable floppy diskettes containing compiled source code (object code).*

4. *Complete source code documentation which shall be such that a programmer experienced with the Pascal language will be able to maintain and alter the Program.*

5. *A draft copy of the User Manual as it exists and which is Attachment B of this contract and is hereby incorporated by reference.*

What actually is provided by the seller will vary from case to case. Sometimes there will be no user manual. Other times there will be advertising materials and market studies which the buyer wants. Whatever the seller has to hand over to the buyer should be included here.

The next section specifies when the items listed in Section III must be delivered. In an outright assignment all the items will usually be delivered at the same time. If this is the case use the following:

IV. Delivery

A. Seller will deliver all items listed in Section III of this agreement on January 4, 198z.

Sometimes a delivery schedule will be more complicated. Perhaps the source code documentation needs to be written or organized. In that case, you might try the following approach. (See Chapter 8 for other delivery schedule techniques.)

IV. Delivery

A. Seller will deliver all items listed in Section III of this agreement on January 4, 198x, except the source code documentation named in III. A. 4, which shall be delivered on March 15, 198x.

After the delivery section should appear an acceptance section. This basically sets a time limit for the buyer to examine and accept the program and other items furnished.

V. Acceptance

A. Buyer shall have five days from the date(s) of delivery to determine whether the delivered items conform with their description under Section III of this agreement. If Buyer rejects an item, such rejection shall be made in writing and shall set forth the reason(s) for the rejection. Seller shall have thirty days from receipt of the written rejection to resubmit the rejected items for acceptance. Buyer shall have five days to inspect resubmitted items.

B. Items that have not been rejected under clause A of this section shall be deemed to have been accepted.

The assignment section appears next. It tells exactly what rights are being assigned to the buyer. It is similar to the license section of a license agreement (see Chapter 8), except that in this situation the buyer is not receiving a license but buying the program outright. In the first example below, I am assuming that all rights in the program are being transferred to the buyer. As I explain later (Chapter 8), it is not necessary to transfer all rights to a program. In fact, you can transfer some rights to one person and keep other rights for yourself or transfer them to other parties at a later time.

VI. Assignment

A. In consideration for the payment described in the section of this agreement titled, "Payment," Seller hereby transfers and assigns all copyrights and all other rights in Program and in all items described in Section III of this agreement to Buyer. Buyer shall have the right to register the copyright to Program in Buyer's own name and shall have the exclusive right to dispose of Program in any way Buyer sees fit. Seller retains no rights in Program whatsoever.

B. The assignment in this section shall take effect on March 1, 198x.

Sometimes, as I just mentioned, you may wish to transfer certain rights and not others. Here is an example of how to assign the rights to the program for use on IBM Personal Computers only:

VI. Assignment

A. In consideration for the payment described in the section of this agreement titled, "Payment," Seller hereby transfers and assigns to Buyer the exclusive *rights to manufacture, publish, and sell the Program for use on the IBM Personal Computer as defined in Section II of this agreement.*

B. *Seller specifically retains all copyrights in the Program that are not assigned by this agreement.*

C. *Buyer may not use any trademarks belonging to Seller.*

Notice that in the above example the buyer may not use the seller's trademarks. If you wish the buyer to be able to use the seller's trademarks, please consult a trademark attorney. This is an area of the law where you can lose your rights if you make a mistake. (See Chapter 9—Trademarks.)

VII. Payment

A. *In consideration of the Assignment described in the section of this agreement titled, "Assignment," Buyer shall pay Seller the sum of $50,000 on March 1, 198x. This shall be the only amount paid to Seller for Program.*

The following warranties are typical in most assignments. They are also included in most license agreements and are fully explained in Chapter 8.

VIII. Warranties

A. *Seller warrants that Seller has the legal right to grant Buyer the assignment set out in Section VI of this agreement and that such assignment does not infringe any third parties' rights.*

B. *Developer warrants that there are no pending lawsuits concerning any aspect of the Program and that the Program has not been published in such a way as to lose any of its copyright protection.*

I usually include an arbitration section in my contracts. Here is the one I use:

IX. Arbitration

Any dispute relating to the interpretation or performance of this agreement shall be resolved at the request of either party through binding arbitration. Arbitration shall be conducted in (city), (state), in accordance with the then-existing rules of the American Arbitration Association. Judgment upon any award by the arbitrators may be entered by the state or federal court having jurisdiction. The parties intend that this agreement to arbitrate be irrevocable.

The last section of the assignment agreement contains the general provisions. These are fairly standard clauses.

X. General

A. *This agreement sets forth the entire understanding between the parties. It may be changed or modified only in writing and such changes must be signed by both parties.*

B. *This agreement is freely assignable by both parties.*

C. *This agreement is binding upon and shall inure to the benefit of the legal successors and assigns of the parties.*

D. *This contract shall be construed under the laws of the State of California.*

_____   _____

(signed)   (signed)

_____   _____

(date)   (date)

If you have any questions about these general provisions, they are probably answered in Chapter 8.

Don't forget to include any attachments you may have referred to in the body of the contract. For a description of the program you may include as an attachment a copy of a user manual, if one exists.

evaluation and beta test agreements

Before publishers will seriously consider a program for potential marketing, they will want to test it. What's more, some publishers will want to enter into a formal evaluation agreement with the developer. From the publisher's perspective the evaluation agreement is important because it legally protects him should he decide to publish a program similar to, and instead of, another program that's already been evaluated. At first glance this seems to benefit the publisher at the expense of the developer. However, the evaluation agreement is also of legal help to the developer (1) it forces the publisher to acknowledge receipt of the program on a certain date, (2) it obligates the publisher not to market it without permission, and (3) it obligates the publisher to return all copies of the program after evaluation. It can also be used to set up a minimum standard of secrecy that the publisher is required to meet. Therefore in my opinion the evaluation agreement is at least as important to the developer as it is to the publisher.

EVALUATION AGREEMENT

I. Introduction

A. *This is an agreement between Marilyn McName (Developer) and Firstware Inc. (Publisher), in which Publisher agrees to evaluate the marketability of JunkMail (Program), a program belonging to Developer.*

II. Agreement

A. *Publisher agrees to evaluate the Program to determine if Publisher wishes to market it.*

B. *Publisher shall offer to enter into a marketing agreement with Developer if Publisher decides on the basis of the evaluation that the Program is sound and that it can be marketed profitably.*

C. *If Publisher decides that the Program cannot be marketed profitably, or if a marketing agreement cannot be reached with Developer, Publisher shall promptly return all copies of the Program to Developer and shall not market the Program.*

D. *Developer agrees that Publisher's acceptance of the Program for evaluation purposes shall not limit the Publisher in any way regarding Publisher's free-dom to develop or release programs similar to the submitted Program, pro-vided, that is, that any similar programs have been obtained independently of the submitted Program.*

E. *Publisher acknowledges Developer's copyrights and other rights in the sub-mitted Program. Publisher agrees to treat Program in the same way Pub-lisher treats its own confidential programs.*

III. Schedule

A. *Publisher agrees to complete evaluation thirty days after receipt of Pro-gram.*

IV. Warranties

A. *Developer warrants that the Program has not been copied from someone else and that Developer is the sole owner of all copyrights and other rights in the Program.*

_____   _____
(signed)   (date)

_____   _____
(signed)   (date)

Section II, clause D. deserves special attention. This is one of the main reasons that some publisher's insist on an evaluation agreement. They are afraid of the fol-lowing scenario: A developer submits a program of marginal value, and the pub-lisher sensibly rejects it. Later the publisher releases a program that was obtained independently of the previously rejected program but that bears some resemblence to it. The disappointed developer of the rejected program sues the publisher for "stealing," his work.

Obviously, a publisher who evaluates any quantity of programs would soon be out of business if it was inadmissible to publish a program that was in some way similar to another program that had been rejected earlier. Since the publisher agrees to respect the copyright and other rights that the developer has in a program (section II E., the developer shouldn't be overfearful of being cheated.

If, however, you consider your program especially valuable because it is an original idea or application, you should be very sure of your publisher's integrity. For instance, if you were the first person to think of using a computer to predict bio-rhythms, you might want to keep the idea itself, in addition to the program, a secret.

Some developers will want more assurance than is offered in section II E. that the publisher will keep the program secret. If you have not already done so, read Chapter 2 on trade secrets and Chapter 3 on copyrights.

For those who want a stronger clause regarding trade secrecy here is an alter-native that may be substituted for clause E:

Section II E.

Publisher acknowledges that Program is a trade secret of Developer and agrees to maintain the secrecy of the Program. Publisher shall restrict access to the Program to those who need to see or use it and shall require those people to sign nondisclosure agreements obligating them not to divulge information relat-ing to the Program to third parties. Publisher also acknowledges Developer's rights, including copyrights, in the Program.

Most publishers are reluctant to sign an agreement containing the above alter-native clause E. However, as you have already learned, everything is negotiable, and if the program is sufficiently valuable or is at a stage (the source-code stage) where it is particularly vulnerable to theft, many publishers will agree to this kind of clause and will handle the program with extreme care. Obviously an experienced program developer with a track record will have a better chance of convincing a publisher to agree to this kind of clause than will a novice.

Whether or not the publisher requires an evaluation agreement, it makes good business sense when evaluating a program to use an evaluation form. The following form is used for evaluating software on a scale of one to ten, where ten is "best." Copy the form and fill out part A. Then have the people evaluating the program fill out part B. If you don't want the last person evaluating the program to be influenced by the others, make separate copies for each evaluator and then combine the results on a master copy. A publisher has no legal obligation to give a completed evaluation form to the developer, though it's professionally courteous to do so. Developers may also wish to use the form in conjunction with beta testing. If you use outside test sites (or any outsiders) to evaluate your programs, be sure they sign either the Beta Test Agreement discussed later in this chapter or a nondisclosure agreement (see Chapter 2) before they receive the software for evaluation.

PROGRAM EVALUATION

Title: _____   Date Received: _____

Author: _____   Date Completed: _____

Street: _____   Computer: _____

City, State: _____   Language: _____

Phone #'s: (___) _____ (___) _____   Memory Used: _____

Previous Author: _____ _____   Program Form: _____

Evaluator #: Date:								Totals	Average
1. Enjoyability:									
2. Originality:									
3. Error Trapping:									
4. Graphics:									
5. Instructions:									
6. Professionalism:									
7. Response Time:									
8. User Friendliness:									
9. Market Sego:									
10. _____:									
Totals									
Average									

COMMENTS

_____
_____
_____
_____
_____
_____
_____

If the publisher decides to reject a program after evaluation, the rejection should be in writing. All copies of the program received by the publisher must be returned to the developer, and any copies made for testing should be destroyed. Do this even if the program is so pathetically awful that no sane person would want to own it—let alone steal it. An efficient office procedure that ensures this being done is very important. If a copy of a program is kept by the publisher and somehow finds its way into the public domain, the publisher could be liable for any damage the developer suffers. In addition, if a programmer claims that a publisher stole or "accidentally released" a program, the publisher will want to be able to point to an effective and well-documented security system.

I advise developers to bury a small piece of nonfunctioning code in a program submitted for evaluation. This piece of code should not appear on any other copies of the program. Carefully keep a log sheet that tells what and where the nonfunctioning code is in the program as well as who has that particular copy of the program. If you submit the program to another publisher, change the code a little and log the change. This way, if there is an unauthorized distribution of your program during or after evaluation, you can look up the nonfunctioning code and trace the leak to a particular source. This kind of proof can be like a "smoking gun" if a dispute should ever lead to litigation.

REJECTION LETTERS

Here is a form rejection letter. Publishers may wish to make their version warmer or more personal. They may also wish to include copies of the evaluation form or a brief comment on the reason for rejection. Do make sure, however, that you cover the basic points contained in this sample.

Dear Mr. McName:

After carefully evaluating JunkMail, we have decided that we cannot market it successfully. Enclosed you will find all copies of the program and documenta-

tion that you submitted to us. We have not retained any copies of the program.

Thank you for allowing Firstware to evaluate your program. We wish you every success in marketing it elsewhere.

Sincerely,

Firstware Corporation

ACCEPTANCE LETTERS

If the program looks acceptable, the publisher will probably want to notify the developer by phone. This call should be followed up by a letter. Here is a sample:

Dear Ms. McName:

After testing JunkMail, we feel that the program has good marketing potential. We would like to enter into a license agreement with you. Enclosed is a copy of Firstware's license agreement. Please read it over carefully. We would like to make an appointment with you as soon as is convenient to discuss the agreement in detail.

Sincerely,

Firstware Corporation

SOFTWARE FIELD-TEST AGREEMENTS (BETA TESTING)

After software has been tested in-house it is desirable to test it under various real-life conditions. This testing in the field is called *beta testing*. I once asked a seasoned programmer why it's called "beta testing" and was informed, "Because in-house testing is called *alpha testing*." This seemed as good a reason as any, so we will call our field-testing agreement a beta test agreement.

There are three purposes of a beta test agreement:

1. To maintain control over the tester's use of the software.
2. To ensure that the tester is obligated to fill out the reports needed by the publisher or developer conducting the test.
3. To keep the testing and the program itself a trade secret.

The test site has no access to the source code, and the object code is a trade secret until it is released. Many competitors would dearly love to have an advance copy of another's software so that they might plan their own strategies accordingly.

Beta testers are sometimes paid, but usually they are compensated with a final copy of the software being tested. I have acted as a beta test site for a well-known microcomputer manufacturer and, in return for testing the software, was given copies of it to use on my computer.

While most beta testing is done in exchange for a copy of the software, publishers should remember that even if they give out only one copy of the software, they will probably have to maintain it just as if someone had really bought it. In some situations maintenance might not involve much, whereas at other times it might involve a good deal. For example, when I beta-tested an accounts-receivable program for one firm, they had to reconstruct my accounts receivable when the program bombed.

The following beta test agreement attempts to limit a publisher's liability. However, just because publishers are not legally responsible for programs when they bomb doesn't mean they can simply dismiss their beta test sites. Life doesn't work that way—law or no law. Therefore do your alpha testing first, and take care of the big bugs before you involve beta testers.

BETA TEST SITE AGREEMENT (WFH-5)

I. Introduction

This is an agreement between Nickaloi Tesla (Tester) and House Electric Inc. (Owner) in which Tester agrees to test a software program known as Power Grid (Program) and to keep Owner informed of the results of the tests.

II. Payment

Tester agrees to accept as payment in full for his/her services a copy of the Program after final testing.

III. Duties

Tester agrees to use the Program as it is intended to be used for a minimum of forty hours per month. If Tester discovers any problem with the Program, Tester shall fill out a Program Report supplied by Owner, documenting to the best of Tester's ability the events that led up to the problem in the Program and the manifestations of the problem. Program Reports shall be mailed to Owner within forty-eight hours of the first noticed occurrence of the problem. (Insert here if you want the Tester to call you.) The test period shall last from April 10, 198x, until August 10, 198x.

Owner shall supply Tester with a copy of the Program and any necessary documentation or instruction regarding its operation. After the test period, Owner shall supply Tester with a final copy of the Program and manual. Tester shall be entitled to the same benefits and the same terms that regular purchasers of the Program are entitled to.

IV. Disclaimer of Warranty

Tester understands that the Program is experimental and that Owner does not warrant the performance of the Program in any way. All warranties regarding fitness and merchantability are hereby disclaimed. The Program is accepted AS IS, and owing to its experimental nature Tester is advised not to rely exclusively on the Program for any reason.

V. Trade Secrets

In accepting the Program, Tester recognizes that the Program is a trade secret belonging to Owner. Tester hereby agrees not to disclose any information relating to the Program (including its existence) to third parties without written permission from Owner.

VI. Limitations on Use

Tester agrees not to sell or transfer any copies of the Program or the original Program to third parties. Tester accepts the Program under the condition that it is for Tester's own use and for no other purpose. Tester hereby acknowledges Owner's copyright in the Program regardless of whether copyright notice appears on the Program or whether it has been filed with the Copyright Office.

_____   _____
(signed)   (signed)

_____   _____
(date)   (date)

The above agreement mentioned a program report form, which, for your convenience, I have included at the end of this chapter. Feel free to tear it out and have it photocopied or printed. Some organizations have it printed on three-part carbonless paper—one copy for the beta test site and two for the publisher. The publisher keeps one copy and gives the second to the programmer so that any bugs can be investigated and fixed. The publisher's copy is marked when the bug has been taken care of.

SOFTWARE REPORT

Name _____

Address _____

City _____ State _____

Zip Code _____ Phone _____

System Name _____

Release Number _____ Serial Number _____

Problem or Suggestion _____
(include examples if possible)

_____

_____

_____

_____

_____

_____

_____

_____

_____

_____

Terminal _____   Printer _____

(Company Use Only)

Date Validated: _____   Date of Response _____

Problem Source: 1 Application   Documentation
(circle one)
                       Hardware   System Software   Other _____

Module Affected _____   Date Fixed/Incorporated _____

Final Disposition _____

_____

_____

_____

_____

                                                                      Report Number

Programmer(s) _____   Fixed Release # _____

_____   Date _____

Keep Part 1 for your records. Send Parts 2 & 3 to _____

BETA TEST SITE USER QUESTIONNAIRE

We at _____ greatly appreciate your taking the time to complete this questionnaire. Your suggestions and comments are very important to us, as they help us to both evaluate and improve our products.

COMPANY _____

PERSON COMPLETING FORM _____ DATE _____

DATE TEST BEGAN _____ DATE TEST ENDED _____

PRODUCT BEING TESTED _____

During the test period, you used this product:

☐ A. more than 4 hours per day
☐ B. 1 to 4 hours per day
☐ C. less than 1 hour per day

Do you have any experience with similar products, on _____ or other computers? _____

If yes, please list all hardware and software used.

_____
_____

Including time spent on your _____ how long have you been using computers? _____

Please give a brief description of your business.

_____
_____
_____

Using a scale of 1 to 10 (1 = terrible, 5 = average, 10 = excellent), please indicate:

Your general satisfaction with this product _____

The ease of using this product _____

The practicality or usefulness of this product _____

The following questions require more lengthy responses. Feel free to use additional sheets of paper if necessary.

What would you say are the _best_ features of this product?

_____
_____

What would you say are its _worst_ features?

_____
_____

Have you noticed any extraneous or useless features of the product (please list)?

_____
_____

Please list suggested enhancements to existing features of the product.

_____
_____

Please list new features that you feel should be added to the product.

_____

_____

_____

Please describe any problems you encountered in using this product.

_____

_____

_____

Would you recommend this product to a good friend?

_____

_____

Additional comments:

_____

_____

license agreements

License (royalty) agreements are the most important and exciting contracts that programmers and publishers sign. A thorough understanding of how a license agreement works is essential if one is to be successful in marketing or writing software. In this chapter I discuss in detail the important aspects of license agreements.

It's a gross understatement to say that writing a marketable program is hard work. Programming is rather like creating motion picture animation. Both processes are often a team effort. The initial idea or vision is only a small part of the creative process. It is the incredibly tedious attention to detail that separates the doers from the dreamers. To accomplish a seemingly simple task can require endless days of work. Just as the animator may draw hundreds of pictures (cells) to achieve a few seconds of laughter, the programmer may write pages of code to solve a task that's taken for granted by the end user. During the detail work neither programmer nor animator can lose sight of the initial vision.

For free-lance developers and animators there are a couple of moments of truth, the first of which, did the program work? did the audience laugh? is decided in an instant. The second moment of truth occurs when the software developer or animator signs on the bottom line of a license agreement. This is the ultimate validation of all those months of effort: someone values your creation enough to devote time, offer talent, and provide money to market it.

The signing of a license agreement isn't important only to the programmer—it's also critical to the publisher. Without exciting new material to sell, the publisher won't be in business long. The publisher is throwing dice because it's never really known if a substantial advance on royalties will be recouped or if the competition will release a better program. Incidentally, here we have an instance of publisher and programmer looking at the same question from different perspectives. The publisher fears that a superior program will hit the market, while the programmer, who doesn't believe in superior programs, fears only that a stronger publisher will reap all the profits from selling a similar one.

CHOOSING A PUBLISHER

I am sometimes asked whether it is better to sign a contract with a large publisher whose terms are more modest than munificent or to sign with a small publisher who at least on paper, is more generous. The small publisher may offer a higher royalty percentage, but a large publisher may sell more programs. Actually this is a false question because most programmers will not have the luxury of choosing from among publishers big and small. After talking with a few you will have an idea of how much they value your work. Assuming your program is marketable, you will probably work with the publisher you feel most comfortable with. Not surprisingly this will most likely be the publisher who is most turned on by your program. Certainly payment terms and percentages are extremely important, but keep in mind that every day your program is not on the market is a day on which you earned no royalties. And every day your program is not being sold is a day on which someone else might release a similar program. It could be inferior to yours in every respect except the most important one: it's out there and yours is not. As a publisher I know is fond of saying, "A percent of something is something, but a percent of nothing is nothing."

Before signing any agreement, however, be certain of three things:

1. *Honesty.* No contract, no matter what it says, will completely save you from a dishonest publisher. If you have any doubts about a publisher's honesty, ask for a list of references, preferably other programmers, and give them a call.

2. *Marketing expertise.* Don't assume that a publisher who was successful at marketing Junk Mail will also be successful with your program. Listen to what the marketing strategy is. The more specific the plans are the better. If what you hear is vague, demand more detail or look elsewhere. It is not too much to expect that a publisher prepare a detailed marketing plan for your program. You should feel confident with your publisher's style. You might, for instance, not want your children's game to be featured in the same advertisement as an x-rated party game. If you have any doubts about the publisher's intentions, ask that the detailed marketing strategy be included in your contract.

3. *The contract itself.* Be sure your license agreement (contract) protects your interests. This seems obvious, yet most programmers are far better at dealing with the two issues just discussed than they are with the terms of the contract itself. This is understandable because few programmers have a legal background, and many don't even know a lawyer. Even those who have lawyers are sometimes reluctant to consult them about a contract. I've seen programmers, on a number of occasions, sign away valuable rights simply because they couldn't be bothered to understand "all that legal garbage" and didn't feel like going to the trouble of hunting up their lawyer to explain it.

So much for the preliminaries. If you've read this far, you clearly want to learn enough law to understand how to approach a license agreement. Now for the specifics.

OUTLINE OF A LICENSE AGREEMENT

A license agreement (also known as license contract, royalty contract, or royalty agreement) usually contains the following sections and clauses. Since each license agreement is (or should be) a negotiated contract, the details will likely vary considerably from contract to contract. The following outline sets out the sections and clauses normally found in a license agreement and serves as an overview of this chapter as well.

Keep in mind that legal terms, like programming commands, sometimes lack standardization. For the purposes of this book the word "section" refers to a major subdivision of a contract. Each section contains one or more clauses, which are really the same as subsections. A clause may be one or more paragraphs long.

Section I—Introduction

A. Who are the parties?
B. What is the program?
C. What type of agreement is it? (e.g., license)

Section II—Definitions

A. Terms with different or ambiguous meanings are defined.

Section III—Items Provided by Developer

A. What exactly is the program that the Developer is licensing to the Publisher?
B. In what form is the program to be delivered?
   1. Does the Publisher get a copy of the source code?
   2. If so, does Publisher get full source-code documentation?
C. Does Developer also furnish a user manual?
D. What does the Publisher *not* get?

Section IV—Delivery Schedule

A. When are the item(s) from Section III due to be delivered to Publisher?

Section V—Program Maintenance, Modification, and Training

A. What, if any, are the Developer's responsibilities once the Publisher takes over?

B. Who pays for fixing bugs and any program recalls?

C. Does Developer have to provide program updates?

    1. If so, does Developer get paid for them?

    2. What if the Developer can't or won't provide updates?

Section VI—The License

A. What exactly is the *subject* of the license?

B. What is the *duration* of the license?

C. What is the geographical and market *scope* of the license?

Section VII—Acceptance

A. What must the Publisher do to show that the program has been accepted?

B. How much time does the Publisher get to evaluate and test the program prior to acceptance?

Section VIII—Royalties

A. What royalty percentage is to be paid the Developer on each program?

    1. Is there a minimum dollar-amount per sale?

B. How are royalties calculated?

C. Is there a minimum guaranteed royalty even if the program doesn't sell well?

D. Is there an advance?

    1. If so, how much?

    2. Is it refundable if the program doesn't sell?

E. When are royalties to be paid?

    1. When do they become owing (accrue)?

F. How many free copies does Publisher get?

G. How many free copies does Programmer get for personal use?

H. Are royalties to be paid on the manual?

    1. How much if the manual is sold with program?

    2. How much if it is sold separately?

I. Are royalties to be paid on dealer demos?

Section IX—Accounting

A. What records must Publisher keep and what access does Developer have to them?

Section X—Warranties

A. What does the Developer warrant?

Section XI—Indemnification

A. Under what conditions will Developer indemnify Publisher?

    1. For suits regarding copyright or trade secret?

    2. For bugs or recalls?

B. Under what conditions will Publisher indemnify Developer?
   1. Law suits concerning the quality of the program?
C. What are the dollar limits to the above indemnifications?

Section XII—Copyrights

A. Who is responsible for copyrighting the program?

Section XIII—Contract Termination

A. Who can terminate the contract?
   1. Why can this be done?
   2. How can this be done?
B. What, if any, contract provisions will survive termination?

Section XIV—Arbitration

A. Do the parties want binding arbitration to govern contract disputes?

Section XV—Source-Code Escrow

Section XVI—General

A. Everything that was not included above.
B. What happens if either party dies or goes under?

Attachments

1. Program description.
2. Delivery timetable (if too complex to fit in main body of contract).
3. Manual description (if too complex to fit in main body of contract).
4. Royalty scales (if too complex to fit in main body of contract).

If you just read Chapter 6, you may be surprised to learn that a royalty agreement is so much more complicated than a work-for-hire agreement. But when you consider it, there is a good reason for the difference in complexity. A work-for-hire contract is little more than an employment contract under which the employer buys out the programmer's interest in the program for either a lump sum or a salary. Once the publisher owns the program that's all there is to it. In contrast, a license agreement establishes an ongoing business relationship. It defines this relationship between publisher and programmer, and it provides the mechanism for resolving future problems if they arise. As you may imagine, the license agreement is longer and more detailed than the work-for-hire contract.

THE LICENSE (OR ROYALTY) CONTRACT IN DETAIL

Let's begin by reviewing the principal clauses in a license contract as well as some of the possible variations. You may want to skim this section for a general picture and reread it later for the specifics. You will find that, while much of what follows requires attention to detail, none of it is truly difficult.

SECTION I—INTRODUCTION

Here is a one-sentence introduction, which is all you really need:

I. Introduction

This is a licensing agreement between John Peterson (Developer) and First-ware, Inc. (Publisher) in which Developer grants Publisher certain rights in the software program Space Race (Program).

Here is another way of saying the same thing. Feel free to choose the version that appeals to you.

I. Introduction

This is a licensing contract between program developer John Peterson, referred to herein as Developer, who owns and has the right to grant licenses in certain computer software, and Firstware Inc., referred to herein as Publisher, who desires to acquire a license to use and market such software. The software that is the subject of this agreement is known as Space Race, but shall be referred to in this agreement as Program.

There is no legal difference between these two introductions, just a stylistic difference. I include both to show that there is no single way of saying something in a contract. The best way is the way that makes sense to both parties. So don't feel you have to copy my style if it isn't yours. What matters most is that the meaning is clear.

SECTION II—DEFINITIONS

In many contracts there is no need for a section of definitions because all meanings are sufficiently clear. However, it never hurts to include them if there is a suspicion that you and the people you are contracting with are saying the same words but understanding them differently. If in doubt, you should always write it down. Here are some sample definitions that might be found in a contract. I am sure yours will be different.

II. Definitions

A. *"Derivative work" shall mean a work that is based on one or more preexisting works and that, if prepared without permission of the program owner, would constitute a copyright infringement.*

B. *"Supporting documentation" shall mean information that describes the format, organization, and content of machine-readable diskettes to be supplied to Publisher under the terms of this contract.*

C. *"Manual" shall mean an instruction manual designed to teach an inexperienced user how to operate the Program.*

D. *"Section" shall mean a part of this agreement that is preceded by a Roman numeral.*

E. *"Clause" shall mean a subpart of this agreement that is preceded by an uppercase Arabic letter.*

One definition that usually should be included in this section is the meaning of "net sales." Net sales can be either the money actually received by the publisher for the sale of a program or the dollar amount charged for a program. This is an instance where a difference of a few words can mean thousands of dollars when the royalty amount is based on net sales. More about this important point will be mentioned later in this chapter. Here are two alternatives:

F. *"Net sales" shall mean the money actually received by the Publisher minus freight, allowances, and returns.*

G. *"Net sales" shall mean the amount billed by Publisher for orders of the Program minus freight, allowances, and returns.*

Remember that the point of a definition is not to arrive at the true definition of a term but at a mutually agreeable definition for the purposes of the contract. For example, one person might think that "documentation" means flowcharts and program notes, but another person might think it means a user manual. Neither is necessarily right—all that matters is that the parties to the contract agree on one meaning for the purposes of the contract.

SECTION III—ITEMS PROVIDED BY DEVELOPER

This section describes what the program developer has to supply to the publisher in order to satisfy the terms of the contract. Maintenance and support are dealt with in section V of the agreement. In legal jargon "Items Provided by Developer" is often called the deliverables section because it contains what the developer has to deliver. If the program already exists, it is usually sufficient to describe it by name and to incorporate by reference a copy of the manual or specification sheet describing its functions. If, however, the program is yet to be written, I prefer to describe what will be developed in a detailed attachment to the contract. This keeps the contract from becoming cluttered with pages of technical specifications. Here are some sample approaches:

III. Items Provided by Developer

A. *Developer shall furnish Publisher a computer-copiable program in object form. This program shall be the Space Race program as it is described in Attachment A.*

Attachment A is discussed in detail later in this chapter.

III. Items Provided by Developer

A. *Developer shall furnish Publisher a computer-copiable program in object form. This program shall be the JunkMail program as it currently exists for the TRS-80 computer. The Program shall have all the features and perform all the functions described in the JunkMail manual, which is incorporated herein by reference.*

The above clause is valuable because it forces the program to live up to its manual. But be sure the manual is thorough. If it is not, include any omitted features as an additional attachment. If the developer has to supply documentation, the following clause may be used.

B. *Developer shall furnish Publisher one set of Developer Computer Program Supporting Documentation, as described in Attachment I.*

Sometimes the publisher will want other items besides the program or documentation. The following clause obligates the developer to provide the results of items like marketing studies that may have been commissioned. In addition, if the program has been advertised by the programmer before the publisher takes it over, the publisher would also want this material.

C. *Developer shall furnish Publisher with any available performance data, productivity data, and economic (marketing) data. At Publisher's request, Developer shall also supply samples of existing advertising, training, or sales material that may aid Publisher in marketing the Program. Notwithstanding the provisions of this clause, Developer shall not be required to furnish nor shall Publisher be allowed to use the advertisement for Program appearing in the July 1981 issue of* Gulp *magazine.*

Notice the last sentence of the preceding sample. It allows the developer to exempt certain things from inclusion in the contract.

Example

Before signing a contract with Firstware John had hired an ad agency to do an advertisement for Space Race that featured Jackie, his wife, standing on a flying saucer in a skimpy mylar flight suit. Jackie never signed a model release and was never paid. She has since divorced John and entered law school. In this situation John would be wise to exempt this ad from the contract.

There are other items that may need to be covered in this section. If the developer has to supply a manual, the source code, source-code documentation, a special copy program, or anything else, it should be written into the deliverables section. Also if the developer is to be the only one with access to the source code, stipulate that in writing here.

Section IV—DELIVERY SCHEDULE

This section sets out a schedule for the delivery of the program and any other items. If the program already exists and can simply be handed over, the delivery schedule can be incorporated into the body of the contract. However, if the program or anything else to be delivered doesn't exist yet and if the delivery schedule is complex, an attachment might be in order.

IV. Delivery Schedule

A. *Developer shall deliver to Publisher at 2555 Virginia Street, Twenty-nine Palms, Maine, all items to be furnished under Section III of this agreement on or before January 3, 1983.*

IV. Delivery Schedule

A. *Developer shall provide all items to be furnished under Section III of this agreement according to the time schedule set out in Attachment II, which is hereby incorporated into this agreement.*

SECTION V—MAINTENANCE, MODIFICATION, AND TRAINING

The type of software usually will dictate what should appear in this section of your contract. For example, if the program is a game and the developer is willing to part with the source code, the publisher may expect nothing in the way of maintenance, modification, or training from the developer. But if the program is designed for business use or is a language or operating system, it is likely the publisher will want to have the technical expertise of the developer available. How much of this the developer is obligated to provide at no extra cost to the publisher is up to the two parties.

The maintenance, modification, and training section comprises three clauses. Let's consider them one at a time.

V. Maintenance, Modification, and Training

A. *For a period of twelve months after January 5, 198x, if Publisher notifies Developer of program error(s) or Developer has other reason to believe that error(s) exist(s) in the Program, Developer shall use his/her best efforts to verify and fix the error(s) within fourteen working days after notification. If a verified error cannot be fixed within fourteen days, Developer shall devote five hours per day toward correcting the error until the error has been corrected. Developer shall promptly notify Publisher if an error cannot be verified within a reasonable time. Error corrections shall be machine-readable and shall be such that Publisher can update the Program immediately.*

This clause specifies the number of months the developer is required to maintain the program after the contract has been signed. Sometimes this is a short period, sometimes the period lasts as long as, or even longer than, the program license. This sample clause only obligates the developer to use his "best efforts." Another publisher may want more, such as a guarantee that the program will be fixed within two weeks even though the reality of the industry is that some bugs are very elusive and could conceivably take months to verify, let alone fix.[1] A programmer or developer who guarantees to fix a yet-to-be-disclosed bug within a certain number of days or weeks is either foolish or crazy. All that a programmar can do is promise what's possible, or, in the language of the sample clause, "use his/her best efforts." "Best efforts" means just that. That there is no penalty should not lead the developer to be lax in his response. A publisher who discovers that the developer is out shooting pool instead of trouble-shooting couldn't be criticized much for rescinding the contract with, or stopping the payment of royalties to, the developer.

Now that you have decided who is responsible and how long is required for fixing bugs, the question becomes: Who pays for the expense of a recall? The publisher is usually the one to send out the updates that fix program errors. Without an agreement, however, there is no set rule on who pays for this. Fortunately, the issue rarely arises since there are very few "pure" recalls. Publishers frequently add an improvement or two to the program at the same time as they fix bugs. The user is charged an update fee—typically not much more than the cost of production and mailing. This way neither the programmer nor the publisher is severely burdened with the cost of fixing a bug. The consumer pays for it, but in return receives an enhanced program at modest cost. Even though publishers are usually willing to accept the responsibility of quality control, when a recall is due to programming error the developer will sometimes be charged as much as the dollar equivalent of royalties already received or still payable. My feeling is that recalling a program is a business risk that the publisher should assume. After all, the publisher owes it to his users to test a program thoroughly before marketing it. If a publisher and programmer get into an argument over who must pay for bugs, it may be settled by rewarding the person who takes the responsibility with a slightly more favorable royalty deal. In this way the person who takes the risk is compensated.

> B. *Publisher shall assume financial and legal responsibility for the quality, reliability, and accuracy of the Program and shall pay all expenses associated with any recalls or updates.*

An alternative sample may read:

> B. *Actual costs incurred as a result of program recalls that are not the fault of the Publisher shall be charged to the Developer. Actual costs shall include materials costs, postage, printing, and labor directly associated with a recall. Publisher's right to collect costs shall be limited as follows: the actual costs recoverable shall not exceed the total amount of royalties already paid or still owing on the software that is the subject of the recall. To collect these costs the Publisher must charge them against future royalty payments due on the software that is the subject of this contract.*

The next sample clause in this section has to do with enhancements or modifications to the program. There are several possibilities.

One approach is to obligate the programmer to provide any improvements to the program at no charge. Notice that the programmer is not obligated to write enhancements or improvements. If the programmer chooses to write them, however, it must be at no charge.

> C. *For a period of thirty-six months after January 23, 198x, Developer shall supply at no charge to Publisher any Program enhancements that improve performance, utility, or existing syntax, and that improve or reduce storage requirements.*

This clause is fairly common, especially in nonexclusive licenses. Let's analyze its logic carefully. At first glance it may seem that the programmer has the short end of the stick. The clause does say that any enhancements will be done gratis. Why should the programmer agree to this? Primarily because improvements help sell the program and increase its market life. This benefits both publisher and programmer. Therefore, there are many instances when a programmer will happily write an enhancement at no cost to the publisher in the hope of being paid back in increased sales. Despite this logic, however, there are times when a programmer is unwilling to do an enhancement without being paid. Perhaps the programmer has other priorities or simply doesn't want to bear the entire cost of the additional programming. I recommend that you don't do any programming without first discussing the proposed improvement with the publisher. Remember, the programmer is not obligated to do any specific enhancement.

A publisher who is lukewarm about the value of an improvement might say, "It looks real nice, go ahead and do it if you want. But since I don't think it will increase sales, we won't pay you extra for it." At this point you decide whether to do the improvement on your own or to shelve the idea.[2]

An alternative in dealing with modifications is the time-and-materials approach, in which the programmer agrees to do any improvements for a flat hourly rate plus the cost of materials. Here is a sample:

> C. Programmer shall write Program enhancements at Publisher's request at the rate of $35 per hour. This hourly rate shall remain in effect for twenty-four months after the date of this Agreement. Thereafter, Programmer shall write Program enhancements at Publisher's request for $50 per hour. Programmer's obligations under this clause shall terminate forty-eight months after the date of this agreement.

This alternative will work for enhancements that are minor or whose scope is easily defined. As a practical matter, however, any large-scale enhancement will have to be renegotiated since no publisher in his right mind would agree to a totally open-ended development project at an hourly rate.

Here is an alternative that works only when the publisher has the source code. It allows the publisher to carry out modifications, including enhancements, but gives the developer the first crack at the job.

> C. Publisher shall have the right to make Program enhancements subject to Developer's approval. Publisher may charge the cost of these enhancements against royalties due to Programmer from the sale of the enhanced program. Before initiating any enhancement, Publisher shall offer Developer the right to do the enhancement at Developer's expense. The Developer retains the right to veto any proposed enhancement.

The above alternative merely sets the ground rules for approaching an enhancement agreement. If the details are complicated, another contract will have to be worked out later. One cannot provide for every possible contingency. Contracts that try to settle every potential issue are invariably long and complex. What's more, the odds increase that there will be contradictory or inconsistent language somewhere in the fine print. Contract writing always involves a trade-off between trying to cover every contingency and having an agreement that is understandable.

The last alternative to handling modifications is to give the publisher carte blanche with the program. That means the developer simply turns over the source code and lets the publisher do with it what he will. Here is the clause that will accomplish this:

> C. Publisher has the right to modify the Program in any way consistent with improving its marketability at Publisher's expense.

The last clause of the maintenance, modification, and training section obligates the developer, at the request of the publisher, to provide training for a specified fee and reimbursement of expenses. Most license agreements do not need this clause.

> D. Should Publisher request training in the use of the Program, Developer shall be paid actual travel expenses and $225 per day for each of Developer's employees who furnish such training.

SECTION VI—THE LICENSE

The license section is the heart of a royalty agreement. It defines exactly what the publisher can do with the developer's program. As you will remember, the existence of the license is the fundamental difference between a royalty agreement and a work-for-hire agreement. Under a license agreement the developer remains the owner of the program and the publisher, the owner of a license which, under certain conditions, allows the program to be marketed. These conditions are entirely dependent on the contract between the publisher and the developer, and can vary dramatically.

The rights that a license confers upon the publisher falls into three broad categories:

1. Subject matter of the license
2. Duration of the license
3. Scope or extent of the license

Let's look at each category separately. The discussion that follows is fairly detailed. In contrast, you will be pleasantly surprised by the brevity of the license itself—most of them are less than a page. It is important to go slowly here because each clause or subpart of the license is a negotiation crossroads that present several paths to choose from. Although Huck Finn found that spitting in his hand was as good a means as any for deciding which path to take, I recommend a less spontaneous approach.

1. Subject matter of the license

This part describes exactly what is being licensed. In most cases it is a program. Sometimes a trademark or a manual are also subjects of the license. It is unnecessary to get into long, elaborate descriptions of the program here, because you have already described the subject of the license in detail in the section "Items to be supplied by Developer."

2. Duration of the license

In addition to identifying the subject, the license should also clearly state how long it lasts. In this respect a publisher is like a leasehold tenant who may use a building for a specified length of time. Two things can cause a license to expire. Either it can expire from old age (like a two-year lease at the end of two years) or it can expire prematurely because certain conditions have not been met by the publisher (perhaps the publisher promised 10,000 sales per year but managed only 3000, or perhaps a lease specified "no dogs" and the tenant ran a kennel on the property). Whatever the reason, when a license expires the rights to the program revert to the programmer. Again this is a key difference between a royalty agreement and a work-for-hire agreement, since under the latter there are no rights to revert to the programmer; they have all been sold to the publisher.

A question frequently asked by programmers is how long a license they should agree to? While most publishers traditionally favor long licenses, many programmers instinctively demand short ones. This is a situation where creative contract-writing can satisfy both parties' concerns without putting a damper on sales. First let's look at the publisher's concerns.

A one- or two-year license gives a publisher the right to market a program for only a short time. After that the publisher has nothing unless a new license is negotiated. If the publisher has a longer time to market the program, recovering an investment in marketing expenses and making a profit are far more likely. Therefore publishers want as much time to sell the software as they can get. In fact many publishers won't consider licenses of less than four or five years—the period they consider to be the useful marketing life of a program. If a publisher does reluctantly accept a short license, you can be sure that less will be done to promote the program than if the publisher had been granted a long license.

Now let's look at the length of a license from a different perspective—the programmer's. What the programmer wants immediately is compensation for months of unpaid programming. Fearing that the publisher may do an inadequate job selling their software, programmers in this situation are often reluctant to grant a long license.

Here is a programmer who carried this reasoning a couple of steps further:

Example

Betty Binary gave her publisher only a short license, thinking the publisher would establish a name for the program and, when the rights reverted to her, she would sell the program herself and, based on the publisher's groundwork, make a fortune. The publisher, however, saw through this scheme and refused to settle for less than a thirty-year term. An impasse was reached and Betty the programmer became Betty the publisher. She has sold some of her programs, but not as many as the program, which is quite good, deserves. The publisher, in the meantime, signed up another program and put his promotional resources behind it.

Most programmers probably don't want to go into the publishing business, but many do want a short-term license, believing that if a program does very well they can negotiate a higher royalty later. This "free-agent" reasoning works about the same for programmers as it does for baseball players or opera singers. If your program is a best-seller, you will be able to negotiate a higher royalty. If your program isn't a bomb, but doesn't quite live up to everyone's expectations (many programs fit this category), the publisher either will drop the program when the short-term license expires or will want to lower your royalty percentage. A good many opera singers and ballplayers who look so promising at the start of a season end up in the chorus or on the bench, wishing they had signed a long-term contract when they had a choice.

Now let's see how some creative contract-drafting can allay the fears of programmer and publisher and simultaneously motivate both parties to do their best for the success of the venture. For instance, instead of limiting the length of the license, allow the publisher as much time as he wants to sell the program. Then you can motivate him to really push your program by including a clause in the royalties section (discussed below) that guarantees you a minimum royalty level. A publisher who doesn't quite manage to meet an agreed-upon sales quota is faced with the choice of making up the monetary difference (in the hope of selling more programs next quarter) or returning the license to the programmer.

Now that we've dealt with the fear of the publisher proving inadequate, let's speak about a more pleasant concern of the programmer's—that a program is a runaway bestseller, but the royalty rate has been set too low. Again, rather than trying to solve this problem by limiting the length of the license in order to attain a sort of free-agent status, it makes more sense to negotiate a royalty rate based on a sliding scale: the more programs sold, the higher the royalty rate. This allows the publisher to recoup expenses early while still allowing the programmer to benefit from an extraordinarily successful program. We will discuss this in detail in the royalty section of this chapter.

It's worth repeating that neither the programmer nor the publisher should ever make it hard for the publisher to justify spending time and money to market the program. A good contract is one that is a strong motivation to both parties to sell as many programs as possible.

Scope or extent of the license

The third area that a license may cover involves any limitations upon where and how the publisher can sell the program. In some contracts there are no limitations, but many others do limit the publisher's sales activities in one or more of the following areas:

- Geography
- Market segment
- Hardware

GEOGRAPHICAL LIMITATIONS

Despite my general predilection toward allowing the publisher latitude, there are often legitimate reasons for strictly limiting the scope of the license as it relates to markets. For example, there is certainly no point in granting a worldwide license to a U.S. publisher that has no dealers in Iceland. It would be far better to grant the publisher only the U.S. rights. Then translate the program into Icelandic and fly to Reykjavik to find a good publisher to market it there. This example is not so frivolous as it might appear. The overseas market for software is expanding rapidly. Germany, the United Kingdom, and Japan are showing great interest in programs. Granting worldwide licenses without the assurance that your program will be marketed worldwide can be like throwing away money.

MARKET-SEGMENT LIMITATIONS

Besides limiting your license geographically, you may also want to limit the markets that the publisher can sell to.

Example

Suppose that *DataBase,* a complex database program, sells best only after a first-rate demonstration in a computer store. You, the programmer, are very much concerned that *DataBase* be demonstrated in as many retail computer stores as possible. To help attain this you may wish to prohibit the publisher from selling *DataBase* directly to the public via mail order.

At first glance this might seem an unnecessary limitation. Why not try to sell as many programs as possible to all comers? The reason is that if the retailers learn the publisher is dealing directly with the public and thereby undercutting their sales, many retailers will refuse to stock the program. There is, from their point of view, no reason to support a publisher that doesn't support them. Since the industry is still relatively small, if even one retail chain won't carry your program, it can mean the loss of a fortune.

As the industry grows, the aforementioned reason for limiting your license may lose significance. But other reasons will appear. If the software publishing industry follows the book industry (where hardback and softcover rights are often divided), you may want to limit one publisher to retail markets, another to educational markets, and still others to rental or network markets. Think especially about the impact of networks.

HARDWARE LIMITATIONS

The last way of limiting a license deals with which machine(s) the publisher can sell the program for. A rough analogy can be found in the film industry. The producer (publisher) of a videotape for television doesn't necessarily own the screen rights and the play rights to the same story. These rights usually are negotiated for on an individual basis. Similarly, you may wish to license a particular publisher to sell programs for the Apple II computer but not for TRS-80 or Horizon computers.

Software publishers tend to have their own specialties. Some of them concentrate on Apples, others on Pets, and still others on CP/M-compatible computers. Therefore unless a programmer is convinced that a particular software publisher will do a credible job in marketing the program for all computers, it makes sense to limit the license to include only those computers that the publisher can handle well. Then look for another publisher to handle the others. If you don't have any luck finding other publishers, you can always expand the license of the first, who isn't likely to complain.

Sometimes publishers, especially large ones, are unwilling to publish a program without an exclusive contract to market it worldwide for use on all hardware. Even though this means that no one else can publish the program, you might want to accept this kind of contract if you feel the publisher will represent your program well in all or most markets. Don't be dogmatic. If the publisher doesn't have a distributor in Iceland but very much wants a worldwide license and is strong in England and West Germany, you might be wise to concede the Icelandic issue (unless of course your program predicts glacial movement). If you have any doubts, though, shop around a little. The biggest software publisher in the world has been quite happy to obtain nonexclusive licenses to market various well-known programs. Hardware manufacturers in particular should not be overlooked. They are searching for programs to run on their machines and don't in the least mind the same programs running on other computers as well. To be able to offer brand name software helps them sell more hardware.

Sometimes a publisher will ask not only for the right to publish your program but also for the exclusive right to sublicense others to do the same.

Example

Firstware demands the right to sublicense JunkMail to other publishers or hardware manufacturers. If Tom grants Firstware this right, it will mean that Bigware, who also wants JunkMail for its new computer, will have to get its license from Firstware, not from Tom.

This area can be quite controversial if it is not expressly settled in the contract.

Example

Bigware approaches Firstware with the intent of sublicensing JunkMail. Since Tom's original agreement with Firstware was silent on the subject of sublicensing, Tom, feeling he could do better financially if he personally negotiated with Bigware, butts into the deal. While Tom and Firstware slug it out, Bigware, smelling the rank odor of a lawsuit, beats a retreat. The result is that Bigware doesn't get to publish JunkMail, and Tom and Firstware have lost a good business opportunity. Even worse perhaps is that they now hate each other.

This is too important a problem not to be solved in advance. You should include a clause that expressly forbids or allows sublicensing. How do you decide what is best? One point to consider is whether the publisher is getting an exclusive license for all types of hardware. If so, the programmer is precluded from sublicensing the program to other publishers. Therefore I can see no reason why a publisher should not be able to sublicense a program if the programmer cannot. On the other hand, if the license is nonexclusive or if the programmer wants to be able to sublicense the program, it might be best to prohibit the publisher from also being able to sublicense.

Assuming that the publisher has been granted the right to sublicense the program, what should the royalty terms be? If the publisher is essentially acting like a broker or an agent and is not incurring publishing costs related to the sublicense, naturally the publisher should get less money. How much less depends on the bargaining abilities of the parties. The publisher will rightfully argue that without the marketing and promotional expertise provided, the program would never have attained the fame that led to the proposed sublicense. The programmer will counter with the equally valid position that the publisher is acting like a broker and should receive a finder's fee, not a substantial profit. The correct position is, as usual, somewhere between the extremes. One possible approach is to invert the royalty percentages. In other words, if the programmer was receiving from the publisher a 20 percent royalty on net sales, and if the publisher then sublicenses the program, the programmer should receive 80 percent of the money from the sublicense agreement and the publisher a 20 percent royalty.

Now that you have a pretty good idea of what a license section should contain, let's look at some samples.

VI. Exclusive License

A. Developer hereby grants to Publisher a worldwide, exclusive license to market copies of the Program for use on all existing or yet-to-be-developed computers. This license shall include the right of Publisher to grant sublicenses to other parties subject to the section of this agreement titled "Royalties" and subject to the limitations of this license.

B. The license granted under clause A of this section shall begin January 4, 198x, and expire January 4, 199x.

C. Upon termination of this license for any reason all rights granted herein shall immediately revert to the Programmer.

D. Developer hereby reserves all rights in the Program not specifically granted by this license agreement.

The preceding license section is quite broad. It essentially gives the publisher the complete rights to the program for all machines, including machines that don't exist yet. In addition, it gives the publisher the power to sublicense the program to other publishers. By itself this license section offers the programmer very little protection. Therefore, any programmer who agrees to this sort of broad license should, for protection, write certain safeguards into the royalties section. I discuss how on page 101 of this chapter.

Here is a sample license section that grants the publisher the exclusive right to publish for a specific machine and also allows the programmer to license the program for other machines.

VI. License

A. Developer hereby grants to Publisher a worldwide, nonexclusive license to market copies of the Program for use on the Apple II computer only. Developer shall not market, or license others to market, Program for the Apple II for the duration of this license.

B. The license granted under clause A of this section shall start January 3, 198x, and shall expire January 3, 198x. Upon expiration or termination all rights granted under this license agreement shall revert to Developer.

Here is a sample of a nonexclusive license section:

VI. Nonexclusive license

A. Developer hereby grants to Publisher a worldwide, nonexclusive license to use, execute, reproduce, sell, lease, or otherwise transfer copies of the Program for use on the Apple II computer only.

B. The license granted under clause A of this section shall start January 3, 198x, and shall expire January 3, 198x. Upon expiration or termination all rights granted under this license agreement shall revert to Developer.

The above sample allows the publisher to publish the program for use on the Apple II computer on a nonexclusive basis. This means that the developer can negotiate with other publishers who may also want to publish for the Apple as well as with publishers who want to sell the program for use on other machines. However, I doubt whether there are many publishers who would be happy with this clause because it would force them to compete with other publishers for the same program on the same machine.

The following sample is a nonexclusive license for a certain geographical area or territory. Sometimes you may want to combine limitations on computers and territories. For example, you may wish to grant only a United Kingdom license for the Apple II.

VI. Nonexclusive License

A. Developer hereby grants to Publisher a nonexclusive license to market the Program within the United Kingdom only. Publisher shall refer sales and inquiries regarding the Program originating from outside the United Kingdom to Developer.

B. The license granted under clause A of this section shall start January 3, 198x, and shall expire January 3, 199x. Upon expiration or termination all rights granted herein shall revert to Developer.

The following sample is a combination of an exclusive license for Apples and a nonexclusive license for other machines.

VI. License

A. Developer hereby grants to Publisher:

1. An exclusive license to publish Program for use on Apple II computers.

2. A nonexclusive license to publish Program for use on computers other than Apple II.

B. The licenses granted under clause A of this section shall start January 3, 198x, and shall expire January 3, 198x. Upon expiration or termination all rights granted herein shall revert to Developer.

The trick to writing a good license section is to first outline exactly what rights you want to assign to the publisher and what rights you want to keep for yourself. Keep in mind the three main variables that we discussed earlier: duration, market segment, and hardware. Once you know what you want to do all that remains is to write it down. And don't forget to include whether the rights are assignable by the publisher. In the appendix to this book I have included a half-dozen sample clauses that you may use or adapt.

SECTION VII—ACCEPTANCE

The acceptance section is not absolutely necessary in all contracts. I recommend including it when the program that is the subject of the license has not been completed or when the publisher wants some time to test and evaluate the program before accepting it for publication.

VII. Acceptance

A. After Developer delivers Program, Publisher shall have thirty days to test Program. If Developer is not notified in writing within forty days of delivery of the Program that the Program is unacceptable, Publisher shall be deemed to have accepted the Program.

B. Publisher shall also be deemed to have accepted the Program if the Publisher makes Program available for sale.

C. If Publisher determines that Program is unacceptable, Publisher shall notify Developer in writing of what changes must be made in the Program to make it acceptable. Developer shall have forty-five days from receipt of the notification to make these changes. If they are not made within the forty-five day period, Publisher may terminate this agreement.

SECTION VIII—ROYALTIES

Finally, it is time to look at the royalties section of our license contract. To the programmer this is usually the most interesting section. There are three main issues that must be dealt with here:

1. How much should a programmer be paid?
2. When should royalty payments be made?
3. What happens if . . .?

In addition there are a few minor issues:

4. Advances
5. Dealer demos
6. Manuals
7. Inflation

1. How Much Should a Programmer Be Paid?

This is usually where all eyes are focused. In fact many programmers get so involved in this question that they lose their perspective and do not pay adequate attention to the rest of the contract. This can be a big mistake, as we will see.

There are two basic approaches to determining how much a programmer gets paid: either pay the programmer a percentage of the net sales price of each program sold, or pay the programmer a fixed amount of the selling price of each program sold.

Which approach is best? Both have their pros and cons. If you feel that the publisher should have maximum flexibility in setting the retail price, then you will ask for a percentage of sales. If you, on the other hand, want to have some control over the retail price, you will demand a fixed amount per sale. For example, if you are given a royalty of twenty-five dollars per program sold, you know that the publisher will not be selling the program for twenty-four dollars; in fact you can predict that the retail price of the program will be at least two-hundred dollars. If, however, you feel that the publisher should be able to set the price freely, adjusting it as the market dictates, you might ask for a 15 percent royalty based on net sales. Net sales are usually defined as the money received by the publisher. Therefore if the publisher sells the program for one-hundred dollars, you would receive a fifteen dollar royalty.

Programmers sometimes ask how they can avoid tieing the publisher's hands by demanding a fixed royalty and still protect themselves from a publisher who insists on selling programs cheaply? Or how can they deal with the publisher who is in effect giving away the programs? Remember, a percentage of nothing is nothing. But wait—since publishers aren't in the business of giving away software, can't you trust them to get the best price they can? This is generally true, but there are exceptions. For example, a publisher who is also a hardware manufacturer might sell software cheaply or even give it away in order to sell hardware. Similarly, it is conceivable that a publisher might give away one program with every purchase of another.

One way to minimize this kind of merchandising is to write a royalty section that guarantees a minimum fixed royalty payment on every program transferred but also contains a provision for a percentage.

Example

Tom demands a 15 percent royalty based on net sales with a $20 minimum for each program transferred. This means that if the program is sold for $100, Tom gets a $20 royalty, not a $15 royalty, as he would under a straight percentage. If the program is sold for $1000, Tom would receive a royalty of $150 (15 percent of 1000). In the unlikely event that the program is given away, Tom still gets $20 per program.

Naturally, the fixed minimum payment will be somewhat less than the programmer hopes to make from the percentage, but at least it guarantees some income if the program is being sold cheaply or given away. Here is a sample of this sort of clause:

VIII. Royalties

A. *In consideration for the rights and license granted by this agreement, and subject to the conditions set forth elsewhere in this agreeement, Publisher shall pay Developer as a royalty a sum equal to 15 percent of the net sales of the Program as defined in Section II of this agreement. Notwithstanding the aforementioned percentage, the minimum royalty amount to be paid shall be $30 per Program sold or otherwise transferred to a third party.*

It may surprise many programmers to learn that, depending on how net sales was defined in section II, a royalty clause can be heavily skewed in the publisher's favor. Notice that the royalty is based on "net sales of the Program actually received." Here is a case where two words can mean a difference of thousands of dollars. When negotiating for a programmer, I invariably insist upon the royalty's being based *not* on money received but on programs shipped. In other words, why should programmers have their royalties dependent on whether the publisher actually gets paid? Studies indicate that every month about 6 percent of the nation's computer stores close down or go bankrupt. An even larger number of them are very slow in paying their suppliers. A wise programmer will therefore try to put the burden of collecting the money on the publisher and will demand immediate payment for programs sold regardless of when the publisher is paid. This really isn't unfair. After all, who, between the publisher and the programmer, is the logical party to collect bad debts? It certainly isn't the programmer's job. I like to use the definition of net sales given earlier in this chapter. This definition is incorporated in the following sample, which specifies that the developer is paid whether or not the publisher collects.

VIII. Royalties

A. *Subject to the conditions expressed elsewhere in this agreement and in consideration for the rights and license granted herein, Publisher shall pay Developer a royalty of 20 percent of net sales of the Program as defined in Section II of this agreement.*

   Notwithstanding the aforementioned percentage, Publisher shall pay Developer a minimum royalty of $45 for each sale or transfer of the Program to third parties.

If for some reason the developer agrees to being paid only if the publisher gets paid, simply use the definition in section II which defines net sales as sales actually received. In this way the royalty section remains the same, and the definition section is the only one that changes.

In addition to combining percentage royalties with a minimum payment, the programmer and publisher may want to put the royalties on a sliding scale similar to the kind usually found in the book industry. To do this the same basic clause can be used, but instead of giving the programmer a flat percentage rate the percentage increases with the number of sales. Here is a sample:

VIII. Royalties

A. *In consideration for the rights and license granted herein, and subject to the conditions set forth elsewhere in this agreement, Publisher shall pay Developer a royalty based on a percentage of net sales, as defined in Section II of this agreement:*

   6% for the first 1000 programs sold or sublicensed,
   10% for the next 1000 programs sold or sublicensed,
   12% for the next 1000 programs sold or sublicensed,
   15% for the next 1000 programs sold or sublicensed.

   Notwithstanding the aforementioned percentage, Publisher shall pay Developer a minimum of $45 for each program sold or transferred.

In negotiating the percentages on the sliding scale, the publisher, seeking to recoup the investment as quickly as possible, will press for low initial percentages. The programmer may wish to accommodate the publisher if, in return, the publisher concedes to the programmer a larger advance or higher subsequent percentages.

2. When Should Royalty Payments Be Made?

After arriving at the royalty amount and deciding whether the amount is based on sales or on money actually received, the programmer is entitled to a small sigh of relief. But there are a couple of very important issues still to be considered, both of which are at the heart of protecting the programmer's interests and both of which can be fairly easily won. The first issue to be decided is exactly when the programmer is to be paid. Publishers in good times and bad have been notorious for borrowing from their authors—at *no* interest. This is accomplished by scheduling royalty payments at long intervals. Some publishers attempt to pay only once or twice a year. Meanwhile the publisher is enjoying the interest-free use of the programmer's money. In our inflationary economy, programmers, by not being paid more frequently, are taking a substantial cut from the real value of their royalty percentage.

How does one write a fair royalty payment clause? First let's define the term *accrue*. A payment is said to accrue when it becomes owing. For instance, suppose we have a royalty agreement based not on money received but on sales. The minute a sale takes place, a royalty accrues based upon the sale. But this doesn't mean the programmer can run over and collect his royalty. When a royalty accrues and when it is due to be paid are two different events. Naturally the programmer would love to be paid as soon as a program is sold. But for accounting purposes this is impractical. The question to be negotiated is, How soon after a royalty accrues is it reasonable to pay the programmer? Once a week? This, too, is impractical. Once a month? Maybe, but this is still a bit short since it will usually take the publisher more than thirty days to collect even from good accounts. Once every three months? This should be enough time for the publisher to collect his money and get his books together and, as a general rule, I recommend it. Once every six months? That's beginning to sound like an interest-free loan, but it might still be reasonable if it's based on the date the program was shipped by the publisher and not on when the publisher got paid. How about once a year? No! If the publisher insists on such an outrageous accrual period, then demand a proportionally higher royalty percentage, or charge interest, or both. There is no reason for programmers to finance publishers at no cost to the publisher. Here is a clause that I think is fair to both parties:

B. *Royalty payments for the preceding calendar quarter shall be made to Developer within forty-five days after the last day of each calendar quarter during the term of this agreement.*

3. What Happens If . . . ?

Now that we know how much is to be paid and when, there is one major issue and a few minor ones still to consider. First let's give the programmer certain guarantees. If the publisher has received a long license and a sliding royalty scale to recoup initial promotion costs, the developer, in return, should insist on a "what if" clause. What if the publisher can't sell many programs? What if the royalty payments are late? Here are some clauses to take care of these questions:

C. *Notwithstanding the provisions of this section, the minimum royalty payment to be made to Programmer every quarter shall be at least $8000. Should the royalties accrued be less than the amount in the preceding sentence, Publisher shall pay, in addition to the accrued royalties, the amount necessary to reach the minimum royalty payment. This additional amount, if paid, shall be regarded as nonrefundable compensation in addition to royalties and shall not be considered an advance on royalties.*

If the situation warrants, the minimum payment may be put on a sliding scale. For instance, the first-quarter minimum could be $2000 and all quarters thereafter $8000. Here is a sample:

C. *Notwithstanding the provisions of this section, minimum quarterly royalty payments shall be due as follows:*
First quarter — $2000
All quarters thereafter — $8000
Should royalties accrued on actual sales be less than the applicable minimum royalty payment, Publisher shall pay in addition to the accrued royalties the amount necessary to reach the minimum royalty payment. This additional amount, if paid, shall be regarded as nonrefundable compensation in addition to royalties and shall not be considered as an advance on royalties.

Clause D simply keeps publishers from dragging their feet in paying:

D. *If Publisher is more than thirty days late on any one payment, Developer may cancel the license granted in Section VI of this contract provided that Developer sends written notice by registered mail to Publisher of his intention to cancel and provided that Publisher does not make full payment within ten days of receipt of notice.*

4. Advances

As I mentioned earlier, there are a few more details to take care of. First is the question of advances. If the publisher is paying an advance, it should be recorded in this section of the agreement. Here is a sample:

E. *Upon execution of this agreement, Publisher shall pay Programmer a $3000 advance on royalties. No further royalty payments shall be made* *until the amount of royalties accrued exceeds the amount of the advance made under this clause.*

One issue to be settled here is whether the advance is refundable or nonrefundable. The question can arise if the publisher doesn't sell enough programs to cover the advance, but it more commonly arises if the advance is paid prior to delivery of the program and the program is ultimately unacceptable to the publisher. In the book business the royalty advance normally must be refunded if an acceptable manuscript is never submitted to the publisher; the risk of the book's not selling after the manuscript is accepted by the publisher is borne by the publisher. The developer and publisher must come to an agreement one way or another, but, unless the advance is huge, I wouldn't spend much time on a question that usually isn't important enough to fight over.

If you decide to make the advance nonrefundable, add the following sentence to clause E:

The advance on royalties shall be nonrefundable.

If, on the other hand, you decide to make the advance refundable, use the following:

The advance on royalties shall be refunded to the Publisher if this agreement should be terminated through no fault of Publisher before the royalties accrued or paid to Developer equal or exceed the amount of the advance. Any refund shall be paid by Developer within sixty days after Developer receives a written demand for payment from Publisher.

5. Dealer Demos—Royalty-free Copies

Next comes the question of dealer demos. I don't think the programmer should inhibit the publisher from distributing as many demos as is possible so long as they are genuine demos and not loss-leaders for another product. If the publisher charges a nominal fee (20 percent) or doesn't charge for them at all, I feel that the programmer should not be entitled to a royalty. However, the programmer would be wise to insist that all demos be labeled "Dealer Demo and Not For Resale." Here is a sample clause:

F. Notwithstanding the other clauses of this section, no royalties shall be paid for dealer demonstration programs. However, Publisher shall keep accurate records of the number of demos released, and all demos shall bear a label on the diskette and on the Manual that reads, "Dealer Demo and Not For Resale."

Another issue that is sometimes important is the number of royalty-free programs that the publisher may have for in-house and promotional use. This isn't as trivial a question as it might appear.

Example

Bigware is so big that it could easily use a few hundred in-house copies of JunkMail. Tom, the programmer, rightfully insists that he be paid royalties on all in-house copies except for a few, say fifty. If Bigware balks at this, Tom might offer a discount for in-house use.

Here is a sample clause:

G. Notwithstanding the other provisions of this section, Publisher shall be allowed fifty royalty-free copies of the Program for in-house use. A royalty payment of $15 shall be paid for each program after the fiftieth program that is put into in-house use.

6. Manuals

When the developer licenses the publisher to distribute a manual along with the program an additional royalty is rarely paid for the manual unless the manual is sold separately from the program. Here is a clause that takes care of this problem:

> H. *No royalties shall be paid to Developer for the sale of any Manuals unless they are sold or transferred independently of the Program. For each copy of the Manual transferred without a simultaneous transfer of a copy of the Program, Publisher shall pay Developer a royalty of $5.*

7. Inflation

The last clause in the royalty section is optional. It's for those contracts that are based on a set payment per sale rather than on a percentage. This clause allows the payment to increase with inflation. (A percentage royalty is theoretically inflation-proof since it increases automatically if the price of the program increases.)

> I. *The fixed-sum royalty amount set out in this section shall be fixed for a period of two years from the date of this agreement. Thereafter, Developer shall be paid an increased royalty should the Consumer Price Index (CPI) published by the Bureau of Labor Statistics of the U.S. Department of Labor increase. The increased royalty shall be computed as follows: On July 1 of each year starting with 198x and continuing for the life of this agreement, the royalty amount due to Developer shall be increased by the same percentage as the CPI measured on February 1 of that year increased over the CPI of February 1 of the previous year.*

You can see that the royalty section does far more than merely state the amount the developer is to be paid. It provides the structural balance to the license section and, if well drafted, can include many reasonable protections for the programmer that could not otherwise be obtained except at the risk of decreasing the publisher's motivation.

SECTION IX—ACCOUNTING

The accounting section simply spells out what records the publisher has to keep and what sort of access the developer is to have to them. All royalty contracts should have an accounting section. Oddly, very few developers take advantage of their right to inspect the records of the publisher. I think more should. While publishers in general are honest, you might be shocked at how poorly some keep records. Often inventory is only loosely accounted for if it's accounted for at all. Developers may find it well worth their while to occasionally scrutinize their publisher's records or to hire an accountant to do so. At the very least, you should familiarize yourself with the reporting methods used so that you will know if your royalty payment was based on a sound sales figure.

IX. *Accounting*

> A. *Publisher shall keep accurate records covering all transactions relating to Program sales and transfers. At the time each royalty payment is due, Publisher shall furnish Developer with a statement setting forth the number of Programs sold or sublicensed, the amount charged, and the net sales received. Developer and/or Developer's agent, upon giving five days written notice, shall have the right to inspect these records during business hours at Publisher's place of business. Developer agrees to sign or require agent to sign nondisclosure agreements obligating Developer and agent not to disclose matters that do not pertain to Developer or Program.*

If there might be some question about the meaning of "accurate records," the term should be explained fully. Here is a sample clause that does this. It may be added immediately after the one set out above.

> B. *Publisher's records shall accurately contain the following information.*
> 1. *The number of copies of the Program that have been sold or transferred to third parties or put into internal use by Publisher.*
> 2. *The number of copies of the Manual sold or transferred to third parties without simultaneous transfer of a copy of the Program.*
> 3. *The number of copies of the Program marked "Not for Resale" or "Dealer Demo" and put into use internally or provided to third parties.*
> 4. *The net sales amounts received from sale of the Program.*

Don't be afraid of deleting or adding to the preceding sample clause. Number 2, for example, should be deleted if a manual is not being licensed along with the program. Number 4 should be deleted if the royalty is a fixed amount instead of a percentage of sales.

SECTION X—WARRANTIES

The warranty section is usually fairly straightforward. A warranty in this context is a promise or guarantee by the developer. The publisher usually will want the developer to make two or three such promises. While theoretically the warranties are separate promises, they are often bundled into one clause. For example, in clause A the developer promises that the program being licensed to the publisher does indeed belong to the developer and that the license does not infringe anyone else's rights. This is to protect the publisher from the possibility of the developer owning only part, or perhaps none, of the program. It is possible that the developer has already licensed part of the rights to the program to another publisher or that the developer had a partner who is now being conveniently ignored.

A. *Developer warrants that Developer has the legal right to grant Publisher the license as set out in Section VI of this agreement and that such license does not infringe any third parties' property or personal rights.*

The next clause warrants that there are no lawsuits pending against the developer for copyright infringement and that the program has not been published in a way that might cause it to lose its copyright.

B. *Developer warrants that there are no pending lawsuits concerning any aspect of the Program and that the Program has not been published in such a way as to lose any of its copyright protection.*

The third warranty clause is optional but can be the most important. It is a promise that the program does everything the developer has claimed it will do. I advise developers to avoid signing this kind of warranty, not because the developer doesn't believe in the program's quality, but because it is impossible to be certain that any program is perfect. The publisher should test the software carefully and ascertain whether it performs properly. Some publishers, however, require this warranty. If this is the case, the developer will have to decide whether to sign the warranty or to find another publisher.

C. *Developer warrants that the Program is fully functional and that it will reliably perform to the standard described in Section III of this agreement.*

Warranties are often construed to be at the heart of a contract. What this means is that if the developer warrants one thing or another and it turns out to be false, the publisher may in many situations be able to void the entire contract. Because of this, it is important not to regard the warranties as boilerplate but as material to be carefully read and evaluated.

SECTION XI—INDEMNIFICATION

There are usually two clauses in an indemnification section. The first obligates the developer to pay the legal fees of the publisher if someone should sue the publisher, claiming that the program has infringed their rights. The persons most likely to sue are other developers or publishers who claim the software is really a theft of their program. This is not much to worry about if the developer is honest. Occasionally, however, problems arise if a former employee of the developer claims to be the true owner of the program. This situation can be avoided by carefully following the work-for-hire procedures in Chapter 6. Some developers balk at agreeing to indemnify the publisher. I don't blame them. However, it is logical that this should be the developer's responsibility because, after all, the publisher has no way of knowing whether the developer came by the program honestly.

XI. Indemnification

A. *Provided that Publisher promptly notifies Developer of all claims, Developer shall defend Publisher against claims that the Program infringes a patent, copyright, trade secret, or other property right of a third party and shall pay the resultant court costs, legal fees, and any damages finally awarded, up to the amount of royalties received or accrued for the Program as of the date of the award or settlement is paid.*

Notice that in the above sample there is a limit on the dollar amount the developer has to spend indemnifying the publisher. The amount is limited by how much money (royalties) has been received or accrued on the program as of the date the claim is paid. I feel this is a sensible limit and a good way of balancing risks.

Example

Fred sues Firstware. His suit claims that Tom stole JunkMail from him and, as a result, Firstware has no right to publish the program. Under the indemnification clause Tom must step in and pay to defend this lawsuit. How much does he have to pay? According to the preceding sample clause Tom has to pay only as much as the amount of the royalties he will have received from Firstware for the program up to the date that the award is paid. After that, Firstware has to take over.

The second indemnification clause obligates the publisher to defend the developer against suits relating to the quality of the program. This means that if someone sues the developer because the program failed and caused substantial damages, the publisher has to pay for the lawsuit and for any damages. Again, there is a limit on how much must be paid. I think it's logical that the publisher should be responsible for the quality of the program. The publisher should test the program, and before it's marketed all warranties to the end user should be properly disclaimed. Since these factors are not in the control of the developer, it makes sense that the publisher should take responsibility for the quality of the program. If publishers are worried about possible legal exposure, they should take out insurance. (See Chapter 11.)

Developers: beware some publishers are now trying to shift indemnification relating to the quality of programs over to you.

Here is a sample of the second indemnification clause:

> B. *Publisher shall indemnify and defend Developer against any claim regarding the quality of the Program up to the total dollar amount received for sale of the Program less the amount of royalties actually paid as of the date the claim is settled or the award paid.*

You may wonder what would happen if, in the above example, Tom really had stolen JunkMail and a court had ordered Firstware to pay Fred damages. Firstware could then withhold all royalty payments and also sue Tom directly for the damages it incurred as a result of Tom's fraud. This might include the damages done to Firstware's reputation. As for a situation in which Tom is sued by a user who experienced damages because of a defect in the program, Firstware's responsibility to indemnify Tom is only up to the amount of net sales minus royalties paid (clause B).

SECTION XII—COPYRIGHTS

The copyright section is routine. It specifies the name that will appear on the copyright notice and requires that someone (usually the publisher) file the material necessary to register the copyright. I discussed how to register a copyright in detail in Chapter 3. The copyright section of the contract also allows the publisher to sue infringers on behalf of the developer, and it obligates the developer to cooperate in supplying anything that's needed to register the copyright.

XII. Copyrights

> A. *All copies of the Program or Manual shall contain an appropriate copyright notice in the name of the Developer.*
>
> B. *If the Program or Manual has not been registered previously in the U.S. Copyright Office, Publisher will register the aforementioned items within thirty days of publication in the name of the Developer. Developer hereby authorizes Publisher to act as Developer's agent for the purpose of registration. Developer shall perform all acts necessary to enable Publisher to register, including signing necessary documents and supplying printouts of the first and last twenty-five pages of the object code of the Program.*
>
> C. *Developer shall enforce its copyrights against infringers or shall authorize Publisher to do so at Publisher's expense.*

The above section includes a provision for the copyright of the manual. If this need not be included in your contract, omit any mention of the manual.

SECTION XIII—TERMINATION

The main reason for a termination section is to tell both parties when and how their contract can be ended and what the consequences of its ending are. Keep in mind, however, that there are situations where your contract will end independent of a termination section. A three-year license, for example, is over when the three years are up—there is no need for any further termination procedure.

When can a party terminate a contract? One occasion is when the other party has committed a breach of contract. A minor breach, however, is not enough to terminate a contract. The breach must be material. A payment that's late by a day or two is a minor, not a material, breach of contract. A payment late by some months, however, would probably be sufficiently material to justify termination. Other reasons to terminate will be found within the contract itself. Minimum sales requirements that have not been met is one reason. If there is a disagreement about whether a breach is minor or material, the party not wanting the termination is likely to take the matter to arbitration or, if there is no arbitration section of the contract, to court.

It's important to realize that merely because a contract is terminated does not mean that all contractual relations between the parties come to an immediate end. Provisions such as payment of accrued royalties, warranties, and indemnification continue and are said to "survive" the contract termination. In addition, the parties may also want to work out an agreement whereby the publisher can sell whatever programs remain in stock.

XIII. Termination

A. *Either party shall have the right to terminate this agreement in the event that the other party commits a material breach of its obligations. Intent to terminate shall be made by a written notice, sent by certified mail to the breaching party, that sets forth the details of the breach. Termination shall become effective thirty days from the date that the notification of intent to terminate was mailed, unless the breaching party has corrected the breach prior to that thirty-day period.*

B. *Notwithstanding clause A above, termination shall be effective immediately if one or more of the following events occurs:*

   1. *A petition of bankruptcy is filed by or against Publisher.*

   2. *Publisher ceases through no fault of Developer to make Program available to buyers for more than thirty consecutive days.*

   3. *Publisher announces that it intends to cease publishing Program.*

C. *Notwithstanding termination of this agreement, the following obligations and rights shall continue in full force:*

   1. *All warranties under the section titled "Warranty" and obligations under the sections titled "Indemnification" and "General" shall survive and continue to bind the parties for five years after the date of termination.*

   2. *Persons and companies who obtained the Program prior to termination shall continue to have the right to use the Program.*

   3. *Publisher shall honor any remaining obligations under the section of this agreement titled "Royalties."*

   4. *Publisher may continue, under the terms of this agreement, to sell copies of the Program and Manual in existence prior to the mailing of the notice of termination.*

When does termination become effective? The preceding sample allows a thirty-day grace period to correct the breach. The length of this period is the decision of the parties. It should be long enough, however, so that any bona fide miscommunications can be cleared up and termination avoided. If you decide not to allow the publisher to see existing stock, omit clause C(4). If the manual is not a subject of the license, omit the word *manual* from clause C(4).

SECTION XIV—ARBITRATION

I discussed the pros and cons of arbitration in Chapter 4. The following general arbitration clause may be used by people who want to have arbitrators decide any contractual disputes.

XIV. *Arbitration*

Any dispute relating to the interpretation or performance of this agreement shall be resolved at the request of either party through binding arbitration. Arbitration shall be conducted in (city), (state), in accordance with the then-existing rules of the American Arbitration Association. Judgment upon any award by the arbitrators may be entered by the state or federal court having jurisdiction. The parties intend that this agreement to arbitrate be irrevocable.

SECTION XV—SOURCE-CODE ESCROW

Often the developer does not want to give the source code to the publisher. Perhaps the publisher won't take the security measures necessary for the preservation of a trade secret. Or perhaps the publisher doesn't want employees "contaminated" with a trade secret (see Chapter 2). Unfortunately, even though it might make sense to the programmer to deny the publisher the source code, this denial can cause the publisher problems. What happens, for instance, if the developer disappears and the program needs maintenance? Maintenance at the object-code level is next to impossible. A wise publisher, therefore, either will require the developer to provide a documented copy of the source code or will require the developer to put the source code where it can be reached in an emergency. Sometimes this means putting the source code in escrow. Escrow in this context means a safe place where the publisher can't get to it unless certain conditions are met. What are these conditions? One condition for a San Francisco developer might be if San Francisco falls into the Pacific. A more common condition could be if the developer dies, becomes incapacitated, or refuses to maintain the program.

An escrow section is purely optional and, unless you feel it's necessary, should be avoided. It requires finding someone who is willing to be an escrow agent—a task that opens the agent to certain potential liabilities. What happens, for example, if the agent accidentally releases the code to the wrong party or for the wrong reason? In finding an escrow agent, your best bet is to try your banker or someone else equipped to provide reasonable security. You may also try a land escrow company, though the ones I have talked to are not enthusiastic.

A good alternative to full-blown escrow is simply to agree to keep an updated copy of the source code in a safe-deposit box. Each party gets a key, but the publisher promises in writing not to use his key unless certain conditions occur. Of course, there is a certain amount of honor involved here, but if the publisher is going to cheat the developer there are easier and more profitable ways to do it than by stealing the source code. I recommend your using a safe-deposit box since it preserves trade secrecy yet is inexpensive and simple. If you don't trust each other enough to share a safe-deposit box, you shouldn't be doing business together.

XV. *Escrow*

A. *Within thirty days of delivery of the Program to Publisher, Developer shall place in the keeping of an independent third party one copy of the Program Source Code and Program Source-Code Documentation for the Program. The independent third party shall be the Bank of _____ located at _____.*

B. *For five years from the date of this agreement, Developer shall update the escrowed Program Source Code and Program Source-Code Documentation within thirty days of supplying Publisher with the object code for any Program updates.*

C. *Developer hereby grants Publisher a contingent license, subject to the conditions in this section, to use the source code for the purpose of maintaining the Program. This contingent license shall become effective only if Devel-*

oper, within five years of the date of this agreement, refuses or is otherwise unable to provide reasonable Program-maintenance support for Publisher. This contingent license shall continue for ten years from the date on which it becomes effective. Should the parties disagree on whether the Developer has refused or become unable to provide maintenance support for the Publisher, the matter shall be decided by binding arbitration as set out in the section titled, "Arbitration."

D. *Developer may terminate the escrow if this agreement is terminated through no fault of the Developer.*

E. *Publisher agrees to pay all fees necessary to maintain the escrow.*

F. *Both parties agree to enter into other terms and conditions with each other or with the third-party custodian of the source code as is necessary to effect the purpose of this section.*

G. *When the escrow terminates, Developer shall regain sole possession of the source code, subject to the provisions of clause C of this Section.*

H. *If the source code in escrow is released to Publisher, Publisher agrees not to publish or disseminate the source code without Developer's written consent.*

Several points have to be negotiated and settled in this escrow section.

- How many days after the contract is signed does the developer have to place the source-code escrow. I put thirty days because this seems reasonable, but it's up to you. (See clause A.)

- Each time the object code is updated, a new copy of the source code has to be sent to the place of escrow. For how many years does the developer have to do this? (See clause B.) And how much time does the developer have to do it in?

- What has to happen before the publisher gets access to the source code? (See clause C.) Once the publisher has access to it, how long may the code be kept?

- Who has to pay the escrow fees? (See clause E.) The sample states that the publisher has to pay fees. However, the developer could pay the fees, or they could be split.

- Clause F obligates the parties to enter into any other agreements that would effectuate this agreement. This is simply a good-faith promise because it is inconvenient to specify in detail all the escrow mechanics that will be worked out later.

- Clause H obligates the publisher not to publish or disseminate the source code. It is important to realize that even though the publisher is legally obligated under this clause, there is still a danger that the trade-secrecy status of the program will be lost if the publisher is careless. One way of dealing with this is to ask the publisher to sign a nondisclosure agreement requiring that the source code be kept secret. For any publishers willing to do this there is the nondisclosure agreement (NDA-3) in the back of this book that they may sign.

Now let's look at a sample section that eliminates the escrow officer and substitutes a safe-deposit box. As I mentioned, this is a streamlined, practical approach with a bit less safety than the full-blown escrow, but it should be adequate for many purposes.

XV. Source Code

A. *Within thirty days of the date of this agreement and for a period of five years thereafter, Developer shall keep a current copy of the Program Source Code and Documentation in a safe-deposit box at the Bank of _____ located at _____ .*

B. *Developer shall update the Program Source Code and Documentation within thirty days after supplying updated Object Code to Publisher.*

C. *Developer shall provide Publisher with a key to the safe-deposit box mentioned in clause A.*

D. Developer hereby grants Publisher a contingent license, which is subject to the conditions in this section, to use the source code for maintenance purposes only. This contingent license shall become effective if Developer within five years of the date of this agreement, refuses or otherwise becomes unable to provide maintenance for Publisher for any reason. This contingent license shall continue for ten years from the date it becomes effective. Should the parties disagree on whether the Developer has refused or become unable to provide maintenance, the matter shall be decided by binding arbitration as set out in the section titled, "Arbitration."

E. Publisher hereby agrees not to open the safe-deposit box unless the conditions noted in clause D are met.

F. Developer agrees to pay all fees associated with the safe-deposit box.

G. When the period mentioned in clause A expires, Developer's obligations under this section of this agreement shall expire.

H. If the Source Code is obtained by Publisher under Clause D, Publisher agrees not to publish or disseminate the source code without Developer's written consent.

SECTION XVI—GENERAL

The last (whew!) section of the license agreement is titled "General" and is basically a catch-all section for items that didn't fit in any of the preceding sections. The general clauses in the following sample can be altered, and in some cases omitted entirely, if they do not apply to your situation. Let's go over them one at a time.

Marketing Restrictions

The first clause I include in the general section defines what sort of freedom the publisher has in establishing marketing strategy and prices. Here is a common clause:

XVI. General

A. Publisher shall have full freedom and flexibility in marketing efforts for the Program, including the freedom to decide its method of marketing, terms, conditions, and prices.

Most publishers will propose a clause like this. A developer who wants some input into the marketing decisions might suggest this alternative clause:

A. Publisher shall consult with Developer regarding marketing plan and prices. However, Publisher shall have final say regarding these items.

If the developer insists on having veto power over the publisher's marketing efforts and can get the publisher to agree to this, the following clause may be used:

A. Publisher shall consult with Developer regarding marketing plan and prices. Should a disagreement arise concerning the items mentioned in the preceding sentence, Developer's position shall prevail.

I do not recommend your using the preceding sample because it limits publishers in an area they know best. It is also the kind of clause that can easily lead to a building up of irritation and frustration. There may be times, however, when a developer has a particular reason for wanting final say in how much a program will sell for or what the advertising copy will look like. Here are a couple of sample clauses that specify this:

A. Publisher shall submit a proposed price schedule to Developer for the Program. Developer retains the right to approve the price schedule, and Pub-

lisher agrees not to release the Program until the price schedule is approved by the Developer.

I do not recommend your using this sample for the same reason I discourage your using the sample before it: it restrains the publisher too much. Here is the second sample:

> A. *Publisher agrees to submit all proposed advertisements and promotional literature concerning Program to Developer. Developer retains the right to reject any advertisement. Rejection must be made in writing within one week of submittal. Developer shall pay actual production costs of any advertisement proposals that are rejected under this clause.*

The above sample makes sense for a developer who is worried about the potential image of the program. If the publisher has a reputation for rather sleazy advertisements, a developer may even want to insist that the publisher pay for rejected ads.

Assignment and Delegation

Another issue often dealt with in this section concerns the ability to transfer (assign) the rights and delegate the obligations under the contract. Assigning rights means allowing someone who is not a party to the contract to step into the shoes of someone who is.

Example

Tom wants to assign, as part of his divorce settlement, the right to receive the royalties to JunkMail to Sally his ex-wife. This doesn't mean, however, that Sally has to assume Tom's responsibilities to maintain and update JunkMail. Tom still has to perform these obligations, but his ex-wife can receive the payments.

What about the obligations or duties? Generally, while the right to receive money is freely assignable, the obligation to perform services is not, unless there is a specific agreement. Suppose Tom plans to leave the country for a year and wants to delegate his duty to maintain JunkMail to Joe. Most software contracts would not allow this without the publisher's permission. If the publisher did give permission, it would normally be granted only if Tom agreed to be liable for maintenance should Joe fail to perform. Here are some sample clauses along with explanations of their effects. If you feel you need something more specialized, you should see a lawyer.

> B. *Neither party may sell, transfer, assign, delegate, or subcontract any rights or obligations under this agreement without the prior written consent of the other party.*
> B. *Neither party may sell, transfer, assign, delegate, or subcontract any rights or obligations under this agreement without the prior written consent of the other party, which shall not be unreasonably withheld.*

The second sample is obviously milder than the first because it specifies that a refusal to assign or delegate any rights or obligations must be reasonable. What is reasonable? I think any assignment or delegation that forces the other party to give up a valuable right is unreasonable. Thus Tom's assignment of his royalties to his ex-wife is reasonable because Firstware isn't likely to care whom it makes the paycheck out to. But Tom's delegation to Joe might be considered unreasonable if Tom does not agree to stand behind Joe and guarantee his maintenance work.

> B. *This agreement is freely assignable by the Publisher.*

This clause would be unwise for the developer since it allows the publisher to assign the license to the program to someone whom the developer may not want to do business with. I would advise against it. Instead, consider the following:

B. This agreement is assignable by the Publisher providing that the Developer gives written consent.

Mailing Addresses

The following clause simply establishes a notice procedure. Since the contract occasionally makes mention of giving notice, this clause tells how to do it.

C. Any notice from one party to the other required by this agreement shall be deemed made on the date of mailing if sent by certified mail and addressed to the address specified below.
[Publisher's Address]
[Developer's Address]

Applicable Law

The next clause tells which state law will apply to this contract. This usually isn't an issue if the parties are located in the same state, but if they are from different states the state law of one state or the other should be chosen. Contrary to popular belief, choosing the applicable state law does not decide where a case will be tried. Where a case is to be tried depends on the facts of the dispute and the rules of civil procedure. Choosing one state law over another simply means that wherever the case is tried, the state law chosen will be the law applied to the case. Suppose Bigware is located in Florida and Tom is in California. The state law chosen in their contract is California, which means that even if the case is tried in Florida, the judge in Florida will have to apply California's state law in deciding the case. In most situations publishers will insist on using the law of the state in which they are located because this is the law they know best. Unless a programmer has a specific reason to object, it makes sense to go along with this since contract law is usually similar from one state to the next.

D. This contract shall be construed under the law of the State of California.

Another clause usually found in the general section is the requirement that all changes to the contract be in writing. This makes some sense, though many people ignore it and make small changes orally. As discussed in detail in Chapter 4, people who don't specify changes in writing take the risk of losing the issue if it should ever be disputed. Also contained in this clause is what lawyers call an "integration clause." This clause asserts that the written agreement is the entire understanding between the parties and attempts to invalidate any oral agreements or understandings between the parties.

E. This agreement sets forth the entire understanding between the parties, it may be changed or modified only in writing and must be signed by both parties.

I usually add one other general clause to cover what happens if, for instance, the developer dies or the publishing company is sold. In most situations you will want the contract to continue to bind the original party (if alive) as well as the succeeding party (the party that takes the place of the original party).

F. This contract is binding upon and shall inure to the benefit of the legal successors and assigns of the parties.

FOOTNOTES

[1] I know of a case where the bug was a result of the combination of hardware and software. Neither the hardware nor the software by itself seemed to be at fault. When they were combined, however, a bug erratically appeared. Needless to say, this was a tough one to verify.

[2] On the other hand, the publisher might love the idea. While the publisher is warming up to the prospect of increased sales, the developer says, "I'd sure like to be able to spend the programming time on this enhancement, but I just can't afford to unless you help pay the way. A one-time $7500 payment will let me do the job." At this point a round of genial negotiations takes place, resulting in an extra $5,000 for the developer.

trademarks

A trademark is a word or graphic symbol used by a manufacturer or merchant to distinguish his goods from the goods of others. This definition of trademark holds true for state as well as federal laws. It doesn't tell the whole story, however, because not every program name will qualify as a trademark.

Kodak is the trademark of a famous film manufacturer. What if you, too, wanted to get into the film business, and decided to call your product "Film"? Most people would instinctively know that you could not use the word *film* as a trademark for the product, film. The reason you cannot do this is that if you owned the trademark to the word other photo-products manufacturers couldn't easily describe their products. The difference between Kodak and Film is that Kodak doesn't describe anything, but film does. In short, you can't trademark a generic name when it describes the item that it is attached to.

Let's carry the example a little further. Suppose you manufacture skin-tight jeans. Your fashion name is—you guessed it—Film. In this context you can indeed trademark the word *film* because it does not describe jeans. Sure, your jeans have a certain filmy quality, but the word is only suggestive of how your jeans fit and is not truly descriptive of the sort of product you sell. So, if you want a trademark, don't pick a generic word that describes your product.

TRADEMARK THEORY IN A NUTSHELL

What's the underlying logic to trademark law? The theory is that a trademark is used to set your product apart from all other similar products. It originally began as a body of law that kept one manufacturer from palming off his products as the products of another. In other words, it was designed to eliminate deception and unfair competition. Today there are three main areas of trademark law: federal law (Trademark Act of 1946, 15 U.S.C. sec. 1051-1127, known as the Lanham Act), the various state laws, and foreign law.

In 1946 Congress passed the Lanham Act. It sets up two registration systems: the Principal and the Supplemental Registers. It is more desirable to register your mark with the Principal rather than with the Supplemental Register. Doing so will provide you with some valuable rights. However, many trademarks are ineligible for the Principal Register although they qualify for the Supplemental Register. Here, in brief, is how the federal registration system works.

The two types of marks protected under the Lanham Act that affect software are trademarks and service marks. Service marks are like trademarks but, rather than identifying a product, they identify a service. (A combination trademark/service mark can sometimes be obtained.) A professional beta-testing service called *Bugzout* would qualify for a service mark. Since trademarks and service marks follow essentially the same rules, we will, for the purpose of this chapter, call both of them trademarks.

TRADEMARK STRENGTHS

Trademarks can be classified according to their strength. A very strong trademark cannot be easily attacked by a competitor, whereas a weak trademark is vulnerable to use by others. How can one tell the relative strength of a mark? The general rule is that the less descriptive the mark is of a certain product, the stronger the mark is. An example of a very strong mark is Kodak. What does Kodak describe? Not a damn thing. It is therefore very strong. It derives much of its strength from other film manufacturers not being able to complain that Kodak has kept them from adequately describing their own products. At the other side of the spectrum are weak marks, which usually are quite descriptive of the products they are applied to. The more descriptive the mark, the weaker it is. An example of a weak mark is *BugKillllller,* when applied to a pesticide.[1]

It might seem a little Alice in Wonderlandish, but a weak mark when applied to one product may be a strong mark when used with another. (Remember our example where Film was a good mark for pants and no mark for camera film.) In most cases a mark is neither simply good nor bad. Instead, its strength may be gauged by a scale that has several subcategories of strength. Here is an illustration of the scale:

Weak Marks			Strong Marks	
(1)	(2)	(3)	(4)	(5)
generic	descriptive	suggestive	arbitrary	coined
nil	may qualify	strong	stronger	strongest

Generic Marks

I already mentioned that generic marks are not eligible for trademark protection when used in connection with the product that they are a generic description of. Sometimes a mark that is generic for one product will qualify as descriptive, suggestive, or arbitrary for use in connection with another product.

Descriptive Marks

A descriptive mark may qualify for trademark protection providing the owner can prove that the mark has secondary meaning in the eyes of the public. Secondary meaning is a question of fact. Are there a large number of buyers who associate the descriptive mark with the manufacturer who uses it? Tender Vittles cat food is an example of a descriptive mark. In order for the cat food company to register it, the company would have to prove to the Patent and Trademark Office (or to a court if the Office was not convinced) that the mark had secondary meaning in the eyes of the public.

Suggestive Marks

Suggestive marks do not have to pass the secondary meaning test. The trademark, "Film" when applied to jeans, is, in my opinion, suggestive. Perhaps you disagree and believe that the mark is descriptive. The difference between descriptive and suggestive is somewhat blurred. Whole briefs are devoted to the semantics of trademarks in an effort to prove that a mark is suggestive rather than descriptive. Instead of trying to duplicate these semantics, let me simply list some suggestive marks: Coppertone suntan oil, Neat hair remover, EasyWriter word processor, Raid bug killer. Now compare them to the following descriptive marks, which do need secondary meaning in order to be registered: Sirloin and Brew restaurant, or Yellow Pages. This, as you may have guessed, isn't a precise area of the law, so try to get a feeling for the difference between descriptive and suggestive marks.

Arbitrary Marks

An arbitrary mark is strong because it does not describe or suggest the product and, therefore, it is unlikely that the public will be confused about who made it. Consider the word *Beans,* for example. Applied to a can of beans, *Beans* is clearly generic and not protectable. In fact, beans sold in cans with plain white labels are said to be generic products. The food packer is not looking for any sort of trademark protection. What happens when you decide to call your clothing line "Beans." This is an example of generic mark for beans becoming an arbitrary mark for clothes. "Apple," as applied to computers, and "Black and White," as applied to scotch, are two more examples of arbitrary marks.

Coined Marks

These marks have no inherent meaning, yet they are the strongest. Kodak, Exxon, Cromemco, Centronics, and Corvus are all coined. They are so strong because they are so unlike a "real" word; there is scarcely a chance that anyone could be misled by them.

Ironically, sometimes a coined mark becomes so successful that it becomes generic and loses its trademark status. Marks that were originally coined but are now generic include aspirin, cellophane, shredded wheat, and trampoline. Xerox is a trademark that may be in danger of becoming generic. As a result of this potential danger, Xerox Corporation is spending thousands of dollars on an ad campaign to remind the public that Xerox is a trademark and does not mean "photocopy." If a company wants to keep its mark from becoming generic, it should always be sure to use the mark as an adjective, never as a noun. Thus Kodak always refers to "Kodak film" in its advertising.

Besides being grouped by type and strength, trademarks may also be classified by appearance (type style, logo design, color, and so forth). There are word marks such as Raid and Xerox. There are symbol marks such as the arm and hammer on baking soda boxes. There can be combinations of words and symbols such as the word "Apple II" emerging from a rainbow apple. The label of a product as a whole, or the shape of the packaging, may also be a trademark. A trade name, however, is not a trademark. Apple Computer, Inc., for example, is not a trademark. But the colored apple with the word *apple* coming out of it is. Sometimes it's hard to know if you are talking about a trademark or a trade name. Sometimes, the names are similar, as is the case with Apple or IBM. The federal trademark laws do not protect trade names. If someone steals your trade name (the name of your business) you will have to pursue the person under your state's unfair competition laws. These laws vary from state to state. If you think you have a problem along these lines, see a lawyer.

Now that you have a general idea of what can be a federal registered trademark, how do you go about choosing a mark and protecting it? First, let's deal with choosing a mark. Suppose your company is Firstware Inc., and you have developed a word-processing program called *The Firstware Word processor*. This mark is not registerable because it's generic—it merely describes the product. This is not to say, however, that Firstware should change the name of its program. Just because a name is not registerable doesn't mean that someone else can use it or that it is a bad name for marketing purposes. State laws, as I will discuss later, would give Firstware some recourse against unfair competition.

You may decide that you don't need or want a mark that is registerable and are content simply with calling a word processor a word processor and with marketing your software under its generic name. This straightforward approach often makes great sense. If you don't have a big advertising budget, you may find it hard to get across exactly what your program is or does if the name isn't descriptive. I often recommend a plain old generic name over a fanciful trademark unless the publisher is convinced that the fancy name will help sales. I can think of dozens of program trademarks that haven't helped sales one bit.

FINDING A TRADEMARK LAWYER

Choosing a trademark is only half the job. Registering it, unfortunately, involves a number of technical steps. Some things you can (and must) do yourself without the aid of a lawyer. However, at certain junctures, expert legal help is invaluable. In trademark law even an innocent and seemingly trivial mistake can prove disastrous. Therefore if after reading this chapter you feel your trademark is valuable, I recommend that you spend the money to retain a trademark attorney. While I don't believe that many trademarks are worth the expense and trouble of registration, if you should decide to register be sure the job is done right.

Another reason lawyers are helpful with registration is that they not only will do the paperwork and correspond with the Patent and Trademark Office but also will be legally responsible for submitting the paperwork necessary to keep your registration active. Trademark lawyers are among the world's great optimists; they keep calendars fifteen years into the future.

It is, I should mention, possible to register your trademark yourself. This chapter will show you how to file. Nevertheless, as I said earlier, I recommend a lawyer, especially if you plan on selling or transferring part or all of your trademark. Trademark lawyers can be found in the Yellow Pages under the heading, "Patent lawyers." This is a certified specialty, which means that the attorney has had to pass an especially tough bar examination given by the Patent and Trademark Office. A general practitioner, who will know no more about trademarks than you do about riparian rights, ought not to be consulted. Trademark lawyers are not inexpensive. Therefore to get the most for your money I suggest you continue reading this chapter. You'll learn how to fill out the registration form and what information you will need to take with you so that when you do consult with your lawyer you won't spend any money needlessly.

CONDUCTING A TRADEMARK SEARCH

After you select your trademark the next step is to conduct a trademark search. You can do it yourself or have your trademark lawyer do it. The purpose of the search is to try to discover if anyone is already using the mark you have selected or if you have inadvertently chosen someone else's mark. If your mark is already being used in the software industry, you'll have to choose another. You could, however, adopt a mark that is being used in another industry so long as there is no likelihood of confusion. For example, you couldn't call your software Kodak software because Kodak is involved in the electronics field, but you might be able to use the name Craftsman software even though there is also a brand of tools of the same name marketed by Sears.

You might be interested in having a search done before involving a lawyer, though a lawyer's feedback on your proposed trademark often will save you the expense of a search. The search itself costs between $45-$65 and takes a week or two. The search firm will report who, if anyone, is using your mark or any mark similar to yours (see page 45 for the name of a firm).

Unfortunately, while the trademark search can turn up bad news (someone else is using your mark), it can't (if apparently no one else is using the mark) assure you that your chosen mark will not be challenged or rejected by the Patent Office. The Patent Office's record system is not computerized. This means that it is possible to miss similar marks, particularly those that are spelled differently but sound the same. In addition, a valid trademark can exist that has not been registered. And just because a mark is not registered does not necessarily mean you can use it. Also, your mark could be generic, immoral, misdescriptive, or deceptive, in which cases the Patent and Trademark Office will refuse you registration as they will have refused registration to anyone submitting a comparable mark.[2]

USING YOUR TRADEMARK

Now let's assume that you have picked a name for your new software, that you have asked yourself (or your lawyer) whether the name can be registered (see the types of marks described above), and that your search indicates no one apparently is using your mark. Your next step is to register, right? Wrong. The law says you can't register a trademark until you first sell the product it is attached to in interstate commerce. One of the biggest differences between trademark law and copyright law is that trademark protection comes from usage, whereas copyright protection comes from an original act of authorship. Or put another way, you could think of the best program name in the history of programming, but unless you sell programs under that name, you don't own a federally protected trademark.

Another key difference between copyright and trademark law is that the person who uses a trademark owns it—not the person who thinks it up. Thus if a developer comes up with a wonderful name and divulges it to a publisher, who uses it, the publisher, not the developer, owns the trademark.

What this actually means is that before you can register your trademark, or even start the filing procedure, you must have labels printed up with your trademark on them, affix those labels to your floppies, and then sell your software across state lines. Don't try to get away with selling your program to a pal across state lines. To qualify a sale has to be for real money, and it must be a legitimate sale, not a sham.

REGISTERING YOUR TRADEMARK

Once you have made your out-of-state sale, you are finally ready to register. Again, if you can afford to, consult a lawyer at this stage. If you don't know whether (1) the program will be a seller or (2) you truly like the trademark you have tentatively selected, I suggest you wait longer before registering. In the United States, while you shouldn't wait longer than you have to, there is really no rush. Registering first doesn't mean you will get onto the Principal Register. Everything depends on who actually first used the mark. Keep sales slips and records of your sales and advertising. Should the issue arise, they may later be used as evidence to determine who first used the mark.

THE TRADEMARK APPLICATION FORM

The trademark application looks easy. It is even shorter than the copyright form. However, there is an important difference. While most copyright mistakes can be corrected fairly easily, even a minute mistake in a trademark application can haunt you for years. Forms may be obtained by writing to:

Commissioner of Patents and Trademarks
Washington, D.C. 20231

Be sure you ask for the form for trademarks for your type of business entity. There are three types of forms—individual, corporate, and firm (unincorporated companies). The only difference between these forms is the heading and footing. The body of the application forms is identical.

Now let's review the form together.

The Heading of the Form

a. At the top right hand corner is a line titled "Mark." Type in the mark you are using. Use all capital letters.

b. Below the mark, type the Class No. In the case of software the class is 9 (when sold with a manual).

c. Your name is next. Again, be sure you have the appropriate form for your type of business entity. If you are incorporated, type in your full legal corporate name as it appears on your stock certificates. On the same line type your state of incorporation. If you are a partnership, type in the name of the firm and, immediately after the firm name, type in your partners' legal names. If you are an individual, type in your full legal name.

d. Your address goes next. On one line type in your business address including street, city, state, and zip.

e. If you are an individual business entity, the next line should contain your full home address. If your company is unincorporated, the next line will contain your firm's domicile, which, if you are located in Chicago, would read, Chicago, Illinois. Corporations have no corresponding line and should go on the body of the form.

```
4.6 Trademark application by a corporation; Principal Register.
                          Mark _____JUNKMAIL_____
                                     (Identify the mark)
                          Class No. __9_____
                                     (If known)
To THE COMMISSIONER OF PATENTS AND TRADEMARKS:
_____Firstware, Inc. A Nevada Corporation_____
          (Corporate name and State or country of incorporation) (10)

_____21 Second Street, Reno, Nevada 77625_____
                        (Business address)
```

The Body of the Form

a. The first line (1) of the body of the form asks for the name of the goods bearing your trademark. Type in "Computer Program and instruction manual sold as a unit with the program."

b. The next line (2) calls for the date that the trademark was first used on the program. This is not the date of the first sale but the date a label was first stuck to a diskette.

c. The following line (3) asks for the type of commerce that the program is being used in. If you have made your out-of-state sale, put down the word "interstate." If you have not yet sold out of state, don't proceed with the form until you have done so. In the next blank enter the date of this first interstate sale.

d. Item (4) assumes that the mark has no requirement of secondary meaning. Skip ahead to (5) if your mark is coined, arbitrary, or suggestive. If, however, the mark does require secondary meaning for registration (if, that is, it's descriptive), you should see a trademark attorney because your application will have to be augmented with evidence that the mark has attained secondary meaning. The one exception to this is if the mark has been used in continuous interstate commerce for more than five years before registration. This, however, is unlikely for any of the readers of this book.

e. Item (5) asks how the mark is applied to the software. In most cases it will be with a label, so type "labels affixed to the goods." If your mark is used on the packaging, you may also wish to state, "packaging containing the goods."

```
   The above identified applicant has adopted and is using the trademark
shown in the accompanying drawing (1) for the following goods:
__Computer_Program_and_Instruction_Manual_sold_as_a_unit_with_the_program,
and requests that said mark be registered in the United States Patent and

Trademark Office on the Principal Register established by the act of July 5,
1946.

   The trademark was first used on the goods (2) on__June 30, 1981__; was
                                                    (Date)
first used in (3)___Interstate_____commerce on __July 25, 1981_____
                (Type of commerce)
_____; and is now in use in such commerce. (4)

   The mark is used by applying it to (5) _labels affixed to the goods and five
specimens showing the mark as actually used are presented herewith.
   (6)

State of__Nevada____ )
                      } ss.
County of__Washoe___ )
```

That's all there is to the body of the form. The foot of the form varies with each business entity.

The Foot of the Form

There are two kinds of form feet. One requires an oath that everything on the form is true, and the other requires a declaration. They amount to the same thing but are filled out a little differently.

Partnerships and Individuals. If your business is unincorporated but is made up of more than one individual, the name of any member of the firm may be listed.

Corporations. If your business is a corporation, the name and title of any corporate officer may be listed.

Next follows a sworn statement by the person whose name was listed. In signing this statement the signatory attests that the trademark belongs to the applicant, that is is not likely to cause confusion with other trademarks, and that everything in the application is true. Then comes a line for a signature. In the case of firms and individuals the person whose name appears above must sign the statement. In the

```
_____Robert Smith_____ states that
          (Name of officer of corporation)

he/she is____President_____of applicant corporation (10) and is
            (Official title)

authorized to execute this affidavit on behalf of said corporation; he/she be-
lieves said corporation to be the owner of the trademark sought to be regis-
tered; to the best of his/her knowledge and belief no other person, firm,
corporation or association has the right to use said mark in commerce, either
in the identical form or in such near resemblance thereto as to be likely,
when applied to the goods of such other person, to cause confusion, or to
cause mistake, or to deceive; and the facts set forth in this application
are true.
                        By___Firstware, Inc._____
                              (Name of corporation)

                        By___Robert Smith, President_____
                             (Signature of officer of corporation
                                  and official title of officer)
JURAT:
Subscribed to and sworn to before me, this _____ day of

_____,_____.

                             _____*
                                   Notary Public
 *The person who signs the jurat must be authorized to administer oaths by the law
of the jurisdiction where executed, and the seal or stamp of the notary, or other
evidence of authority in the jurisdiction of execution, must be affixed.
```

case of corporations the name of the corporation appears first, followed by a corporate officer's signature, which is preceded by the word "by." This makes it clear that the person signing is doing so on the corporation's behalf and not as an individual. The following footer must be signed before a notary. If you use a form that contains a declaration rather than an oath, you needn't use a notary. Your trademark lawyer will be able to advise you.

THE DRAWING

The Patent Office requires that a drawing accompany the application form. If your trademark is a word mark, simply type the word in capital letters on a piece of paper. This is your drawing. Marks other than word marks should have a drawing that conforms to the Patent and Trademark Office's regulations. Your lawyer will tell you more about this. You must put a heading at the top of the paper with your name, address, date of first use, and the goods as named in the application (see sample below). Each of these pieces of information must be typed on a separate line.

```
Firstware, Inc.
21 Second Street
Reno, Nevada  77625

June 30, 1981 (first date of use)
July 25, 1981 (interstate commerce)

For: Computer Program and Instruction Manual
                              JUNKMAIL
```

FILING

Now it's time to file. The drawing, the application, a money order for one hundred seventy-five dollars made out to the Patent and Trademark Office, and five specimens of the mark as you have used it must be sent to the Patent Office. These specimens should be the actual diskette labels applied to individual 8½ × 11 sheets of paper.

Registration is good for five years and can be renewed. If any of you should be fortunate enough to have a trademark in use for five years, your trademark lawyer will remind you when it is time to renew.

THE PATENT AND TRADEMARK OFFICE RESPONSE

To say that the Patent and Trademark Office is slow is to understate the situation. Eventually you will get a little blue slip acknowledging your filing. When will you hear next from the office? Don't hold your breath. Current backlog for a first response is more than a year, with complete registration taking approximately twenty-five months. This is not to say that the Patent Office is inept. Quite the contrary. There are more than 100,000 applications ahead of yours. The office is simply overworked and understaffed. When they receive your application, it will be assigned a serial number and given to an attorney for examination. This examination consists of a trademark search and a review of your application. If all goes well (usually it does not) your mark will be published in the *Official Gazette* (see below). If all does not go well, you will receive a letter that, after the eighth or ninth reading, may start to take on some meaning. With the receipt of this letter it is time, if you have not already done so, to go to a trademark lawyer. While sometimes your confusion will dissipate as quickly as a word has been explained, more frequently there are all sorts of other complications. It is, I am afraid, beyond the scope of this book to deal with all the questions that an examiner, in the letter sent to you, could conceivably ask. I can give you a couple of hints, however: You will, first of all, have six months to respond to the examiner's letter, after which time the registration is considered dead and you will have to start all over again if you want to pursue the matter. Secondly, in most circumstances if you prepare your own response and don't have it checked by your lawyer, you are asking for trouble.

After you make your response the examiner takes some more months and may raise more objections. Again, the help of a lawyer is invaluable. Your second response may draw still another letter from the examiner requesting more information or a clarification. And so it goes.

TRADEMARK PUBLICATION

I mentioned earlier that if your application is approved, it will be published in the *Official Gazette*. The purpose of this is so that the rest of the world can have a chance to oppose your trademark registration if anyone should feel that it infringes on a mark already in use. In the meantime you may want to oppose (again a lawyer is necessary) any trademark published in the *Gazette* that is similar to yours. For a fee your lawyer will watch the *Gazette* for you and can also advise you on how best to deal with situations in which someone else is using your mark or a mark similar to yours.

If no one successfully challenges your right to the trademark, it is entered into the Principal Register. Now what has all this gotten you?

The Principal Register

I mentioned that having a mark listed in the Principal Register confers certain advantages on the trademark owner. One of the main advantages of a Principal Register mark is that, should you ever find yourself in court, you are entitled to certain legal presumptions. If your mark is in the Principal Register, the court presumes that the trademark is yours. If this doesn't seem like a big deal, consider the following:

Example

Firstware followed the necessary steps to get its trademark, "Wordrite," onto the Principal Register. Wordrite is a spelling program that proofreads text files. A few months after Firstware registered Wordrite, Barnware a South Dakota firm, files suit claiming that Wordrite is in fact the trademark for its software program that checks spelling. What, if anything, does Firstware's Principal Register status do to help its legal position? Because Firstware is on the Principal Register, it has the powerful presumption that it is the true owner of Wordrite. Barnware will have to show that it used the mark Wordrite before Firstware, and it will have to prove that Firstware's use of the name misleads the public. However, if the public hasn't heard much about Barnware's Wordrite but has heard a good deal about Firstware's program of the same name, it will be unlikely that Barnware could win its case even though it may have been the first to use Wordrite.

If, after five years of Principal Register status, Firstware files the appropriate form, it can achieve Incontestable Status for its mark, which means that the aforementioned legal presumption is almost challenge-proof. In addition to initial legal presumption and eventual Incontestable Status, a listing in the Principal Register provides you with the federal remedies listed under the Lanham Act. Included among these remedies are federally enforceable injunctions to stop infringers, triple damages (sometimes), and court orders calling for the destruction of infringing labels or packaging.

Supplemental Register

Now let's examine what happens if your mark doesn't qualify for inclusion in the Principal Register. You may still qualify for the Supplemental Register, the main requirements of which are that your mark be capable of distinguishing your goods or services from similar goals or services by other manufacturers and that it not be a generic mark. The benefits, however, are not so great as those of the Principal Register. One attorney even goes so far as to suggest that Supplemental Register status is more for the client's psychological well-being than for anything else.

Although the Supplemental Register does not have the advantages of the Principal Register, it does convey some real benefits, such as the following:

- You can keep any other similar marks from being registered on the Principal or the Supplemental Register.
- You can take your case to federal court.
- You can seek remedies under the Lanham Act.
- You can register in any foreign country whose law specifies your having first registered in your home country.
- You can (and will) get a certificate—suitable for framing—for your office.
- You can use the ®

Before being allowed onto the Supplemental Register you first must have used the mark for a year in interstate commerce—unless, that is, you are registering for the purpose of obtaining foreign registration, in which case the Patent Office will make an exception.

Returning for a moment to the question of whether registration is worth the hassle, you might consider how valuable your mark would likely be to a competitor. Just because a mark is not registered does not mean that it is up for grabs (see State Laws). Federal registration does give you the advantage of using the power of the nationwide federal court system. A federal court decision in your favor regarding a trademark is enforceable throughout the United States. In contrast, if you had to rely solely on state law, you would have to file a lawsuit in every state in which you wished to prevent someone from using your trademark. The whole thing boils down to a business decision. If after you use the mark awhile it becomes more valuable to you, you can always register it.

STATE LAWS

Each state has its own trademark protection law. Often one may file a form with the state in which you want protection that is similar to the federal form. If you are doing business in only one state, you should consider filing in that state. (A payroll program is a perfect example of this, because withholding tax requirements are different for each state.)

The particulars of the various state laws stem from the common law of unfair competition but, while generally accomplishing the same thing, vary enough so that it would be futile to go into state-by-state detail here. The underlying theory of all these laws is similar to the Lanham Act. The requirements for proving a case are similar. In each state a court for people is provided to litigate over the ownership of trademarks. Trade names also are often covered by state law. In simplified terms, the person who first used the mark in connection with a particular product will be the one who wins the case. This may seem straightforward and easily settled, but the actual cases (federal and state) are rarely open and shut. For example, expensive public-opinion surveys are often used to prove or disprove public confusion over a trademark. In addition, there is often expert testimony on public perception of one mark or another. The question before the court sometimes revolves around whether two marks are similar and sometimes around who used a mark first. Usually a great deal of time is spent arguing over how similar the two products are to each other and whether the public would be confused by allowing both companies to simultaneously use similar marks.

Example

Suppose Smallware, a small software company, sells a word-processing program for use on the Pet computer. The product consists of a floppy disk and a three-ring instruction manual. It sells for $79 under the trademark "Word-o-rama." A year after Smallware began its sales, Giantware, a hardware company, announced the introduction of a stand-alone word processor, complete with printer, for $7500. This stand-alone wordprocessor is called "WORD-A-RAMA." Smallware feels that this is a clear infringement of its trademark and takes the case to court. What are some of the things a judge should consider?

There are several issues here. The most easily resolved is that Smallware did indeed use the trademark first, which means that if the court decides the rest of the issues in Smallware's favor, it should impose an injunction prohibiting Giantware from further use of the trademark. This, however, is only the first issue. You undoubtedly noticed the differences between "Word-o-rama" and "WORD-A-RAMA." Not only is the spelling slightly different, but one is in uppercase and lowercase letters while the other is entirely capitalized. Does this mean that these two names are the same for trademark purposes? The legal test is whether the public would likely be confused by thinking that the two names were the same. There is not much doubt that confusion would exist, since the two words are almost identical. Generally speaking, trademarks that sound, look, or mean the same are considered too close for comfort. E-Z writer, EasyWriter, Easy Writer and EZWRITER are all regarded as so close to one another that the public would be confused.

So far the case seems to be tilting toward Smallware. We have determined that Smallware used the mark first and that the two marks are similar enough to cause confusion. Now for the difficult question: Are the uses of the two marks so close as to confuse the public? Remember that although both products are used in word processing, one is merely a floppy disk that costs $79 while the other is a hunk of hardware that costs considerably more, $7500. I'm not entirely sure how a court would decide this issue. My feeling is that most people would not be confused by the simultaneous use of the marks. But you might disagree, especially if you were Smallware's attorney. The question could be argued for days. Smallware could hire a firm to poll shoppers at a mall. Giantware could commission a telephone survey of the entire state of Rhode Island to determine who, if anyone, has heard of Smallware's program.

If you should discover someone using your trademark who refuses to voluntarily cease and desist (as lawyers say), you will have to consult a trademark lawyer for advice on what course to take.

FOREIGN LAWS

Despite its shortcomings, the United States has one of the most sensible trademark laws in the world. In most other countries trademark registration comes *not* from use but from registration, which means that anyone can think up a trademark and race to the trademark office and register. There are even people who specialize in finding trademarks in the United States and registering them abroad in their own names. When a U.S. firm tries to sell its program abroad, its floppies are stopped in customs because they invariably infringe a trademark registered in the destination country. You probably guessed it. Just behind the customs inspector is the foreign "trademark owner" who, for a fee, is willing to sell the U.S. firm back its own trademark.

To make matters worse, many foreign countries require that a trademark be registered in the company's own country before allowing pursuit of the foreign registration. This means that prior to its being accepted, and while it is being published in the *Gazette*, someone could be registering your trademark abroad—and not in your name! Again, this is a complex and specialized area. If you want foreign registration for your trademark, see a trademark lawyer, for advice on how to minimize your exposure and properly time the filings. Foreign filings cost about five hundred dollars.

Even though the registration system in other countries is poor, this does not mean that you lose all your rights if you can't get registered or if someone beats you to the registration office. As does the United States, other countries have laws that protect a person who is actually using the mark and who used it first. The disadvantages for the nonregistered party are simply that 1) those legal presumptions that come with registration are absent, and 2) a legal procedure rebutting the presumption that a registered owner is the true owner of the mark must be endured.

You can assign and license a trademark. However, in contrast to copyright transferral, transferring a trademark right is a bit tricky because all rights to a trademark stem from usage. A person who is not using the mark cannot transfer it, let alone own it. This means that when a mark is transferred, the goodwill associated with the mark must be transferred with it, which may seem a bit vague if not altogether abstract. Perhaps an illustration will clarify matters.

Example

JunkMail is a trademark. Tom has been selling JunkMail for a couple of years for use on the Apple III. Firstware arrives on the scene and wants to buy all rights to JunkMail. Tom can assign the trademark rights to JunkMail along with the actual program if he also assigns the goodwill of his business.

But what if Tom wants to keep partial ownership of the trademark for himself and license Firstware to use it too? To do this he must maintain some control over the manufacture of JunkMail. Suppose Firstware wants to publish JunkMail for the TRS-80, and Tom still wants to publish it himself for the Apple. Unless he maintains a certain measure of control over the manufacture of TRS-80 program, there is a danger that the mark, as it applies to TRS-80s, will be lost to him through lack of use. In trademark terms this is known as *abandonment*. One must continually use a trademark in order to keep it.

How much control does Tom need to keep over the manufacture of JunkMail in order to maintain his ownership of the trademark? This is a tough question to answer precisely. Some experts feel, and I agree, that enough control is maintained if Tom merely obligates himself to fix any bugs in the program that is manufactured by Firstware. This is still a gray area of the law. For now just be aware that this is a problem area, and be careful when transferring trademark rights.

HOW TO USE YOUR TRADEMARK

If your mark is on the Principal Register or Supplemental Register you should use an ® in conjunction with it. The purpose of the ® is to put the public on notice that your mark is really a trademark and that it is registered. Do you have to use the ® every time your mark appears? It can't hurt, but it is unnecessary. If your mark appears many times in a book, manual, or ad, you may use the ® only the first time the mark appears. You might even place an asterisk next to the first appearance of the mark and include a footnote saying, "This mark is the property of [your name] and is registered in the United States Patent and Trademark Office."

If your mark is not on the Principal or Supplemental register, you must not use the ® or otherwise falsely indicate that it is registered. You may, however, put TM or tm next to your mark if it is not registered. If it is registered in a particular state, mention this in a footnote:

Crackies TM *

* Crackies is a trademark belonging to the Firstware Corporation and is registered In Vermont.

How to Use Others' Marks

Sometimes, for one reason or another, you may need to refer to another company's trademark (perhaps in an advertisement or in your manual). It is an advisable courtesy to acknowledge the owner of the mark with a small asterisk and footnote. If you follow this practice, you can avoid potential nasty letters and lawsuits arising from the claim that you are using someone else's mark to confuse the public.

FOOTNOTES

[1] Weakmarks can also be overly-used marks such as "Acme."
[2] There are other reasons for the Patent Office's refusing to register a mark. Among marks that are refused registration are "mere surnames," disparaging marks, false marks, names of living individuals, tradenames, and geographical names.

chapter 10
patents

Patent protection is the equivalent of a monopoly on your program. If you own a valid patent you can prevent people from making and selling your program for seventeen years. In addition, you can prevent people from using unauthorized copies. Sound inviting? Unfortunately, despite this potentially powerful protection, in most cases patents are not for software.

In Chapter 1, I mentioned that the excessive time and money that the patent application process consumes are drawbacks to patenting software. The patent application process is even more technical, time-consuming, and frustrating than the trademark registration process discussed in Chapter 9. Don't expect your lawyer to patiently wait until your patent is approved before insisting on being paid. Patent lawyers could not long remain in business if they had to wait for results before billing for their time. Throughout the patent application process you will be required to shell out substantial sums to cover legal and registration fees.

There are other drawbacks even more fundamental than time and money. The principal one is that the law is extremely unclear on exactly what sorts of programs are patentable. To understand this problem it is necessary to briefly review the three criteria that must be met before an invention can receive patent protection.

PATENT REQUIREMENTS

Subject Matter

The first condition is that the invention must fall within one of the classes specified by Congress (35 U.S. Code [USC] 101). Among the classes allowed are processes, machines, and manufactured items. "Newly discovered laws of nature" and "mental processes" are specifically excluded. The Patent Office has traditionally refused to allow applications for software patents, claiming that programs, because they are mathematically based, fall within the law of nature exclusion. It has been contended that since the square root of 4 couldn't be patented, neither could a computer program that calculated it.

Two cases decided by the U.S. Supreme Court in 1981 have changed the position of the Patent Office regarding the law of nature exclusion. *Diamond* v. *Bradley* and *Diamond* v. *Diehr* stand for the proposition that a program is no longer excluded from patent protection simply because it is a program. These two cases involved a patent application for a computer-controlled rubber-curing process. A computer was used to monitor and continually calculate the exact curing time and temperature for rubber oil seals. The program used was based on a well-known formula or *algorithm.* The claimants, however, did not ask for a patent on the formula itself but on the entire process, which they claimed was unique. The Supreme Court held in a 5 to 4 decision that the process as a whole was a proper subject for patent protection even though part of the process (the algorithm) was clearly not patentable by itself.

What these decisions apparently mean is that a computer program might be patentable if the patent does not attempt to monopolize a formula but instead uses the formula to solve a task in a new way. Despite this decision, programmers have not been beating a path to the Patent Office looking for protection. Why? Aside from the time and money constraints, most programmers want to be able to protect the very thing the Supreme Court has said is not protectable, namely, the algorithm. When you stop to think about it, the court's decision, which was initially heralded by the news media, is meaningless to most programmers for at least two reasons. First of all, in many situations if the programmer can't patent the formula or algorithm the patent protection is worthless. What's more, even if a program doesn't attempt to monopolize a formula, and thus qualifies under the new Supreme Court ruling there are still two more tough patent hurdles to jump. These are discussed below.

Novelty

Suppose you have met the first requirement of the Patent Office, which stipulates that your program is a process that does not attempt to claim a monopoly on an algorithm. The second requirement is that the program must be novel (35 USC 102). By "novel" the Patent Office means that the program must be different from previously discovered or known programs. How different is hard to say. Since the Patent Office has no history of patented programs (prior art) in its files, it is impossible to foresee what will be required in terms of novelty. If you came up with a new gadget to peel and core apples, the Patent Office could search its records and compare it with the 2,345,012 other apple peelers that have been invented before deciding where your peeler stands in terms of novelty. How they will accomplish this task when it comes to computer programs remains to be seen.

Lack of Obviousness

Finally, assuming your program has met the first two requirements, there is one more hurdle to clear: the program must not be obvious. "Obvious" in the jargon of patent law, means that an ordinary skilled programmer (whoever that is) would not consider whatever it is that makes your program novel to be anything more than an obvious logical extension of the current art of programming. In other words, the question becomes, Is your program a true innovation meriting a seventeen-year monopoly or is it just one more logical development in the art of programming? Again, the Patent Office has no history of dealing with programs to aid it in making a determination on what is obvious and what is not.

WHAT IS PATENTABLE?

Other than rubber-curing programs, what software is patentable? Because of the shaky state of the patent law regarding software, there is no definitive answer. In my opinion the most likely candidates for patent protection will be programs, such as operating systems and languages, that are integrally related to hardware. Most application software, however, will surely fail the second and third conditions. In fact, the patent law specifically excludes methods of doing business, and that exclusion might be interpreted as covering all business-application software.

Example

JunkMail contains innovative sorting algorithms. Tom is considering taking the patent route. Should he? In this case what Tom wants to protect are his algorithms. Patent law will not do this because he is attempting to protect a law of nature.

Example

Firstware wants to patent GENERAL LEDGER accounting system. Can it? No, because business systems are not patentable, and an accounting system would almost certainly fail the requirements of novelty and obviousness.

Example

Jackie has developed a computer program called GimmeFive, which controls the operations of automatic bank tellers. A bank customer who wants to make a withdrawal goes to the robot teller and gives its mechanical hand a firm handshake. Since everyone has an individual handshake (as everyone has a particular voice and a unique fingerprint), the program can identify the customer by sensing the movement, strength, and sincerity of the handshake. If the handshake is not recognized by the program, the mechanical hand relentlessly grasps the would-be embezzler until the police arrive. This is a program that might be patentable since it doesn't attempt to claim an algorithm and relies on common statistical methods for its logic. It is also novel and not obvious. It could, therefore, probably pass the three patent requirements.

WHAT DOES A SOFTWARE PATENT ACHIEVE?

Suppose for a moment that you succeed in obtaining a patent for your software. What kind of legal protection has your patience and money bought you? In some respects your protection will be stronger than copyright protection, and in other respects it will be weaker. A valid patent is stronger than a copyright in that it covers the idea and not merely the expression of the idea (see Chapter 3 for a discussion of this distinction). This means that if you own a patent on a program and someone makes, markets, or uses substantially the same program without your permission, you would not have to prove that the other person actually copied your program to win your case, as you would if it were a matter of copyright infringement. If you own a valid patent, even subsequent independent inventors cannot legally produce infringing programs.

DISADVANTAGES OF PATENT PROTECTION (THERE'S NO SUCH THING AS A FREE LUNCH)

Despite its theoretical strengths, the patent, when it is applied to actual programs, loses much of its attractiveness. As I mentioned earlier, it is clear that you can't claim a patent on an algorithm. In many cases this is exactly what the programmer wants to protect. An algorithm can be protected by using trade-secret law. However, patent protection and trade-secret law don't mix because in order to get a patent you must make public the inner workings of your program, and to do so would immediately terminate your trade-secret protection. Why this painful public disclosure? The basic reason for the government's granting a seventeen-year monopoly on an invention is to promote the interchange and development of ideas and inventions. In return for complete disclosure, the government grants the monopoly.

Another problem with patents is that they are subject to challenge in the courts. The outcome of each challenge will depend on the facts of each case. What seems novel and not obvious to one court might seem the opposite to another. This is especially true when one program is compared to another. An example will clarify this.

Example

Suppose you patent an operating system for a new microcomputer. At the time, no one opposes your patent and everything seems in order. A year later another programmer markets a similar operating system. This second system was independently developed. What are your patent protection options?

You can't simply ignore the problem because, unlike copyright law where a copyright owner can safely ignore small-fry infringers, a patent owner runs the risk of losing the patent unless all infringers are pursued. If you sue the infringer, you must first prove that the new program actually infringes your patent. The infringer will surely claim that the programs (which look different) are different. If you succeed in proving that the programs are similar enough to constitute an infringement, the infringer will next attack the validity of your patent. This is entirely aboveboard and to be expected, the validity of your patent will be questioned every time you sue an infringer. Finally, the infringer will likely claim that your program is obvious and not novel and therefore not patentable.

You can see how expensive and bothersome this whole process can become. Since most programmers only want to protect the expression of their ideas, copyright law normally will meet this goal more cheaply and easily than patent law. In addition, copyright protection does not (in my opinion) preclude trade-secret protection, which can be used to protect unique algorithms. (See Chapter 2.)

CONCLUSION

Because there is much uncertainty and inconvenience in the current state of patent law, it is probably fruitless to pursue this route further unless your program is part of a larger unique process and meets the other requirements discussed above. It will take some time—perhaps a very long time—for the whole question of patent protection for software to even begin to be settled. Meanwhile, if you are adventuresome, patient, young, and decidedly wealthy, you may want to help resolve some of these questions. To do this you only need to retain a patent lawyer (preferably also young) who can apply for a patent for your program. Naturally, I can't predict what the Patent Office's response will be, but my guess is that the application will be rejected. At that point you can take the matter to court, and several years and many thousands of dollars later there is a small chance that you will find yourself before the U.S. Supreme Court. You may win your case, but don't count on it. The *Diamond v. Diehr* case was decided by a majority of merely one vote, which in itself doesn't inspire much confidence in the stability of software patent law. Most readers of this book, however, are more interested in writing and marketing their programs than in making legal history. If you fall into the first group, I suggest that you protect your program by using techniques other than patent law.

chapter 11
limiting liability

I have devoted two chapters to showing you how to legally protect your software from pirates. Unfortunately, there is another and often more dangerous group from whom you will need to protect yourself: unhappy customers.

In some ways software is like photographic film. The raw material is cheap and easily replaceable, but that which is stored on the film or disk can be priceless. Also, no matter how stringent the quality control, with film and floppies you never really know if the product will work until it is in the customer's camera or computer. Suppose, after spending a year and $20,000 photographing the quetzal bird in the jungles of Guatemala, you find that, because of a film defect, most of your color slides have a badly fogged background. Do you think the film manufacturer is going to reimburse you for your travel expenses? Not likely. At most you can expect some fresh film and a terse letter referring to a small disclaimer of warranty printed on every box of film.

This isn't as harsh as it might seem. In return for cheap film, users bear the risk of a bad roll. If the manufacturer of film had to pay full damages for the consequences of a roll of film's failing, the price of film would be substantially higher than it is now.

Example

Ledger Corp. manufactures bookkeeping software. It sends a case of program disks to a retailer. In transit the disks have a brief encounter with a box of magnetic pot holders. Although the magnetism damages the disks, this is not immediately apparent to users. Aldo buys one of the damaged Ledger programs and uses it for a while. Everything seems fine, so he invests $24,000 to convert his old bookkeeping system to the new software. When it comes time to close out his fiscal year, the whole program bombs and the data is lost. Aldo is annoyed. Not only has he lost his $24,000 and the $250 he paid for the program, but his books are in a mess and he can't tell who owes him money or what he owes others. The IRS is unamused and decides to audit Aldo after he files a late return. Aldo retains a CPA to clean up the mess and then hires a lawyer to clean up Ledger Corp. What is Ledger's liability?

Admittedly, this is an example that has a few problems. For instance, all computer accounting systems do include backup procedures, and the user should be advised to keep printouts of all data. But for the sake of the example, let's assume that a court determined the blame rests on Ledger Corp. If Ledger's floppies were sold with no valid warranty disclaimer, there is a possibility that Aldo could successfully recover in excess of $25,000 from Ledger Corp., the retail store, or both of them. This is a lot of potential liability considering the original program cost only $250. What can a software publisher do to protect itself besides closing shop?

Most software publishers take the same approach to programs that film manufacturers take to film. They will replace faulty media (floppies), but they will not pay any extra damages that arise because of a defective product. This can be accomplished legally by disclaiming several warranties. In order to understand how to disclaim a warranty, you must first know something about how they can be created.

CREATING A WARRANTY UNDER THE UNIFORM COMMERCIAL CODE

The Uniform Commercial Code (UCC) is a law that has been adopted by most states. Among other things it governs warranties, of which two main types have been established: express and implied.

EXPRESS UCC WARRANTIES

According to UCC Section 2-313, an express warranty is, in effect, an affirmation of fact or promise as to the quality of a program which is made by the seller and that becomes a part of the basis of the bargain. The first thing to notice is that the express warranty must be made by the seller. This seems to suggest that retailers, not publishers, have to worry about express warranties. However, a publisher who sells by direct mail or even advertises a program also might be held to have made an express warranty. Remember that the publisher is selling to the retailer, and the retailer might demand that the publisher honor any warranty that the publisher has made. At the risk of making this discussion seem like one of those endless sets of wooden nestling dolls, let's now examine the three types of express warranties that are possible under the UCC. Most people in the software industry are unaware of these warranties.

Affirmations of fact or promises   This type of express warranty normally develops out of sales literature, verbal sales pitches, packaging, instruction manuals, and so forth. One example might be a package that reads, "Data Bash, the database manager that holds 3560 addresses per floppy disk." This sort of warranty needn't even be made in writing. If a salesperson states "Data Bash will hold 3560 addresses on a single disk," the legal effect is as though it were a statement in writing. If someone buys the program partly as a result of this statement, a warranty has been created. If the program fails to live up to the statement, the warranty has been breached.

If you are selling programs, don't make claims that you can't support. Sure, you can say, "This is the best doggone program west of the Farallons." This is known in law as *puffing* and is considered the sort of sales pitch that no one should take too seriously. But when you make a statement that can be taken literally, such as "This program will sort 5000 fields using ten sort keys in seconds," be prepared to defend it.

Description of the goods   This type of express warranty is similar to the first. It is a description—usually a spec sheet, a table, or a chart—of the program. If Data Bash's product spec sheet reads, "This program generates Applesoft Basic files," this may be a form of warranty. If the program really generates Microsoft Basic files and if this specification can be said to be part of the basis of the bargain, the warranty will have been breached.

Sample or model   The last type of express warranty under the UCC arises from the use of a sample model to sell software. Retailers often demonstrate software in the store and therefore create this warranty—often without realizing it. This type of warranty promises that the software will work as well as it did during the store demonstration and is breached if it does not.

Now that you know the three types of express warranties, you might want to know what all this has to do with you. After all, isn't it the retailer who gets stuck in most cases? Not always. In creating the warranty the retailer has probably relied on your literature and your promises. While you might not be sued by the end user, you might be liable to the retailer, who can possibly claim that the warranty you offered was relied on when the warranty was made to the end user. It is, therefore, clearly in your interest to be careful not to make unintentional warranties since the retailer might rely on them and, in turn, pass them on to consumers. As noted before, you should be even more careful if you sell directly to end users.

How to Disclaim Express Warranties

The best way to disclaim an express warranty is not to make one in the first place. There is no legal requirement for you to make an express warranty, so if you don't want to make one, don't. One reason for telling you about the three ways of making an express warranty was to give you the information you need to avoid making one accidentally. However, if an ambitious employee is consumed with enthusiasm for a new program and promises the customer that it will do everything from bookkeeping to babysitting, a warranty may have been made and you may be stuck unless you specifically disclaim that warranty.

IMPLIED UCC WARRANTIES

Unlike an express warranty, an implied warranty needn't be a direct statement or demonstration. There are two important types of UCC implied warranties: the implied warranty of merchantability and the implied warranty of fitness for a particular purpose. Everyone in the software business tries to disclaim these warranties. Sometimes the disclaimers are effective; other times, especially if the matter goes before a consumer-oriented court, they are not. The last time I checked the warranty disclaimers at my local computer store I found only a few that I thought would stand up in court.

Implied warranty of merchantability   Unless this warranty is correctly disclaimed, it is automatically created every time a program is sold. It promises the user that the program will perform as well as programs of its type should perform. I know this is vague, but rather than dwelling on its nuances, let me tell you exactly how to disclaim this warranty. The point to remember is that if you do not properly disclaim the implied warranty of merchantability, it will automatically attach itself to your software.

Implied warranty of fitness   This warranty is not automatically created. It comes into play only if the seller (again, we are referring mainly to retailers) recommends a specific program for a customer's particular needs. For example, if a customer comes in and says "I need a payroll program to handle my fifty employees," and the retailer replies, "Payola will do the trick," the implied warranty of fitness has been created. If Payola actually can handle only twenty employees, the warranty has been broken.

Again, it is the retailers who will usually be stuck with defending themselves against lawsuits involving implied warranties. But as I mentioned before, publishers should do what they can to disclaim these warranties. The courts are becoming increasingly willing to allow consumers to sue manufacturers, so don't think you can successfully hide behind the retailer.

STEPS YOU CAN TAKE TO LIMIT YOUR LIABILITY

You now are convinced, I hope, that it makes sense to take steps to limit your liability. There are no totally foolproof ways of guaranteeing that your liability will be limited. If a liability issue should ever go to court, the court has fairly broad discretion in making its ruling. But here are some ideas that will certainly help reduce your potential legal exposure:

1. Make sure your software is reliable and fully tested. If you are a publisher, be certain one of your own programmers has tested the software thoroughly. Before releasing programs for business and industry, do a thorough beta testing. (See Chapter 7 for a sample beta test site contract.)

2. Make sure your advertising and sales claims for the program match its capabilities. Don't claim that even a child can learn it when it takes a Ph.D. If your ads have been deceptive, the court is permitted to treat the ads as if they were warranties made by you. You could then be held legally responsible for their veracity. In some cases, claims that you make for your product are held to be warranties. This, of course, doesn't mean you can't enthusiastically market your programs; just don't cross the fine line between salesmanship and deceptive advertising.

Example

You advertise that your bookkeeping program, Accounter, will handle everything from a personal checkbook to a large corporation's accounts-payable ledgers. A million-dollar company buys your software only to discover three months later that the program truncates all amounts over six digits.

In this instance you might be in trouble. Even though Accounter was fine for home use, it apparently was inadequate for a business application. Would you be in a better legal position if you had disclaimed all liability? The answer is "no." Warranty disclaimers do not usually shield sellers from the consequences of false advertising.

3. If, despite your rigorous quality-control system, which extends from program development to manufacturing, a customer reports a serious bug, what should you do to protect yourself? Immediately consider a program recall. A recall is indicated particularly if the defective program is one on which the end user's reliance is likely to produce real losses. Accounting, word processing, and data processing programs are some examples of the kinds of programs where defects can cause serious problems. Defective games and other consumer programs are less likely to cause serious problems; the consumer can return the program with little or no loss. Retailers are equipped to deal with these situations.

As every programmer knows, some bugs are very difficult to locate. And the fixing of one bug can introduce another. Therefore don't, in your eagerness to please your customers, send replacement software prematurely. Test and retest "fixed" software before re-releasing it. I know of one case where there were four releases before a bug was really fixed. With each release the company added a minor enhancement which was given to the customer at no charge. This helped to reestablish the lost goodwill, but the bug should have been fixed correctly the first time.

4. During a recall situation I advise you to document all the work done and every effort made to fix the problem, and keep a file of it. This documentation will be invaluable if a customer sues you or if your programmer sues you because you withheld any royalty payments until the bug was fixed.

THE DISCLAIMER

So far I have discussed how to minimize the chances that a customer will sue you and have suggested several ways to demonstrate your good faith if he should. Besides following these guidelines, you should use a warranty disclaimer. The warranty disclaimer serves to limit the customer's legal remedies should the matter ever go to court. In addition, the disclaimer should contain a limitation on damages. This is your last line of defense. It means that if the matter goes to court and if the customer wins, the amount of the damages may be limited to the amount set forth in the disclaimer.

It's important to remember that the disclaimer of warranty is not a magic charm that will protect you from all lawsuits. In fact many consumer-oriented courts will seek to invalidate a disclaimer if they possibly can. This is especially so if the case involves false advertising, a shoddy product, or poor customer relations.

Here is a sample disclaimer of warranty. Because the effectiveness of a disclaimer has much to do with how a program is packaged and presented to the buyer, you may wish to consult your attorney before using this one. This is especially true if you sell software which people rely on for important business uses.

THIS SOFTWARE AND MANUAL ARE SOLD "AS IS" AND WITHOUT WAR-RANTIES AS TO PERFORMANCE OR MERCHANTABILITY. THE SELLER'S SALESPERSONS MAY HAVE MADE STATEMENTS ABOUT THIS SOFT-WARE. ANY SUCH STATEMENTS DO NOT CONSTITUTE WARRANTIES AND SHALL NOT BE RELIED ON BY THE BUYER IN DECIDING WHETHER TO PURCHASE THIS PROGRAM.

THIS PROGRAM IS SOLD WITHOUT ANY EXPRESS OR IMPLIED WARRAN-TIES WHATSOEVER. BECAUSE OF THE DIVERSITY OF CONDITIONS AND HARDWARE UNDER WHICH THIS PROGRAM MAY BE USED, NO WAR-RANTY OF FITNESS FOR A PARTICULAR PURPOSE IS OFFERED. THE USER IS ADVISED TO TEST THE PROGRAM THOROUGHLY BEFORE RELY-ING ON IT. THE USER MUST ASSUME THE ENTIRE RISK OF USING THE PROGRAM. ANY LIABILITY OF SELLER OR MANUFACTURER WILL BE LIMITED EXCLUSIVELY TO PRODUCT REPLACEMENT OR REFUND OF THE PURCHASE PRICE.

If your program doesn't have a manual you may delete the words, AND MANUAL ARE and substitute the word IS. Again, consult your lawyer if you want to make even a slight change. Disclaimers are trickier than they look; a small word change can have a big effect.

Let's look at the disclaimer point by point. The first sentence disclaims the implied warranty of merchantability. The words AS IS are a legally recognized way of disclaiming this warranty. The second and third sentences disclaim any express warranties made by salespeople. The fourth sentence disclaims all other express and implied warranties. The fifth sentence disclaims the implied warranty of fitness for a purpose. The sixth advises the buyer to test the program, which is good general advice and further strengthens the disclaimer. The seventh sentence summarizes the disclaimer by telling the user, "Use this program at your own risk." The last sentence limits the amount of damages should the matter get to court by telling the user that any liability will not extend beyond a replacement of the program or a refund of the price.

WHERE TO PUT THE DISCLAIMER

I mentioned earlier that many disclaimers are legally inadequate. While sometimes the defect has to do with the wording of the disclaimer, more often the disclaimer fails because it is not correctly presented to the buyer. If someone must actually buy the program in order to see its disclaimer, the disclaimer is invalid. In order to dis-claim a warranty, the buyer must be clearly notified of the disclaimer before the sale takes place. Obviously, for this advance notice to occur the warranty disclaimer should be printed where it can be read without the necessity of unpackaging the program. A good place is on the back of a shrink-wrapped package (make sure your packing person puts the disclaimer facing out, not in). It's also a good idea to print the disclaimer on the inside or back cover of the manual, or if there is no manual on the instruction sheet. You might be wondering about those dozens of warranty dis-claimer cards piled in a shoe box in your closet. Some of these undoubtedly were packed in the box of the item that you bought. I'm sure you didn't even see the card until you got home. These cards are invalid attempts to disclaim warranties. True, they might discourage a consumer from trying to obtain satisfaction, but legally most of them are meaningless.

It's critical that you print the disclaimer in a type size that is readable. Contrary to the belief of some people, a disclaimer must be readable to be valid. The theory behind a disclaimer is that the person buying the product has in fact read it before buying the product, or, if not, that it is no one's fault but the buyer's. Some people worry about discouraging customers by printing a prominent disclaimer. This is not a realistic worry. The American public is used to disclaimers. Consider the health warnings on cigarette packages. And when was the last time you didn't buy a roll of film because of the warranty disclaimer on the box?

Until now our discussion has dealt with the Uniform Commercial Code warranties. There is, however, another area that is also of importance in connection with liability. The personal computer and its software come within the reach of various consumer protection laws. This is true even when the personal computer is used solely for business purposes. The most important of these laws is known officially as The Magnuson-Moss Warranty—Federal Trade Commission Improvement Act, 15 USC 2301. First, the bad news. This is a complex piece of legislation that is controlled by equally complex Federal Trade Commission (FTC) rules. The good news is that you can keep your software out of reach of this act if you do not warrant it in any way. We have just discussed how to avoid creating express warranties and how to disclaim those created automatically. Do this properly and you shouldn't have to worry about the Magnuson-Moss Act.

This act does come into play if you sell your program with a written warranty. While, at this writing, there are not yet any legal decisions on this point, it is believed that the act will generally apply only to the magnetic media, that is to the physical product, and not to the program it contains unless you make specific claims about the workings of the program. I should point out that this is a changing area of the law, and what is true today may be false tomorrow.[1] The act's definition of what constitutes a written warranty includes some of the written warranties that would arise under the UCC, as well as written promises by suppliers to refund, repair, replace, or take other remedial action if the program fails to meet the specs set out in the written warranty. There are a couple of types of warranties that arise under the UCC that are not considered warranties under the act. For example, spec sheets and the right to return the product, even if written, are not, by themselves, written warranties for the purpose of the act, though they might be under the UCC.

Notice that I have used the word supplier not seller. It's important to realize that this act applies not only to retailers but also to publishers.

Before going further, keep the following in mind:

1. You can keep free of the act by validly disclaiming all warranties and by making sure you don't promise to repair and replace. If you promise to replace defective disks, don't make statements about the quality of the program; simply state that disks that do not boot will be replaced.

2. The act will generally apply only to the media, which is quite inexpensive, unless you specifically warrant the program itself.

3. The act requires a written warranty to trigger it.

You might at this point ask, "Although this act seems technical, my exposure is pretty limited since it covers only the media, so why worry?" A good question. One answer is that the act provides that, if you do offer what amounts to a warranty as defined by the act, you cannot validly disclaim implied UCC warranties. This might seem a bit technical, but what it amounts to is that, if you make a warranty that triggers the act, you may also automatically trigger the UCC implied warranties which you so conscientiously tried to disclaim. These UCC warranties, remember, are not limited to just the media, as the act warranties are.

There is another important twist to the act. If you provide a service contract for free or for a fee, and it involves servicing the software within ninety days of its sale, this offering will be considered a written warranty under the act. Therefore, unless you plan on creating a warranty and running the risk of triggering the UCC implied warranties, don't offer service contracts within ninety days of the sale of the program.

CLASSES OF WARRANTIES—FULL AND LIMITED

If you don't wish to avoid the act's warranties altogether, you should know that there are two classes of act warranties. You have undoubtedly seen them often. One is a full warranty and the other is a limited warranty. The limited warranty allows you to limit the UCC implied warranties provided that the limitation is for no shorter a period than the length of time that the limited warranty itself is effective.

Full Warranties. I can state with confidence that no one in the software industry is offering or is likely to offer a full warranty. To do so involves offering free replacements, no limitations on damages, and no limitations of implied warranties, among other things. Therefore, I do not think it is necessary to discuss the detailed requirements for full warranties.

Limited Warranties. Some publishers offer limited warranties. These warranties should extend only to the media itself and not to the program. Rather than offering a detailed discussion of the limited warranty, I have included a sample for you to use if you want to. Remember that you don't have to use it. If you do, you are only warranting the diskette itself and not the program contained on it. This limited warranty contains a disclaimer which, if you choose to use it, should replace the disclaimer given above. As with that disclaimer, you should discuss this limited warranty with your lawyer to make sure it fits your requirements.

LIMITED WARRANTY

THIS PROGRAM, INSTRUCTION MANUAL, AND REFERENCE MATERIALS ARE SOLD "AS IS," WITHOUT WARRANTY AS TO THEIR PERFORMANCE, MERCHANTABILITY, OR FITNESS FOR ANY PARTICULAR PURPOSE. THE ENTIRE RISK AS TO THE RESULTS AND PERFORMANCE OF THIS PROGRAM IS ASSUMED BY YOU.

HOWEVER, TO THE ORIGINAL PURCHASER ONLY, THE PUBLISHER WARRANTS THE MAGNETIC DISKETTE ON WHICH THE PROGRAM IS RECORDED TO BE FREE FROM DEFECTS IN MATERIALS AND FAULTY WORKMANSHIP UNDER NORMAL USE FOR A PERIOD OF NINETY DAYS FROM THE DATE OF PURCHASE. IF DURING THIS NINETY-DAY PERIOD THE DISKETTE SHOULD BECOME DEFECTIVE, IT MAY BE RETURNED TO THE PUBLISHER FOR A REPLACEMENT WITHOUT CHARGE, PROVIDED YOU HAVE PREVIOUSLY SENT IN YOUR LIMITED WARRANTY REGISTRATION CARD TO THE PUBLISHER OR SEND PROOF OF PURCHASE OF THE PROGRAM.

YOUR SOLE AND EXCLUSIVE REMEDY IN THE EVENT OF A DEFECT IS EXPRESSLY LIMITED TO REPLACEMENT OF THE DISKETTE AS PROVIDED ABOVE. IF FAILURE OF A DISKETTE HAS RESULTED FROM ACCIDENT OR ABUSE THE PUBLISHER SHALL HAVE NO RESPONSIBILITY TO REPLACE THE DISKETTE UNDER THE TERMS OF THIS LIMITED WARRANTY.

ANY IMPLIED WARRANTIES RELATING TO THE DISKETTE, INCLUDING ANY IMPLIED WARRANTIES OF MERCHANTABILITY AND FITNESS FOR A PARTICULAR PURPOSE, ARE LIMITED TO A PERIOD OF NINETY DAYS FROM DATE OF PURCHASE. PUBLISHER SHALL NOT BE LIABLE FOR INDIRECT, SPECIAL, OR CONSEQUENTIAL DAMAGES RESULTING FROM THE USE OF THIS PRODUCT. SOME STATES DO NOT ALLOW THE EXCLUSION OR LIMITATION OF INCIDENTAL OR CONSEQUENTIAL DAMAGES, SO THE ABOVE LIMITATIONS MIGHT NOT APPLY TO YOU. THIS WARRANTY GIVES YOU SPECIFIC LEGAL RIGHTS, AND YOU MAY ALSO HAVE OTHER RIGHTS WHICH VARY FROM STATE TO STATE.

WARRANTY REGISTRATION CARD
NAME: _____
COMPANY: _____
ADDRESS: _____
CITY: _____
STATE: _____
TYPE OF BUSINESS: _____
PROGRAM PURCHASE: _____
SERIAL NUMBER: _____
DATE PURCHASED: _____
COMPUTER BRAND: _____

Notice that the warranty form includes a registration card. Since it is only a limited warranty, this card is fine to use. If you don't plan to use this limited warranty form, or plan to disclaim all warranties, don't use this card. Instead, if you want to use a registration card for creating mailing lists, consider something like the following form. It has been carefully worded to avoid raising or triggering warranties.

USER FEEDBACK CARD

We want to keep in touch with users. Please fill out and mail this card immediately.
Name: _____
Address: _____
City: _____
State: _____ *Zip:* _____ *Phone (   )* _____
Where did you buy the program? _____
When? _____
How much did you pay? _____
How would you rate the user manual? /   /excellent   /   /good   /   /poor
How would you rate the program? /   /excellent   /   /good   /   /poor

Feel free to add any other questions you feel appropriate.

As you should now realize, warranties are an extremely tricky and technical area of the law. As applied to software, warranty law is a new field, so expect the rules to change without warning. In addition, the existence or nonexistence of a warranty is totally dependent on the specific facts of each person's situation. Therefore, let me give you a disclaimer of my own. Do not rely on the information in this chapter without having a knowledgeable lawyer review it in connection with your specific situation. The fact that you will have read this chapter should help you keep out of trouble (your lawyer can't do that for you) and will help you communicate with your lawyer.

INSURANCE AS A PROTECTION DEVICE

ERRORS AND OMISSIONS

Insurance is a common device that companies use to limit the risk of financial loss. The name of the coverage available for the software industry is "errors and omissions" insurance. Coverage is specialized, so it's available from only a handful of companies. Most contracts are designed for data processing service centers that produce computerized data on their own equipment from their customers' source material. There are, however, two or three insurers that offer coverage for programmers and publishers who design software for specific applications.

Most errors and omissions policies protect you against claims arising out of negligent acts and errors or omissions committed or alleged to have been committed by the insured. The legal defense of a claim typically is handled by the insurance company as part of the coverage. Usually coverage will not cover claims that arise for any of the following reasons:

- Delay
- Dishonest, fraudulent, criminal, or malicious acts or omissions by the insured
- Loss or damage of other peoples' property, including loss of use
- Tax returns or balance-sheet preparation
- Bodily injury
- Claims by anyone with a financial interest in the insured
- Punitive or exemplary damages imposed by a court or jury
- Claims involving disclosure or unauthorized use of confidential data (trade secrets)

Depending on your needs some of these exclusions could be modified or deleted, though this may make the policy more expensive. Most policies contain a deductible that must be paid by the insured. Usually it is at least one thousand dollars but, depending on the nature of your business, it can be more. Here are some of the items a typical errors and omissions policy covers:

- Income lost by others resulting from your negligent act
- Expenses incurred by the claimant (the person suing you) in an effort to maintain normal operations during the problem
- Cost of reprocessing to correct your negligent actions
- Loss of a customer's vital records
- Loss of control of a customer's inventory or accounts-receivable

Premiums vary depending on the nature and size of the insured, the limitations of the policy, and the amount of the deductible. Usually the premium is based on a certain amount per one thousand dollars of gross sales.

Those who want errors and omissions insurance should carefully choose an independent insurance broker who knows about this form of coverage and who has access to the few companies that offer it. Interview the broker, and check references. Since errors and omissions coverage is specialized and highly negotiable, a knowledgeable broker will be in the best position to find and negotiate the proper coverage at a competitive price. This negotiation process may involve persuading the underwriters to modify or delete certain exclusions and in general to tailor the insurance coverage to fit your needs. If you can get this coverage, it is likely that the insurance company will have specific requirements regarding disclaimers of warranty. Obviously the decision whether or not to buy insurance has to take into account the reliability of your software and your ability to either recover from, or pass on, the fallout from faulty software[2].

---

[1] Turnkey systems may fall under the act, in which case both software and hardware would be covered as a single product.

[2] Thanks to William L. Pope of John Burnham and Company, Newport Beach, CA 92660. They can provide errors and omissions coverage.

chapter 12
remedies

Until now I've focused on measures you may take to minimize the chance you will face a serious legal problem. As you have undoubtedly inferred, I believe that the adage "An ounce of prevention is worth a pound of cure" is appropriate to law and doubly so to software law. Even if you've done what you can to avoid trouble, there is no guarantee that trouble won't find you. In this chapter I will discuss how to approach legal problems and review some of the strategies available to you.

The first impulse of some people faced with a legal problem is to call in a lawyer and charge into battle. The first reaction of others is to bury their heads in the nearest sandbox and hope that the trouble will disappear. The problem with the aggressive approach is that you may find yourself involved in an expensive, lengthy, and enervating lawsuit. On the other hand, hiding and hoping that the problem will evaporate is also far from ideal. The unaggressive approach can easily lead to the loss of valuable rights, and ultimately may land you in court.

What should your response be when confronted with a legal problem relating to your software? As an alternative to immediately initiating legal action or simply ignoring the problem, I recommend the following approach.

HOW TO APPROACH A LEGAL PROBLEM

1. *Define the problem.* Often the appropriate response to a legal problem will become clear if you sit down and, as rationally as possible, try to define it in writing. Your written definition should include all the ramifications of the problem that you can foresee. First, be sure that you have a good working understanding of the legal issues. If you are unclear about a point of law either you can research it yourself or you can consult a lawyer. While it does cost to have a lawyer educate you, don't, if the stakes are high, let a couple of hundred dollars stand between you and a clear understanding of your case. Remember that buying a legal opinion is far less costly than retaining a lawyer by saying, "Take over this case and let me know in a few months how it goes."

   Once you have an understanding of the legal rules that affect your case, try to estimate how much it might cost you if it remains unresolved. Then try to figure out how much time and money it would cost to resolve it. These two

141

financial forecasts may be off the mark, but at least they are an early attempt to quantify your problem. Finally, decide how much psychic value the problem has; that is, what it is worth to your peace of mind to have the situation resolved.

2. *Decide on a course of action.* Now it's time to ask yourself what specifically you want in terms of measurable results. Again, depending on what you decide, this may or may not involve hiring a lawyer. You may decide that a simple letter or phone call will do the trick or, when a dispute can't be settled informally, you may want to suggest binding arbitration. Perhaps you'll be happy with a written apology and a bottle of wine from the other side. (I suspect this solution would satisfy fifty percent of all potential litigants.) Or you may decide to call in the guns and do legal battle.

3. *Pursue your course of action.* Try to structure your response so that you will be able to measure quickly whether it was successful. This will usually involve establishing a deadline for the other side's response. For instance, if you write a letter to a person who has been illegally selling copies of your program, include in the letter a date by which that person must, in writing, promise to stop the illegal conduct. That way you will know quickly what, if anything, you should do next.

4. *Evaluate your results.* Periodically monitor the situation and review your strategy. Again, it's easier to do this if you have written things down and assigned deadlines for responses. If the problem isn't on the way to being resolved, you will have to go through the subroutine discussed under "Define the Problem." This time you may decide to take firmer action; you may decide to hire a lawyer. On the other hand, you may decide to let the matter drop because solving it, you feel, will take more time and money than it is worth. Either way you will have approached the problem logically, with the result you want to achieve and the resources you want to allocate in clear view.

1. *Open up a case file.* As elementary as this may sound, many people don't take the simple step of getting a manila folder and putting all the items relating to a case in it. I know of instances where correspondence that would have been valuable evidence wound up in the wastebasket because no one felt like filing it. So be sensitive (without being paranoid) to potential legal problems by setting up a case file promptly. Even if nine times out of ten the potential issue dissipates, that tenth time will make it all worthwhile.

2. *Get it in writing.* One important reason for setting up a case file is to collect evidence that may be useful in proving your case or at least in showing the other side that you could prove your case should you choose to do so. Conversations don't fit into files and are hard to prove (don't tape them) if the other party doesn't follow through on a verbal commitment. Whenever you think you have reached a verbal settlement, try to have it put in writing and have both parties sign it. At the very least send a letter to the other side confirming your settlement or conversation. Keep a photocopy in your file. When you receive a letter, staple it to the envelope. The postmark showing when the letter was mailed may come in handy. Also, buy a "RECEIVED" stamp, and stamp everything you get in the mail with the date on which it was delivered.

It is impossible to cover every kind of legal problem that one might encounter. The possibilities are as infinite as the number of ways one person can annoy another. Equally numerous are the possible responses to a problem. There is never a response that will always be right. I will, therefore, outline the kinds of legal problems that most commonly affect software and some options that may be chosen to deal with them.

TRADE SECRETS

There are two principal threats to a trade secret. The most devastating is disclosure. Someone may get hold of your source code and publish it in a computer magazine or pass it out in a computer class. Once your trade secret is disclosed, it is generally lost as a trade secret. (If the disclosure is to a very limited group, you may be able to salvage it.) When a trade secret is lost there is not much you can do about it except seek recompense from the person who disclosed the secret. The key to doing this is to prove that the trade secret was disclosed wrongfully.

Example

Gulp magazine publishes the source code of a program designed to do very fast record sorts. It was developed by Jane Adams. Jane considered this program, called Sorty, to be her most valuable trade secret. Jane's assistant mailed the source code of Sorty to *Gulp* magazine in place of another program that Jane wanted to publish. *Gulp* was not aware of the mistake and published the source code. In this case it is clear that *Gulp* did not obtain the program wrongfully and therefore owes Jane nothing.

Example

Suppose *Gulp*'s editor found Jane's program under a chair where Jane had accidentally dropped it. This situation is less clear, although one certainly couldn't say that *Gulp* came by the program wrongfully. Again, *Gulp* would not owe Jane anything for disclosing her trade secret, but she might be able to sue for copyright infringement.

Example

Now suppose *Gulp* bribed Jane's secretary, Jim, to transmit a copy of Sorty over the phone. The trade secret in this situation was obtained wrongfully. Jane could justifiably demand damages should *Gulp* disclose or use the program. In addition, she can sue Jim, who might also be prosecutable under criminal law. Should Jane immediately start the court process? It depends on whether the magazine has yet printed the program. If it has not, but intends to, she should immediately see her lawyer about obtaining an injunction against *Gulp* to stop the presses.[1] If the damage is already done because the program has been printed, Jane might want to try negotiating a settlement herself for the damage she sustained. She might, for example, settle for a year's full-page color ads in *Gulp* magazine in lieu of or in addition to monetary damages. Before doing anything, however, she should evaluate her legal problem, as I suggested earlier in this chapter. If the damage is significant enough for her to feel justified in hiring a lawyer, she should do so and hope that the amount awarded will be enough to cover her attorney's fees. In some cases the court will award attorney's fees, but one's assessment of the need to go to court should not depend on the assumption that attorney's fees will be awarded. Of course, hiring a lawyer does not mean Jane will necessarily or even probably wind up in court. A good lawyer will explore with her all the options that may achieve the results she wants.

Generally, people who approach a legal problem with the hope of achieving justice in some cosmic sense end up disillusioned and somewhat poorer for the experience. While it is undoubtedly satisfying to nail someone who deserves it, you will always pay some sort of price in money and time. Be certain the potential results are at least as valuable as the price you will pay.

The second threat to a trade secret is usually a dispute which does not center on disclosure per se, as in the preceding examples. Instead the dispute will revolve around whether or not someone who has had legitimate access to a trade secret can use it. The usual scenario of such a software trade-secret problem runs like this:

Example

Jane's programmer, Ross, decides that he's had enough of Jane's autocratic ways and, after taking a matchbook-cover course. "Be Your Own Boss," opens up a software business of his own. He sells a program named Sifty that looks, feels, and smells very much like Sorty. Jane naturally want to put a stop to this. What are her options? Much depends on the position Ross takes. Suppose he claims that Sifty was his own creation and is unrelated to Sorty. If he is telling the truth, there is nothing that Jane can do. If Ross is lying, then Jane may be able to get an injunction keeping him from using or disclosing Sorty. The trade secret in this case could be saved if Ross has not already disclosed it.

Example

Now suppose Ross claims that Sorty is his program or at least partly his because he helped Jane invent it. This may be true. It depends on his arrangements with Jane. As you can see, if she had taken the preventative steps of having Ross sign nondisclosure agreements and a work-for-hire agreement, she would have a better case. Courts have occasionally held that a trade secret belonged to both the employee and employer.

Employees are not the only ones who can cause problems. Licensees and customers who have had legitimate access to a trade secret may suddenly decide to compete with you. In this case the existence of well-drafted license agreements may be instrumental in showing that a trade secret belongs to you.

Generally trade secret infringement problems are such that it's a good idea to have a lawyer working with you from the start, unless the secret you are trying to protect has no more than sentimental value. This is because you are dealing with a property right which can be lost entirely if you don't act quickly and forcefully. A warning letter to someone who is about to abuse a trade secret will put them on notice, but once the secret is out, it's out. In other areas of law, it is less important to come on so strong and fast.

COPYRIGHTS

The first thing to be sure of before dealing with a potential copyright problem is that your program is registered with the Copyright Office. As was discussed in detail in Chapter 3, copyright law specifically requires registration before you can even go to court (17 USC 411).

Next, decide how large the problem is. If a small user group is passing out a few copies of your program to its members, you may wish to send them a stern letter or you may wish to have your lawyer do so. This puts the infringers on notice that the copying is illegal. Later, if you should take them to court, they will not be able to plead innocent because of ignorance. In many cases a letter pointing out the criminal and civil sanctions against copying will be enough to stop the casual infringer.

Sometimes a letter may not be the best approach, as with a profiteering pirate who would be likely to pack up and sail away in response to it. There is a fairly rare procedure called a "writ of seizure," by which you can have a U.S. marshall seize the infringing copies, provided that you post a bond equal to twice the value of the material seized. This is used in extreme cases. The nice thing about it is that the procedure is *ex parte,* in other words, the pirate doesn't even have to be advised in advance of any court hearing (17 USC 501 Rules 3-4 [*Rules of Practice for Copyright Cases*]). See a lawyer about this one.

In some cases it's difficult to know when to sue and when not to. Suppose a computer store gives away free bootleg copies of your program with the purchase of certain computers. In this situation you may want to sue if you can prove the facts of the case. Once you institute a suit you may, through a common legal technique known as "discovery," be able to obtain a list of the customers who have been given your software. These people can be made to surrender their copies. You can see how a suit like this can become very ugly very fast. Always keep in mind the potential negative impact of throwing the book at someone. I'm not suggesting that you should let infringers go; I simply suggest that you shouldn't pick on ninety-seven-pound weaklings.

Even in the previous situation in which a computer store is giving away your software there are plenty of creative ways of obtaining satisfaction without suing. For example, you might get on the phone and tell the dealer that you are aware of what's going on. Don't threaten the dealer, but use a little leverage short of filing suit. Even after filing (should you decide to do so), but before going to court, you can always try to come to a settlement with the infringer. A substantial order of your programs may be a good settlement. There is a certain justice in forcing an infringer to buy your programs. They are now stocked in such abundance that the dealer will have to sing your praises in order to sell them. This might be a way of turning an enemy into a good customer. Naturally, when dealing with someone of dubious character, you should demand your money up front.

The legal remedies for copyright infringement are found in Chapter 5 of Title 17 of the U.S. Code, and are discussed in greater detail in Chapter 3. They include:

- Injunctions (17 USC 502)
- Impounding and destroying infringing articles (17 USC 503)
- Damages (17 USC 504)
- Discretionary costs and attorney's fees (17 USC 505)
- Criminal penalties (17 USC 506)

One remedy that is often overlooked, but is useful when the infringing software is being imported into the United States, is to have customs stop the software when it arrives. You can't use this remedy unless the software has already been registered with the Copyright Office. For a fee, you can even have customs notify you if they see anything that looks like your software (labels or manual) being brought into the country (17 USC 602, 603).

While I don't recommend allowing a person to copy large numbers of your programs without a challenge, it is important to realize that the copyright law does not require you to pursue every infringer. As a practical matter you will want to let the small fry go with a letter of warning and thus save your energy for the medium-size and big-time operators.

CONTRACTS

Sooner or later just about everyone involved with software will have a contract problem. It may be as simple as a late royalty payment or as complicated as a question over whether an ambiguously worded license agreement gives the publisher the right to market software for a new computer.

Suppose, for example, that a license read "Firstware has the right to market JunkMail on the Nutrino Computer." A year later Nutrino announces the Mutrino, a new machine jointly produced with an English computer firm. Can Firstware sell JunkMail for the Mutrino even though it did not exist at the time of the agreement? Your guess is as good as mine. A well-drafted contract should address the issue of machines that do not yet exist, but no one can write a perfect contract every time.

Contract disputes seem to fall into a couple of broad categories. Let's call the first good-faith disagreements, which occur when both parties sincerely believe they are right. The key to resolving this sort of problem is to keep the channels of communication open. If you can keep a good-faith disagreement from escalating into open warfare, there is a chance that you can settle the problem in the same way you wrote the initial contract—through negotiation. If negotiation fails, arbitration sometimes succeeds as an alternative to a full-blown lawsuit. You can use arbitration either if both parties agree to it after the problem arises or if both agreed to it in writing when the original contract was signed.

One suggestion I have found valuable in trying to settle a good-faith dispute is to NEVER mention the words "court" or "lawyer" unless you really intend to go that route. Nothing brings negotiations to a halt faster than the whisper of lawsuits. Again, remember to get any settlement in writing and to keep a case file on all disputes. This is true even if the dispute-resolution process seems to be going smoothly and amicably.

The other kind of contract dispute is a bad-faith dispute. This occurs when one party decides to break the contract. A money problem or any of a number of other reasons could be behind the party's decision. Some people, following the lead of entertainers and sports heroes, perhaps, feel it is all right to break a contract when it becomes economical to do so. A publisher, for instance, might owe a programmer royalties that simply cannot be immediately paid. Rather than settling the problem in a straightforward manner, the publisher accuses the programmer of having delivered a poor-quality program. If there is a significant amount of money involved in a bad-faith dispute or a significant property right at stake (ownership of the copyright, for instance), then swift recourse to the courts may be the best and most direct solution. There is no point in prolonging negotiations with someone who does not feel bound to honor commitments.

Sometimes the difference between good- and bad-faith disputes is blurred.

Example

Suppose Tom and Firstware disagree on whether Tom should be paid royalties on programs that Firstware sold to a computer store that went bankrupt before paying for them. Tom feels he is entitled to a royalty and that bad debts are Firstware's problem. Unfortunately, the contract is silent on the matter. Right now this is a good-faith dispute which, if possible, should be settled through negotiation.

Instead of negotiating, however, Tom hires a lawyer to threaten Firstware with the loss of its exclusivity rights in JunkMail unless it pays the disputed amount. Firstware responds through its own lawyer by announcing it will stop selling JunkMail. Now that both sides have retained lawyers, direct communication between Tom and Firstware ceases (at the insistence of both attorneys). Tom further escalates the problem by selling JunkMail directly to retailers in order to make up for Firstware's no longer selling it. The matter winds up in court. What should have been resolved simply has turned into a nightmare. At this point the lawyers start preparing their cases. They take the most extreme positions possible. Questions about the quality of JunkMail are raised now that were never raised before. Questions about the quality of Firstware's marketing efforts are raised by Tom's lawyer, even though until the dispute arose Tom was delighted with the size of his royalty checks. Once this process starts, it takes on a momentum of its own; anything becomes fair game. Both Tom and Firstware lost sight of the simple fact that it is in neither's economic interest to hurt the other.

There are, of course, many other types of contract disputes. Rather than try to deal with them all here, I suggest that, if you find yourself in the middle of a contract dispute, you follow the general procedures specified earlier in this chapter. In addition, do the following:

1. Reread the contract carefully. The subject of the dispute may be covered in the contract but overlooked by one or both sides. Or you may notice that there are obligations under the contract that the other party has failed to fulfill. This information will serve as a bargaining chip during settlement negotiations.

2. If the dispute is in good faith, try negotiating a settlement. I do not recommend involving lawyers initially unless you feel that the relevant law is technical or that the sides have become so distant that face-to-face negotiations have little value. You may wish to hire a lawyer for consultation without having to turn the whole process over to one.

3. Consider arbitration. Arbitration has its pros and cons, but I think it is generally a good way of arriving at a fair, reasonably quick, and inexpensive result. Some of the court formalities, however, relating to evidence and discovery are lacking, and this may or may not be to your benefit. Also, there is no possibility for the loser to appeal the case unless gross misconduct by the arbitrators can be proved. Finally, arbitration often results in compromise, where there is no clear-cut victor. Depending on the circumstances both parties may be unhappy with the result, since neither actually has won the case.

4. Realize that winning the battle over a contract dispute may result in your losing the war. If the other side is so alienated by your position that it will no longer trust you enough to do business with you, you may, win or lose, find yourself in an unenviable position. Try to win your point without losing the relationship. This may mean compromise even if you believe in your heart that you are right.

TRADEMARKS

As I stated before, trademark law is an area for specialists. If you feel that someone is violating your trademark rights, you probably should see a patent and trademark lawyer. If you care to, you can send letters to the infringers telling them to stop, but if you really want action, spend the money on a lawyer.

One trademark problem that crops up often in the software business has to do with using someone else's trademark in an advertisement. Publishers who sell software designed to run on an Apple, for example, have to be able to use the word "Apple" in advertisements in order to sell their software. Technically, they are allowed to do so as long as they don't give the impression in the ad that the program is endorsed or published by Apple Computer. In addition, it is wise to footnote at least the first mention of "Apple," thereby acknowledging that the trademark "Apple" belongs to Apple Computer, Inc.

Example

Ross has succeeded in proving to the courts that he owns all rights in his sorting program called Sifty. Next, he launches into an aggressive ad campaign, which includes full-page color ads in *Gulp* magazine. His ad is a "no holds barred" feature-by-feature cost comparison of Sifty and Sorty, Jane's program. In addition, Ross hired a famous ad agency to write a jingle, which now appears at the top of each ad and on Ross's business card:

SORTY is nifty but
SIFTY is thrifty

Jane is more than irritated. She hires a lawyer to sue Ross for trademark infringement. Has Ross committed anything worse than bad taste? The answer depends on whether the public is likely to be confused by the ad into thinking that Sorty and Sifty are published by the same company. In this case, there might be some confusion. A court could hold that Ross must acknowledge in a footnote on each future ad and on his business cards that Sorty is a trademark belonging to Jane.

COLLECTING MONEY

Partly because the software industry is so young, there are a good many programmers, computer stores, and publishers going in and out of business on almost a daily basis. Often a dispute will arise over nothing more than one person's owing another money and being unable or unwilling to pay it. Here are a few techniques for dealing with this sort of problem:

1. Send statements. If you are a publisher, you should send monthly statements to all accounts over thirty days. This might seem an obvious step, but one reason for sending statements is less than obvious. Sometimes when a retailer owes money, if the matter gets to court, counsel will attempt to raise defenses relating to the quality of the merchandise received but not paid for. In other words, you will suddenly start hearing about short shipments, defective disks, and damaged merchandise. If you can show, however, that you sent statements on a regular basis and that the retailer accepted them, it will be much harder to bring up defenses relating to the merchandise. The retailer can be said to have acquiesced to the accuracy of the statement.

2. Cash on Delivery (COD). While no retailer likes paying cash up front for merchandise, don't be afraid of putting customers on a COD basis before they have the opportunity to fall too far behind in their payments. It might seem a little strange, but my experience has been that customers are often less offended by having to pay COD if the policy is made sooner rather than later. If you wait month after payless month until you blow up and send a nasty letter, your customer won't be grateful for your former easygoing attitude. Instead, you will have made an enemy.

3. Copy all incoming checks. Even though it might seem tedious, you should copy and file all incoming checks. Checks contain the customer's bank account number and, of course, the bank's name. This information may come in handy if you want to find out whether the customer has money in the account. Call the bank, read the bookkeeper the account number, and ask if there is enough money in the account to clear your check. Also, if you ever have to sue your customer, collecting the judgment can be expedited if you know the name of the bank and the account number. Incidentally, the reason for copying all checks rather than just recording the customer's bank account number is that companies in financial trouble often switch banks, leaving you (and other creditors) wondering where to find the money.

4. Get written payment schedules from late payers. You should persuade late payers to commit to a written payment schedule. If they do this and still miss a payment, they will have broken a written commitment to you. At this point you can decide whether to sue or grant an extension. The written payment schedule avoids the problem of vague promises such as "Next week I think I can get some money to you." One never really knows where to draw the line unless a written commitment is broken.

5. Charge interest. The interest charged on late payers can sometimes be enough to pay your bookkeeper's salary. Before charging interest, call a late payer and explain that you simply can't afford to lend money interest-free. If you explain it

in these terms, the customer will be more likely to pay than if an item titled "interest" just appears on the statement. After calling the customer, write a note confirming your conversation. Besides earning money on your receivables, charging interest will also encourage late payers to pay you before they pay another publisher who doesn't charge interest. Finally, a customer who pays interest on an invoice will be less likely to dispute the amount of the invoice later on.

6. Don't be afraid to sue, especially in small-claims court. Sometimes customers are so impervious to pleas and threats that it becomes less of a headache to sue them than to send out still another photocopy of their outstanding invoices. If the debt is small and you are in the same state as the debtor, consider small-claims court. If the amount owed is more than the small-claims court allows (usually $750–$3000, depending on the state), try suing once for each outstanding invoice starting with the oldest one. If small-claims court is not for you, hire an attorney to file in the appropriate court. This need not be expensive since the debtor may not even show up. The quicker you sue, the more likely you will be able to collect a judgment before the debtor disappears.

7. Don't be afraid to collect your judgments. Contrary to popular belief, collecting a judgment is not all that difficult if the debtor is still in business. You can attach the debtor's bank account. (You know the bank and account number from the check you copied and you can call the bank to see if the account contains enough money to cover the judgment.) If the account is empty, you can send a sheriff to the debtor's business to seize various items of value, which will be sold to satisfy the judgment. In most states you can order the sheriff to send in a "keeper" who will stand patiently by the cash register to collect all money being paid for merchandise until your judgment is satisfied. The debtor is charged for these collection tactics.

PROVING INFRINGEMENT

One of the biggest practical problems with squashing an infringer is proving your case. This has led many lawyers and programmers to the cynical view that if you have to go to court you may as well forget it. I think this overstates the problem a bit, though it certainly can be hard and sometimes even impossible to prove certain types of infringement.

The first problem lies in the nature of software itself. If one has the source code, cosmetic changes are easily made. Even with the object code and a disassembler it is possible to make changes. Moreover, it is possible to use just a small piece of central code in another type of program. This can be impossible to detect. While it is relatively easy to disguise software, it is often difficult to unmask the deception. If detection is difficult, imagine trying to explain to a jury, which has been expressly chosen for its ignorance about software, that though the two printouts before them look totally different, they are substantially the same.

This brings us to the second problem. Not only are juries unfamiliar with computers and software, but so too are most judges. You can spend weeks boring everyone in the court to tears with definitions of hardware, firmware, software, boards, machine code, ad infinitum. Even after many weeks of education you are apt to be asked questions such as, "How much C/PM does a ram have?"

Unfortunately, neither problem can be solved entirely. Nevertheless, it may help to examine some approaches lawyers have used to prove copyright and trade-secret infringement.

1. The "smoking gun". This approach is used when the defendant is caught holding a smoking gun. In one case the defendant was a former employee of the plaintiff. Shortly after quitting, the defendant began to sell software similar to that which had taken the plaintiff years to develop. The burden of proof was put on the defendant to prove how in the world he could have legally obtained this software in a month when similar software had taken years to program. In this case the defendant could not come up with a reasonable explanation, and the plaintiff won.

2. Bugs and nonfunctioning code. Much stolen software is cosmetically changed in an effort to conceal it. This doctored software, however, contains the same bugs or idiosyncrasies that were in the original software. It may become embarrassing for the defendant to explain this kind of coincidence. A similar result may sometimes be obtained by placing nonfunctioning code in the program. This code, it is hoped, will remain even if the rest of the program is changed cosmetically. The defendant may be forced to explain what a non-functioning algorithm for computing pi to 10,000 (or even ten) decimal places is doing in a sorting program.

3. When approaches 1 and 2 are not enough. You can still try to show that the infringing program is a copy of yours by demonstrating that it works the same way and is really a progeny of your program. This sort of case is usually presented with flowcharts, and will necessarily be quite technical. Unfortunately, this kind of evidence is highly vulnerable to attack from the defendant, who will present bundles of flowcharts that seemingly contradict yours.

CHOOSING A LAWYER

I think that everyone in the software business should have access to a lawyer. In most business situations a general business lawyer who can handle corporation formation or problems, debt collection and litigation, and advice on general business subjects is adequate. When your problem involves matters such as copyrights, trade secrets, trademarks, and license agreements, you should consult a specialist.

1. Patent and Trademark Lawyers

Patent and trademark lawyers are also very familiar with trade secrets. In fact, their field is known in law as "intellectual property rights." They know the ins and outs of the Copyright and Trademark offices, where a general lawyer will be of little help. You can find a patent and trademark specialist in the Yellow Pages under "Patents," or "Trademarks," or "Attorneys—Patents." Obviously you should ask friends in the industry for recommendations. Ask prospective lawyers if they represent others in your field. Many lawyers are still unfamiliar with software.

2. Art and Entertainment Lawyers

A lawyer who specializes in art and entertainment law may be a good choice for copyright problems, assignments, and contract and license agreements. These lawyers understand intellectual property and are often good negotiators.

3. Computer Lawyers

There are not many computer-law specialists yet, though in a year or two there will be plenty. Finding a lawyer familiar with the demands of the software industry would be a plus. But as with any lawyer, be sure the fee and working arrangements are satisfactory to you. It would be better to find a patent and trademark lawyer you feel comfortable with (and can teach a little) than to hire a computer expert you can't tolerate.

WORKING WITH A LAWYER

I've already indicated that using the services of a lawyer does not mean you must lose control over your case. Lawyers usually charge by the hour and are willing to act as consultants without insisting on running the show. When it comes to lawsuits, some lawyers are willing to represent you for a percentage of the money won. This is called a *contingent fee* since the lawyer is only paid contingent upon winning some money from the defendant. Generally, contingent fees are about a third of the money collected.

If you want to save time and money and gain the respect of your lawyer, do your best to come to your consultation prepared. Shoe boxes of unorganized receipts and folders with unrelated documents are frustrating to deal with, and take up costly time. Also, if you have outlined your problem in writing, the lawyer will be spared some groundwork and can get to the heart of the issues more quickly.

I recommend that you not talk computerese unless you are dealing with a lawyer who knows the jargon. I have heard what should have been conversations turn into existential plays with the programmer talking at 9600 baud and the lawyer speaking in Latin. Explain technical terms to your lawyer and ask that the same be done for you. You'll find that lawyers are experts at picking up jargon and, in a short time, will be speaking the language of computers like a native.

Situations to Avoid

Don't use a lawyer who is too busy for you. If your calls go unanswered, call another lawyer. In your first interview, arrive at an understanding of how much your lawyer will charge you. Lawyers are supposed to talk price from the beginning, but if yours forgets, don't be embarrassed to ask. If you feel the price is too high and you can't afford the services, say so before work begins on your project. Also, ask for an estimate of how long the project should take in billable hours and of when you can expect results. Obviously, you shouldn't be pushy, but do try to get an idea of what to expect and when to expect it so that you will later be able to tell whether you've gotten what you bargained for.

---

[1] An injunction is a court order to do or not to do something. If one violates the injunction, the court has the power to fine and imprison the violator.

appendix a
trade secret agreement and non-disclosure agreement

NOTICE

THIS PROGRAM BELONGS TO _____ . IT IS CONSIDERED A TRADE SECRET AND IS NOT TO BE DIVULGED OR USED BY PARTIES WHO HAVE NOT RECEIVED WRITTEN AUTHORIZATION FROM THE OWNER.

SAMPLE TRADE SECRET STATUS REMINDER LETTER

Dear _____ :

This letter is to remind you of _____ position regarding the trade secret status of the following items:

_____

_____

_____

_____ owns all rights, including trade secret rights, in the above-listed item(s). This means that you may not legally divulge or discuss the item(s) with third parties without our written permission. This obligation to keep the items confidential will continue to exist even if you are no longer connected with _____ .

Please don't hesitate to ask any questions you might have regarding trade secrets, ownership rights, or anything else related to this subject. If you have no questions, please sign the acknowledgment at the bottom of this letter and return it to me, keeping the copy for your own records.

Thank you for your cooperation.

Sincerely,

Chief Executive Officer

ACKNOWLEDGMENT

I have read and agree with the statements in the above letter.

_____   _____
SIGNED   DATE

SAMPLE PROJECT LOG

DATE	NAME	TIME IN	TIME OUT	COMMENTS

NOTICE

THIS PROGRAM BELONGS TO (insert your name or company). IT IS CON-
SIDERED A TRADE SECRET AND IS NOT TO BE DIVULGED OR USED BY
PARTIES WHO HAVE NOT RECEIVED WRITTEN AUTHORIZATION FROM
THE OWNER.

(T-1) NONDISCLOSURE AGREEMENT

I. INTRODUCTION

This is an agreement between _____ (Employee) and _____ (Company) in which the employee agrees not to disclose trade secrets or other confidential information belonging to Company.

II. AGREEMENT

In consideration of Employee's employment by Company, Employee agrees to keep all trade secrets and/or proprietary information of Company in strict confidence.

III. TRADE SECRETS

A trade secret is any information, process, or idea that is not generally known in the industry, that Company considers confidential, and that gives Company a competitive advantage. Examples of trade secrets include:

Computer program listings, source code, and object code.

All information relating to programs now existing or currently under development.

Customer lists and records.

Employee understands that the above list is intended to be illustrative and that other trade secrets which will also be held confidential may currently exist or arise in the future. In the event that Employee is not sure whether certain information is a trade secret, Employee will treat that information as confidential unless Employee is informed by Company to the contrary.

Employee agrees to surrender to Company all notes, records, and documentation that was used, created, or controlled by Employee during employment upon termination of that employment.

IV. ATTORNEY FEES

If any legal action arises relating to this agreement, the prevailing party shall be entitled to recover all costs, expenses, and reasonable attorney's fees incurred because of the legal action.

V. DURATION

This agreement is considered by both parties to be a binding contract and shall remain in effect indefinitely, even if Employee's employment with Company terminates.

VI. EXECUTION

This agreement is executed on _____ (date) and covers all Company trade secrets currently known to Employee as well as all trade secrets that shall become known during Employee's tenure at Company.

_____ Employee   _____ Company
SIGNED   SIGNED

(T-2)   NONDISCLOSURE AGREEMENT

I. INTRODUCTION

This is an agreement between _____ (Employee) and _____ (Company) in which Employee agrees not to disclose certain confidential information and/or trade secrets belonging to Company.

II. AGREEMENT

In consideration of Employee's employment by Company, Employee agrees to hold the following information belonging to Company in strict confidence.

(1) All information relating to the program development of _____ .

(2) All algorithms and internal workings of all Company programs, especially _____ .

(3) _____

III. In fulfilling Employee's obligations under this agreement, Employee promises not to divulge Company trade secrets unless authorized in writing by Company. This agreement shall remain in force even after employment at Company has been terminated.

IV. Employee agrees to surrender to Company upon termination of employment all notes, records, and documentation that was used, created, or controlled by Employee during employment.

V. ATTORNEY FEES

If any legal action arises relating to this agreement, the prevailing party shall be entitled to recover all costs, expenses, and reasonable attorney's fees incurred because of the legal action.

VI. EXECUTION

This agreement is executed on _____ (date) and covers all Company trade secrets and proprietary information currently known to Employee as well as all trade secrets that will become known during Employee's tenure at Company.

_____ Employee   _____ Company
SIGNED   SIGNED

(T-3) NONDISCLOSURE AGREEMENT

I. INTRODUCTION

This is an agreement between _____ and _____ (Company) in which _____ agrees not to disclose trade secrets belonging to Company.

II. AGREEMENT

In consideration of being made privy to trade-secret information belonging to Company, _____ hereby agrees not to disclose this information to third parties and to treat this information as a trade secret belonging to Company.

III. TRADE SECRET

The information to be treated as a trade secret is all confidential information relating to

_____ .

IV. ATTORNEY FEES

If any legal action arises relating to this agreement, the prevailing party shall be entitled to recover its court costs, expenses, and reasonable attorney's fees.

V. EXECUTION

This agreement is executed on _____ and shall remain in effect until the information included herein is no longer a trade secret or until Company sends _____ written notice releasing him/her from the obligations of this agreement, whichever event occurs first.

_____   _____
SIGNED   Employee   SIGNED   Company

(T-4)   NONDISCLOSURE AGREEMENT

I. This is an agreement in which _____ (User) acknowledges receipt of certain trade secrets of _____ (Company) and agrees to hold these trade secrets confidential.

II. AGREEMENT

In consideration of being made privy to secret information belonging to Company, User hereby acknowledges receipt of the information listed in Section III of this agreement. User also agrees not to disclose this information to third parties and to treat this information as a trade secret belonging to Company.

III. TRADE SECRET

The information to be treated as a trade secret is all confidential information relating to

_____ .

IV. ATTORNEY FEES

If any legal action arises relating to this agreement, the prevailing party shall be entitled to recover its court costs and reasonable attorney's fees.

_____ User   _____ Company
SIGNED   SIGNED

_____   _____
DATE   DATE

appendix b
assignment of copyright agreement

ASSIGNMENT OF COPYRIGHTS

I. INTRODUCTION

_____ (Seller) owns all copyrights and other rights to a computer program (Program) and wishes to assign those rights to _____ (Buyer).

II. DEFINITIONS

A. "Program" shall mean the computer program described in Attachment A to this contract, which is hereby incorporated by reference.

III. ITEMS PROVIDED BY SELLER

A. Seller shall deliver to Buyer the following items:

IV. DELIVERY

A. Seller will deliver all items listed in Section III of this Agreement on _____ _____ , 198____ .

V. ACCEPTANCE

A. Buyer shall have five days from the date(s) of delivery to determine whether the delivered items conform with their description under Section III of this agreement. If Buyer rejects an item, such rejection shall be made in writing and shall set forth the reason(s) for the rejection. Seller shall have thirty days from receipt of the written rejection to resubmit the rejected items for acceptance. Buyer shall have five days to inspect resubmitted items.

B. Items that have not been rejected under Clause A of this section shall be deemed to have been accepted.

VI. ASSIGNMENT

A. In consideration for the payment described in the section of this agreement titled, "Payment," Seller hereby transfers and assigns all copyrights and all other rights in Program and in all items described in Section III of this agreement to Buyer. Buyer shall have the right to register the copyright to Program in Buyer's own name and shall have the exclusive right to dispose of Program in any way Buyer sees fit. Seller retains no rights in Program whatsoever.

B. The assignment in this section shall take effect on _____ _____ , 198____ .

VII. PAYMENT

A. In consideration of the Assignment described in the section of this agreement titled, "Assignment," Buyer shall pay Seller the sum of $_____ on _____ _____ , 198____ . This shall be the only amount paid to Seller for Program.

VIII. WARRANTIES

A. Seller warrants that Seller has the legal right to grant Buyer the assignment set out in Section VI of this agreement and that such assignment does not infringe any third parties' rights.

B. Developer warrants that there are no pending lawsuits concerning any aspect of the Program and that the Program has not been published in such a way as to lose any of its copyright protection.

IX. ARBITRATION

Any dispute relating to the interpretation or performance of this agreement shall be resolved at the request of either party through binding arbitration. Arbitration shall be conducted in _____ , _____ , in accordance with the then-existing rules of the American Arbitration Association. Judgment upon any award by the arbitrators may be entered by the state or federal court having jurisdiction. The parties intend that this agreement to arbitrate be irrevocable.

X. GENERAL

A. This agreement sets forth the entire understanding between the parties. It may be changed or modified only in writing and such changes must be signed by both parties.

B. This agreement is freely assignable by both parties.

C. This agreement is binding upon and shall inure to the benefit of the legal successors and assigns of the parties.

D. This contract shall be construed under the laws of the State of _____ .

_____   _____
SIGNED   SIGNED

_____   _____
DATE   DATE

appendix c

work-for-hire contracts for independent programmers and staff programmers

WORK-FOR-HIRE CONTRACT FOR INDEPENDENT PROGRAMMERS (WFH-1)

I. INTRODUCTION

This is a work-for-hire agreement in which _____ (Programmer) agrees to provide programming services to _____ (Company). Company shall pay Programmer according to the payment schedule set forth in Attachment A of this contract, which is incorporated by reference herein.

II. DUTIES

Programmer shall create a computer source code and complete documentation for Company as per the specifications set forth in Attachment B to this contract, which is incorporated by reference herein.

Company shall supply Programmer all items listed in Attachment B prior to _____ _____ , 198____ .

III. OWNERSHIP

In consideration for payment as set forth in Attachment A of this contract, Programmer hereby assigns all rights in the Program to Company, including the right to copyright the program in Company's name. Programmer understands that Program is a work made for hire which shall be the exclusive property of the Company.

Consistent with Programmer's recognition of Company's complete ownership rights in the Program described in Attachment B, Programmer agrees not to use the Program created under this contract for the benefit of any party other than Company.

IV. COMPLETION DATE

Programmer agrees to complete all work as per the schedule set forth in Attachment D of this contract, which is hereby incorporated by reference herein.

V. TRADE SECRETS

All types of information relating to the Program, including this contract and its attachments, are to be considered the trade secrets of Company. Programmer shall keep all trade secrets of Company confidential, and shall sign nondisclosure agreements when requested by Company.

VI. ARBITRATION

Any dispute relating to the interpretation or performance of this agreement shall be resolved at the request of either party through binding arbitration. Arbitration shall be conducted in _____ , _____ , in accordance with the then-existing rules of the American Arbitration Association. Judgment upon any award by the arbitrators may be entered by the state or federal court having jurisdiction. The parties intend that this agreement to arbitrate be irrevocable.

VII. GENERAL PROVISIONS

a. Programmer may neither subcontract nor hire persons to aid in the programming work without the prior written consent of Company.

b. Any modifications to this agreement must be in writing and signed by both parties.

_____   _____
SIGNED   SIGNED

_____   _____
DATE   DATE

ATTACHMENT A—PAYMENT SCHEDULE

(CHOOSE ONE OF THE FOLLOWING ATTACHMENT A ALTERNATIVES OR WRITE YOUR OWN. IN EITHER CASE, RETYPE THE ATTACHMENT ON A SEPARATE SHEET OF PAPER.)

(ALTERNATIVE ATTACHMENT A)

Programmer shall be paid on the first and fifteenth day of each month until the work is completed. Payment shall be $_____ per month.

(ALTERNATIVE ATTACHMENT A)

Programmer shall be paid $_____ every _____ day beginning on _____ _____ , 198_____ , and continuing until _____ _____, 198_____ . No further payments shall be made after _____ _____ , 198_____ , until all duties as described in Attachment B are performed to Company's satisfaction, at which time Company will pay Programmer a final payment of $_____ .

(ALTERNATIVE ATTACHMENT A)

Programmer shall be paid $_____ for completing all work as detailed in Attachment B. Payment of $_____ will be made on the first of each month, starting _____ _____ , 198_____ , and continuing for _____ months thereafter.

ATTACHMENT B—DUTIES

(TYPE OUT AN ATTACHMENT B ON A SEPARATE SHEET OF PAPER.)

Programmer will be responsible for:
(Here you must insert what the programmer has to produce by describing the program in detail. Besides the actual program, the programmer might be expected to deliver detailed specifications, documentation, a copy-protection scheme, a source diskette from which object diskettes will be made, and so forth. Describe in detail exactly what is expected. For a sample of this kind of attachment refer to the discussion on royalty deliverables in Chapter 8.)

Company will be responsible for:
(List here what the Company's responsibilities, other than payment, will be. Is the Company expected to provide hardware, technical specifications, a work space?)

ATTACHMENT C—WORK SCHEDULE

(TYPE UP ATTACHMENT C ON A SEPARATE SHEET OF PAPER.)
Programmer agrees to complete the programming according to the following schedule:

WORK-FOR-HIRE CONTRACT FOR STAFF PROGRAMMERS (WFH-2)

I. INTRODUCTION

This is an agreement whereby _____ (Programmer) acknowledges that any programming done for _____ (Company) is the exclusive property of Company.

II. PROGRAM OWNERSHIP

In consideration of employment by Company, Programmer hereby agrees that any programming done during employment shall be considered a work for hire for the exclusive benefit of the Company. This means that Company shall own all rights to any programs developed, including all copyrights and the right to market (or not to market) the programs. Programmer also agrees not to use the program or any of its parts for the benefit of other employers or for the benefit of anyone other than the Company.

Programmer agrees to sign upon request any documents affirming that any particular program written during employment by Company is in fact a work for hire and belongs exclusively to Company.

III. PAYMENT

Programmer specifically acknowledges that his/her normal salary is full payment for any programming done for Company and understands that this salary is in lieu of any royalties.

IV. TRADE SECRETS

Programmer understands that Company considers all programming to be a trade secret belonging to Company. Programmer, therefore, will neither divulge nor discuss with third parties matters relating to programs on which Programmer is working or any other programs belonging to Company without written permission of Company. In addition Programmer agrees to sign, upon request, nondisclosure agreements relating to any aspect of Company's business.

_____   _____
SIGNED   SIGNED

_____   _____
DATE   DATE

WORK-FOR-HIRE CONTRACT FOR FREE-LANCE MANUAL WRITERS (WFH-3)

I. INTRODUCTION

This is an agreement in which _____ (Writer) agrees to write a software instruction manual as a work for hire for _____ (Company).

II. DUTIES

Writer shall write an instruction manual for the _____ (Program). The manual shall be of professional quality and shall be designed to teach persons unfamiliar with the Program how to operate it. The chapter titles and an outline of the information that must be included in the manual are in Attachment A of this Agreement and are incorporated by reference herein. Writer shall submit to Company chapters of the manual as they are completed according to the schedule set out in Attachment A of this Agreement.

Company shall provide Writer all information necessary for writing the manual including:

_____

III. TERMINATION

Company shall review each chapter within one week of receipt. If Company is dissatisfied with the quality of the writing or information presented, Company shall notify Writer and arrange a conference with Writer so that the problems can be corrected. If the problems cannot be corrected to Company's satisfaction, both parties agree that Writer shall stop writing the manual and shall accept as payment in full for his services the money he received up to the date that Company notified Writer in writing of its dissatisfaction. Company may use any parts of Writer's writing as it sees fit.

IV. PAYMENT

Company shall pay Writer as per the payment schedule set out in Attachment A.

V. OWNERSHIP

The Program manual is a work for hire. Company shall be considered sole owner of all rights to the manual and has the right to publish and copyright it in its name. Writer's name shall appear on a cover page identifying him as the author. Company has the right to change, edit, and add to the manual in any way it sees fit.

VI. TRADE SECRETS

Writer acknowledges that all information concerning the Program, including information relating to the manual (prior to its being made public), are the trade secrets of the Company. Writer agrees to hold confidential all trade secrets of Company and all matters relating to Program, manual, this contract, and Company's business. Writer agrees to sign nondisclosure agreements relating to the items named in the preceding sentence as required by Company.

VII. GENERAL PROVISIONS

a. Modifications to this agreement must be in writing and signed by both parties.

b. Neither party may assign this agreement without the consent of the other. Writer shall not subcontract with other persons in fulfilling this contract without the express permission of company.

_____   _____
SIGNED   SIGNED

_____   _____
DATE   DATE

ATTACHMENT A—PAYMENT SCHEDULE

(TYPE UP ATTACHMENT A ON A SEPARATE SHEET(S) OF PAPER. DESCRIBE THE MANUAL IN AS MUCH DETAIL AS IS NECESSARY FOR BOTH PARTIES TO HAVE A GOOD UNDERSTANDING OF WHAT THE MANUAL SHOULD BE.)

Chapter titles	Date due	Payment	Payment due

(insert descriptions of the manual if necessary)

WORK FOR HIRE AGREEMENT FOR IN HOUSE MANUAL WRITERS (WFH-4)

I. INTRODUCTION

This is an agreement whereby _____ (Employee) agrees that all writing done for _____ (Company) will be a work for hire.

II. OWNERSHIP

In consideration of employment by Company, Employee hereby agrees that any writing done for Company during employment, including writing done after business hours, shall be considered a work for hire for the benefit of Company. Company shall own all rights in the Employee's work product, including the copyrights and the right to use or not to use the writing. Company shall have the right to change, alter, or edit the writing as is seen fit. Employee agrees to sign, upon request, any additional documents affirming that any particular writing done during employment is in fact a work for hire and belongs exclusively to Company.

III. PAYMENT

Employee acknowledges that his/her normal salary is full payment for any writing done for Company and understands that this salary is in lieu of any royalties.

IV. TRADE SECRETS

Employee agrees that if in the course of writing access to trade secrets of Company is given, Employee will hold Company's trade secrets confidential and not discuss them with third parties without the written consent of Company. Employee also agrees to sign nondisclosure agreements relating to Company's business whenever required by Company.

_____   _____
SIGNED   SIGNED

_____   _____
DATE   DATE

appendix d
evaluation agreement and beta test site agreement

EVALUATION AGREEMENT

I. INTRODUCTION

A. This is an agreement between _____ (Developer) and _____ (Publisher) in which Publisher agrees to evaluate the marketability of _____ (Program), a program belonging to Developer.

II. AGREEMENT

A. Publisher agrees to evaluate the Program to determine if Publisher wishes to market it.

B. Publisher shall offer to enter into a marketing agreement with Developer if Publisher decides on the basis of the evaluation that the Program is sound and that it can be marketed profitably.

C. If Publisher decides that the Program cannot be marketed profitably, or if a marketing agreement cannot be reached with Developer, Publisher shall promptly return all copies of the Program to Developer and shall not market the Program.

D. Developer agrees that Publisher's acceptance of the Program for evaluation purposes shall not limit the Publisher in any way regarding Publisher's freedom to develop or release programs similar to the submitted Program, provided, that is, that any similar programs have been obtained independently of the submitted Program.

E. Publisher acknowledges Developer's copyrights and other rights in the submitted Program. Publisher agrees to treat Program in the same way Publisher treats its own confidential programs.

III. SCHEDULE

A. Publisher agrees to complete evaluation thirty days after receipt of Program.

IV. WARRANTIES

A. Developer warrants that the Program has not been copied from someone else and that Developer is the sole owner of all copyrights and other rights in the Program.

_____   _____
SIGNED   DATE

_____   _____
SIGNED   DATE

ALTERNATIVE CLAUSE FOR SECTION II. E

Publisher acknowledges that Program is a trade secret of Developer and agrees to maintain the secrecy of the Program. Publisher shall restrict access to the Program to those who need to see or use it and shall require those people to sign nondisclosure agreements obligating them not to divulge information relating to the Program to third parties. Publisher also acknowledges Developer's rights, including copyrights, in the Program.

PROGRAM EVALUATION

Title: _____   Date Received: _____

Author: _____   Date Completed: _____

Street: _____   Computer: _____

City, State: _____   Language: _____

Phone #'s: (___) _____ (___) _____   Memory Used: _____

Previous Author: _____ _____   Program Form: _____

Evaluator #:									Totals	Average
Date:										
1. Enjoyability:										
2. Originality:										
3. Error Trapping:										
4. Graphics:										
5. Instructions:										
6. Professionalism:										
7. Response Time:										
8. User Friendliness:										
9. Market Size:										
10. :										
Totals										
Average										

COMMENTS

_____

_____

_____

_____

_____

_____

_____

SAMPLE FORM REJECTION LETTER

Dear _____ :

After carefully evaluating _____ , we have decided that we cannot market it successfully. Enclosed you will find all copies of the program and documentation that you submitted to us. We have not retained any copies of the program.

Thank you for allowing us to evaluate your program. We wish you every success in marketing it elsewhere.

Sincerely,

_____

SAMPLE FORM ACCEPTANCE LETTER

Dear _____ :

After testing _____ , we feel that the program has good marketing potential. We would like to enter into a license agreement with you. Enclosed is a copy of our license agreement. Please read it over carefully. We would like to make an appointment with you as soon as is convenient to discuss the agreement in detail.

Sincerely,

_____

BETA TEST SITE AGREEMENT (WFH-5)

I. INTRODUCTION

This is an agreement between _____ (Tester) and _____ (Owner) in which Tester agrees to test a software program known as _____ (Program) and to keep Owner informed of the results of the tests.

II. PAYMENT

Tester agrees to accept as payment in full for his/her services a copy of the Program after final testing.

III. DUTIES

Tester agrees to use the Program as it is intended to be used for a minimum of forty hours per month. If Tester discovers any problem with the Program, Tester shall fill out a Program Report supplied by Owner, documenting to the best of Tester's ability the events that led up to the problem in the Program and the manifestations of the problem. Program Reports shall be mailed to Owner within forty-eight hours of the first noticed occurrence of the problem. The test period shall last from _____ _____ 198_____ , until _____ _____ , 198_____ .

Owner shall supply Tester with a copy of the Program and any necessary documentation or instruction regarding its operation. After the test period, Owner shall supply Tester with a final copy of the Program and manual. Tester shall be entitled to the same benefits and the same terms that regular purchasers of the Program are entitled to.

IV. DISCLAIMER OF WARRANTY

Tester understands that the Program is experimental and that Owner does not warrant the performance of the Program in any way. All warranties regarding fitness and merchantability are hereby disclaimed. The Program is accepted AS IS, and owing to its experimental nature Tester is advised not to rely exclusively on the Program for any reason.

V. TRADE SECRETS

In accepting the Program, Tester recognizes that the Program is a trade secret belonging to Owner. Tester hereby agrees not to disclose any information relating to the Program (including its existence) to third parties without written permission from Owner.

VI. LIMITATIONS ON USE

Tester agrees not to sell or transfer any copies of the Program or the original Program to third parties. Tester accepts the Program under the condition that it is for Tester's own use and for no other purpose. Tester hereby acknowledges Owner's copyright in the Program regardless of whether copyright notice appears on the Program or whether it has been filed with the Copyright Office.

_____   _____
SIGNED   SIGNED

_____   _____
DATE   DATE

BETA TEST SITE USER QUESTIONNAIRE

We at _____ greatly appreciate your taking the time to complete this questionnaire. Your suggestions and comments are very important to us, as they help us to both evaluate and improve our products.

COMPANY _____

PERSON COMPLETING FORM _____ DATE _____

DATE TEST BEGAN _____ DATE TEST ENDED _____

PRODUCT BEING TESTED _____

During the test period, you used this product:

☐ A. more than 4 hours per day
☐ B. 1 to 4 hours per day
☐ C. less than 1 hour per day

Do you have any experience with similar products, on _____ or other computers? _____

If yes, please list all hardware and software used.

_____
_____

Including time spent on your _____ how long have you been using computers? _____

Please give a brief description of your business.

_____
_____
_____

Using a scale of 1 to 10 (1 = terrible, 5 = average, 10 = excellent), please indicate:

Your general satisfaction with this product _____

The ease of using this product _____

The practicality or usefulness of this product _____

The following questions require more lengthy responses. Feel free to use additional sheets of paper if necessary.

What would you say are the *best* features of this product?

_____
_____

What would you say are its *worst* features?

_____
_____

Have you noticed any extraneous or useless features of the product (please list)?

_____
_____

Please list suggested enhancements to existing features of the product.

_____
_____

appendix e
license agreement

OUTLINE OF A LICENSE AGREEMENT

USE THIS OUTLINE AS A CHECKLIST FOR ASSEMBLING YOUR OWN LICENSE AGREEMENT.

SECTION I—INTRODUCTION

A. Who are the parties?

B. What is the program?

C. What type of agreement is it? (e.g., license)

SECTION II—DEFINITIONS

A. Terms with different or ambiguous meanings are defined.

SECTION III—ITEMS PROVIDED BY DEVELOPER

A. What exactly is the program that the Developer is licensing to the Publisher?

B. In what form is the program to be delivered?
    1. Does the Publisher get a copy of the source code?
    2. If so, does Publisher set full source-code documentation?

C. Does Developer also furnish a user manual?

D. What does the Publisher not get?

SECTION IV—DELIVERY SCHEDULE

A. When are the item(s) from Section III due to be delivered to Publisher?

SECTION V—PROGRAM MAINTENANCE, MODIFICATION, AND TRAINING

A. What, if any, are the Developer's responsibilities once the Publisher takes over?

B. Who pays for fixing bugs and any program recalls?

C. Does Developer have to provide program updates?
    1. If so, does Developer get paid for them?
    2. What if the Developer can't or won't provide updates?

SECTION VI—THE LICENSE

A. What exactly is the *subject* of the license?

B. What is the *duration* of the license?

C. What is the geographical and market *scope* of the license?

SECTION VII—ACCEPTANCE

A. What must the Publisher do to show that the program has been accepted?

B. How much time does the Publisher get to evaluate and test the program prior to acceptance?

SECTION VIII—ROYALTIES

A. What royalty percentage is to be paid the Developer on each program?
   1. Is there a minimum dollar amount per sale?

B. How are royalties calculated?

C. Is there a minimum guaranteed royalty even if the program doesn't sell well?

D. Is there an advance?
   1. If so, how much?
   2. Is it refundable if the program doesn't sell?

E. When are royalties to be paid?
   1. When do they become owing (accrue)?

F. How many free copies does Publisher get?

G. How many free copies does Programmer get for personal use?

H. Are royalties to be paid on the manual?
   1. How much if the manual is sold with program?
   2. How much if it is sold separately?

I. Are royalties to be paid on dealer demos?

SECTION IX—ACCOUNTING

A. What records must Publisher keep and what access does Developer have to them?

SECTION X—WARRANTIES

A. What does the Developer warrant?

SECTION XI—INDEMNIFICATION

A. Under what conditions will Developer indemnify Publisher?
   1. For suits regarding copyright or trade secret?
   2. For bugs or recalls?

B. Under what conditions will Publisher indemnify Developer?
   1. Law suits concerning the quality of the program?

C. What are the dollar limits to the above indemnifications?

SECTION XII—COPYRIGHTS

A. Who is responsible for copyrighting the program?

SECTION XIII—CONTRACT TERMINATION

A. Who can terminate the contract?
    1. Why can this be done?
    2. How can this be done?

B. What, if any, contract provisions will survive termination?

SECTION XIV—ARBITRATION

A. Do the parties want binding arbitration to govern contract disputes?

SECTION XV—SOURCE-CODE ESCROW

SECTION XVI—GENERAL

A. Everything that was not included above.

B. What happens if either party dies or goes under?

ATTACHMENTS

1. Program description.

2. Delivery timetable (if too complex to fit in main body of contract).

3. Manual description (if too complex to fit in main body of contract).

4. Royalty scales (if too complex to fit in main body of contract).

LICENSE AGREEMENT

How to use this section: Because license agreements vary depending on the software and people involved, I have used a menu approach so that you can create your own license agreement. Read each section and clause carefully. If you have a question about any particular clause, refer back to Chapter 8. Some sections will be unnecessary and can be left out entirely. In other cases you will want to add a section of your own. Feel free to modify sections to suit your circumstances. Whenever you create your own license agreement, it is important that you check it over carefully, making sure that you have not included contradictory sections or clauses and that, if a section refers to another section or to an attachment, there is indeed a section or attachment that corresponds to the reference. If you encounter areas where you have questions that are not answered by this book, consult a lawyer.

I. INTRODUCTION

This is a licensing agreement between _____ (Developer) and _____ (Publisher), in which Developer grants Publisher certain rights in the software program _____ (Program).

ALTERNATIVE INTRODUCTION

I. INTRODUCTION

This is a licensing contract between program developer _____ , referred to herein as Developer, who owns and has the right to grant licenses in certain computer software, and _____ referred to herein as Publisher, who desires to acquire a license to use and market such software. The software that is the subject of this agreement is known as _____ , but shall be referred to in this agreement as Program.

THE FOLLOWING DEFINITIONS ARE SAMPLES ONLY. INSERT DEFINITIONS THAT MAKE SENSE TO YOU.

II. DEFINITIONS

A. "Derivative work" shall mean a work that is based on one or more preexisting works and that, if prepared without permission of the program owner, would constitute a copyright infringement.

B. "Supporting documentation" shall mean information that describes the format, organization, and content of machine-readable diskettes to be supplied to Publisher under the terms of this contract.

C. "Manual" shall mean an instruction manual designed to teach an inexperienced user how to operate the Program.

D. "Section" shall mean a part of this agreement that is preceded by a Roman numeral.

E. "Clause" shall mean a subpart of this agreement that is preceded by an uppercase Arabic letter.

F. "Net sales" shall mean the money actually received by the Publisher minus freight, allowances, and returns.

ALTERNATIVE DEFINITION OF "NET SALES"

F. "Net sales" shall mean the amount billed by Publisher for orders of the Program minus freight, allowances, and returns.

III. ITEMS PROVIDED BY DEVELOPER

A. Developer shall furnish Publisher a computer-copiable program in object form. This Program shall be the _____ Program as it is described in Attachment A.

ALTERNATIVE SECTION III. A.

III. ITEMS PROVIDED BY DEVELOPER

A. Developer shall furnish Publisher a computer-copiable program in object form. This Program shall be the _____ Program as it currently exists for the _____ computer. The Program shall have all the features and perform all the functions described in the _____ manual, which is incorporated herein by reference.

OPTIONAL CLAUSE B. FOR SECTION III.

B. Developer shall furnish Publisher one set of Developer Computer Program Supporting Documentation, as described in Attachment I.

OPTIONAL CLAUSE C. FOR SECTION III.

C. Developer shall furnish Publisher with any available performance data, productivity data, and economic (marketing) data. At Publisher's request, Developer shall also supply samples of existing advertising, training, or sales material that may aid Publisher in marketing the Program.

OPTIONAL SENTENCE FOR OPTIONAL CLAUSE C.

Notwithstanding the provisions of this clause, Developer shall not be required to furnish nor shall Publisher be allowed to use _____ .

IV. DELIVERY SCHEDULE

A. Developer shall deliver to Publisher at _____ , _____ , _____ , all items to be furnished under Section III of this Agreement on or before _____ , 19_____ .

ALTERNATIVE SECTION IV. TO BE USED WITH A TIMETABLE ATTACHMENT

IV. DELIVERY SCHEDULE

A. Developer shall provide all items to be furnished under Section III of this agreement according to the time schedule set out in Attachment II, which is hereby incorporated into this Agreement.

V. MAINTENANCE, MODIFICATION, AND TRAINING

A. For a period of _____ months after _____ _____ , 198_____ , if Publisher notifies Developer of program error(s) or Developer has other reason to believe that error(s) exist(s) in the Program, Developer shall use his/her best efforts to verify and fix the error(s) within _____ working days after notification. If a verified error cannot be fixed within _____ days, Developer shall devote five hours per day toward correcting the error until the error has been corrected. Developer shall promptly notify Publisher if an error cannot be verified within a reasonable time. Error corrections shall be machine-readable and shall be such that Publisher can update the Program immediately.

B. Publisher shall assume financial and legal responsibility for the quality, reliability, and accuracy of the Program and shall pay all expenses associated with any recalls or updates.

ALTERNATIVE SECTION V. B.

B. Actual costs incurred as a result of program recalls that are not the fault of the Publisher shall be charged to the Developer. Actual costs shall include materials costs, postage, printing, and labor directly associated with a recall. Publisher's right to collect costs shall be limited as follows: the actual costs recoverable shall not exceed the total amount of royalties already paid or still owing on the software that is the subject of the recall. To collect these costs the Publisher must charge them against future royalty payments due on the software that is the subject of this contract.

C. For a period of _____ months after _____ _____ , 198_____ , Developer shall supply at no charge to Publisher any Program enhancements that improve performance, utility, or existing syntax, and that improve or reduce storage requirements.

ALTERNATIVE SECTION V. C.

C. Programmer shall write Program enhancements at Publisher's request at the rate of $35 per hour. This hourly rate shall remain in effect for _____ months after the date of this Agreement. Thereafter, Programmer shall write Program enhancements at Publisher's request for $50 per hour. Programmer's obligations under this clause shall terminate _____ months after the date of this agreement.

ALTERNATIVE SECTION V. C.

C. Publisher shall have the right to make Program enhancements subject to Developer's approval. Publisher may charge the cost of these enhancements against royalties due to Programmer from the sale of the enhanced Program. Before initiating any enhancement, Publisher shall offer Developer the right to do the enhancement at Developer's expense. The Developer retains the right to veto any proposed enhancement.

ALTERNATIVE SECTION V. C.

C. Publisher has the right to modify the Program in any way consistent with improving its marketability at Publisher's expense.

D. Should Publisher request training in the use of the Program, Developer shall be paid actual travel expenses and $_____ per day for each of Developer's employees who furnish such training.

VI. EXCLUSIVE LICENSE

A. Developer hereby grants to Publisher a worldwide, exclusive license to market copies of the Program for use on all existing or yet-to-be-developed computers. This license shall include the right of Publisher to grant sublicenses to other parties subject to the section of this agreement titled "Royalties" and subject to the limitations of this license.

B. The license granted under clause A of this section shall begin _____ ____ , 198____ , and expire _____ ____ , 19____ .

C. Upon termination of this license for any reason all rights granted herein shall immediately revert to the Programmer.

D. Developer hereby reserves all rights in the Program not specifically granted by this license agreement.

ALTERNATIVE SECTION VI.

VI. LICENSE

A. Developer hereby grants to Publisher a worldwide, nonexclusive license to market copies of the Program for use on the _____ computer only. Developer shall not market, or license others to market, Program for the _____ for the duration of this license.

B. The license granted under clause A of this section shall start _____ ____ , 198____ , and shall expire _____ ____ , 198____ . Upon expiration or termination all rights granted under this License Agreement shall revert to Developer.

ALTERNATIVE SECTION VI.—NONEXCLUSIVE LICENSE

VI. NONEXCLUSIVE LICENSE

A. Developer hereby grants to Publisher a worldwide, nonexclusive license to use, execute, reproduce, sell, lease, or otherwise transfer copies of the Program for use on the _____ computer only.

B. The license granted under clause A of this section shall start _____ ____ , 198____ , and shall expire _____ ____ , 19____ . Upon expiration or termination all rights granted under this License Agreement shall revert to Developer.

ALTERNATIVE SECTION VI.—NONEXCLUSIVE LICENSE

VI. NONEXCLUSIVE LICENSE

A. Developer hereby grants to Publisher a nonexclusive license to market the Program within _____ only. Publisher shall refer sales and inquiries regarding the Program originating from outside _____ to Developer.

B. The license granted under clause A of this section shall start _____ _____ , 198____ , and shall expire _____ _____ , 19____ . Upon expiration or termination all rights granted herein shall revert to Developer.

ALTERNATIVE SECTION VI.—HYBRID LICENSE

VI. LICENSE

A. Developer hereby grants to Publisher:
  1. An exclusive license to publish Program for use on _____ computers.
  2. A nonexclusive license to publish Program for use on computers other than _____ .

B. The licenses granted under clause A of this section shall start _____ _____ , 198____ , and shall expire _____ _____ , 19____ . Upon expiration or termination all rights granted herein shall revert to Developer.

VII. ACCEPTANCE

A. After Developer delivers Program, Publisher shall have _____ days to test Program. If Developer is not notified in writing within _____ days of delivery of the Program that the Program is unacceptable, Publisher shall be deemed to have accepted the Program.

B. Publisher shall also be deemed to have accepted the Program if the Publisher makes Program available for sale.

C. If Publisher determines that Program is unacceptable, Publisher shall notify Developer in writing of what changes must be made in the Program to make it acceptable. Developer shall have _____ days from receipt of the notification to make these changes. If they are not made within the _____ day period, Publisher may terminate this Agreement.

VIII. ROYALTIES

A. In consideration for the rights and license granted by this Agreement, and subject to the conditions set forth elsewhere in this Agreement, Publisher shall pay Developer as a royalty a sum equal to _____ % of the net sales of the Program as defined in Section II of this Agreement. Notwithstanding the aforementioned percentage, the minimum royalty amount to be paid shall be $_____ per Program sold or otherwise transferred to a third party.

ALTERNATIVE SECTION VIII. A.

VIII. ROYALTIES

A. Subject to the conditions expressed elsewhere in this agreement and in consideration for the rights and license granted herein, Publisher shall pay Developer a royalty of _____ % of net sales of the Program as defined in Section II of this Agreement.

Notwithstanding the aforementioned percentage, Publisher shall pay Developer a minimum royalty of $_____ for each sale or transfer of the Program to third parties.

ALTERNATIVE SECTION VIII. A.

VIII. ROYALTIES

A. In consideration for the rights and license granted herein, and subject to the conditions set forth elsewhere in this agreement, Publisher shall pay Developer a royalty based on a percentage of net sales, as defined in Section II of this agreement:

_____ % for the first _____ programs sold or sublicensed
_____ % for the next _____ programs sold or sublicensed
_____ % for the next _____ programs sold or sublicensed
_____ % for the next _____ programs sold or sublicensed

Notwithstanding the aforementioned percentage, Publisher shall pay Developer a minimum of $_____ for each program sold or transferred.

B. Royalty payments for the preceding calendar quarter shall be made to Developer within _____ days after the last day of each calendar quarter during the term of this agreement.

C. Notwithstanding the provisions of this section, the minimum royalty payment to be made to Programmer every quarter shall be at least $_____ . Should the royalties accrued be less than the amount in the preceding sentence, Publisher shall pay, in addition to the accrued royalties, the amount necessary to reach the minimum royalty payment. This additional amount, if paid, shall be regarded as nonrefundable compensation in addition to royalties and shall not be considered an advance on royalties.

ALTERNATIVE SECTION VIII. C.

C. Notwithstanding the provisions of this section, minimum quarterly royalty payments shall be due as follows:

First quarter — $_____
All quarters thereafter — $_____

Should royalties accrued on actual sales be less than the applicable minimum royalty payment, Publisher shall pay in addition to the accrued royalties the amount necessary to reach the minimum royalty payment. This additional amount, if paid, shall be regarded as nonrefundable compensation in addition to royalties and shall not be considered as an advance on royalties.

D. If Publisher is more than _____ days late on any one payment, Developer may cancel the license granted in Section VI of this contract provided that Developer sends written notice by registered mail to Publisher of his intention to cancel and provided that Publisher does not make full payment within _____ days of receipt of notice.

E. Upon execution of this agreement, Publisher shall pay Programmer a $_____ advance on royalties. No further royalty payments shall be made until the amount of royalties accrued exceeds the amount of the advance made under this clause.

OPTIONAL SECOND PART TO SECTION VIII. E.

The advance on royalties shall be nonrefundable.

ALTERNATIVE OPTIONAL SECOND PART TO SECTION VIII. E.

The advance on royalties shall be refunded to the Publisher if this agreement should be terminated through no fault of Publisher before the royalties accrued or paid to Developer equal or exceed the amount of the advance. Any refund shall be paid by Developer within _____ days after Developer receives a written demand for payment from Publisher.

F. Notwithstanding the other clauses of this section, no royalties shall be paid for dealer demonstration programs. However, Publisher shall keep accurate records of the number of demos released, and all demos shall bear a label on the diskette and on the Manual that reads, "Dealer Demo and Not For Resale."

G. Notwithstanding the other provisions of this section, Publisher shall be allowed _____ royalty-free copies of the Program for in-house use. A royalty payment of $_____ shall be paid for each program after the fiftieth program that is put into in-house use.

H. No royalties shall be paid to Developer for the sale of any Manuals unless they are sold or transferred independently of the Program. For each copy of the Manual transferred without a simultaneous transfer of a copy of the Program, Publisher shall pay Developer a royalty of $_____ .

OPTIONAL SECTION VIII. I.—TO BE USED FOR FIXED-SUM ROYALTY AMOUNTS

I. The fixed-sum royalty amount set out in this section shall be fixed for a period of _____ years from the date of this agreement. Thereafter, Developer shall be paid an increased royalty should the Consumer Price Index (CPI) published by the Bureau of Labor Statistics of the U.S. Department of Labor increase. The increased royalty shall be computed as follows: On _____ _____ of each year starting with 198_____ and continuing for the life of this Agreement, the royalty amount due to Developer shall be increased by the same percentage as the CPI measured on _____ _____ of that year increased over the CPI of _____ _____ of the previous year.

IX. ACCOUNTING

A. Publisher shall keep accurate records covering all transactions relating to Program sales and transfers. At the time each royalty payment is due, Publisher shall furnish Developer with a statement setting forth the number of Programs sold or sublicensed, the amount charged, and the net sales received. Developer and/or Developer's agent, upon giving _____ days written notice, shall have the right to inspect these records during business hours at Publisher's place of business. Developer agrees to sign or require agent to sign nondisclosure agreements obligating Developer and agent not to disclose matters that do not pertain to Developer or Program.

OPTIONAL CLAUSE B.

B. Publisher's records shall accurately contain the following information.
1. The number of copies of the Program that have been sold or transferred to third parties or put into internal use by Publisher.
2. The number of copies of the Manual sold or transferred to third parties without simultaneous transfer of a copy of the Program.
3. The number of copies of the Program marked "Not for Resale" or "Dealer Demo" and put into use internally or provided to third parties.
4. The net sales amounts received from sale of the Program.

X. WARRANTIES

A. Developer warrants that Developer has the legal right to grant Publisher the license as set out in Section VI of this agreement and that such license does not infringe any third parties' property or personal rights.

B. Developer warrants that there are no pending lawsuits concerning any aspect of the Program and that the Program has not been published in such a way as to lose any of its copyright protection.

OPTIONAL SECTION C.—NOT ADVISED

C. Developer warrants that the Program is fully functional and that it will reliably perform to the standard described in Section III of this Agreement.

XI. INDEMNIFICATION

A. Provided that Publisher promptly notifies Developer of all claims, Developer shall defend Publisher against claims that the Program infringes a patent, copyright, trade secret, or other property right of a third party and shall pay the resultant court costs, legal fees, and any damages finally awarded, up to the amount of royalties received or accrued for the Program as of the date the award or settlement is paid.

B. Publisher shall indemnify and defend Developer against any claim regarding the quality of the Program up to the total dollar amount received for sale of the Program less the amount of royalties actually paid as of the date the claim is settled or the award paid.

XII. COPYRIGHTS

A. All copies of the Program or Manual shall contain an appropriate copyright notice in the name of the Developer.

B. If the Program or Manual has not been registered previously in the U.S. Copyright Office, Publisher will register the aforementioned items within _____ days of publication in the name of the Developer. Developer hereby authorizes Publisher to act as Developer's agent for the purpose of registration. Developer shall perform all acts necessary to enable Publisher to register, including signing necessary documents and supplying printouts of the first and last twenty-five pages of the object code of the Program.

C. Developer shall enforce its copyrights against infringers or shall authorize Publisher to do so at Publisher's expense.

XIII. TERMINATION

A. Either party shall have the right to terminate this agreement in the event that the other party commits a material breach of its obligations. Intent to terminate shall be made by a written notice, sent by certified mail to the breaching party, that sets forth the details of the breach. Termination shall become effective _____ days from the date that the notification of intent to terminate was mailed, unless the breaching party has corrected the breach prior to that _____-day period.

B. Notwithstanding clause A above, termination shall be effective immediately if one or more of the following events occurs:

    1. A petition of bankruptcy is filed by or against Publisher.
    2. Publisher ceases through no fault of Developer to make Program available to buyers for more than _____ consecutive days.
    3. Publisher announces that it intends to cease publishing Program.

C. Notwithstanding termination of this agreement, the following obligations and rights shall continue in full force:

    1. All warranties under the section titled "Warranty" and obligations under the sections titled "Indemnification" and "General" shall survive and continue to bind the parties for _____ years after the date of termination.
    2. Persons and companies who obtained the Program prior to termination shall continue to have the right to use the Program.
    3. Publisher shall honor any remaining obligations under the section of this agreement titled "Royalties."
    4. Publisher may continue, under the terms of this agreement, to sell copies of the Program and Manual in existence prior to the mailing of the notice of termination.

XIV. ARBITRATION

Any dispute relating to the interpretation or performance of this agreement shall be resolved at the request of either party through binding arbitration. Arbitration shall be conducted in _____ , _____ , in accordance with the then-existing rules of the American Arbitration Association. Judgment upon any award by the arbitrators may be entered by the state or federal court having jurisdiction. The parties intend that this agreement to arbitrate be irrevocable.

OPTIONAL SECTION. IF NOT USED CHANGE SECTION NUMBER XVI TO XV

XV. ESCROW

A. Within _____ days of delivery of the Program to Publisher, Developer shall place in the keeping of an independent third party one copy of the Program Source Code and Program Source-Code Documentation for the Program. The independent third party shall be the Bank of _____ located at _____ .

B. For _____ years from the date of this agreement, Developer shall update the escrowed Program Source Code and Program Source-Code Documentation within _____ days of supplying Publisher with the object code for any Program updates.

C. Developer hereby grants Publisher a contingent license, subject to the conditions in this section, to use the source code for the purpose of maintaining the Program. This contingent license shall become effective only if Developer, within _____ years of the date of this agreement, refuses or is otherwise unable to provide reasonable Program-maintenance support for Publisher. This contingent license shall continue for _____ years from the date on which it becomes effective. Should the parties disagree on whether the Developer has refused or become unable to provide maintenance support for the Publisher, the matter shall be decided by binding arbitration as set out in the section titled, "Arbitration."

D. Developer may terminate the escrow if this agreement is terminated through no fault of the Developer.

E. Publisher agrees to pay all fees necessary to maintain the escrow.

F. Both parties agree to enter into other terms and conditions with each other or with the third-party custodian of the source code as is necessary to effect the purpose of this section.

G. When the escrow terminates, Developer shall regain sole possession of the source code, subject to the provisions of clause C of this section.

H. If the source code in escrow is released to Publisher, Publisher agrees not to publish or disseminate the source code without Developer's written consent.

ALTERNATIVE LESS FORMAL ESCROW (OPTIONAL)

XV. SOURCE CODE

A. Within _____ days of the date of this agreement and for a period of _____ years thereafter, Developer shall keep a current copy of the Program Source Code and Documentation in a safe-deposit box at the _____ located at _____ .

B. Developer shall update the Program Source Code and Documentation within _____ days after supplying updated object code to Publisher.

C. Developer shall provide Publisher with a key to the safe-deposit box mentioned in clause A.

D. Developer hereby grants Publisher a contingent license, which is subject to the conditions in this section, to use the source code for maintenance purposes only. This contingent license shall become effective if Developer, within _____ years of the date of this agreement, refuses or otherwise becomes unable to provide maintenance for Publisher for any reason. This contingent license shall continue for _____ years from the date it becomes effective. Should the parties disagree on whether the Developer has refused or become unable to provide maintenance, the matter shall be decided by binding arbitration as set out in the section titled, "Arbitration."

E. Publisher hereby agrees not to open the safe-deposit box unless the conditions noted in clause D are met.

F. Developer agrees to pay all fees associated with the safe-deposit box.

G. When the period mentioned in clause A expires, Developer's obligations under this section of this agreement shall expire.

H. If the source code is obtained by Publisher under clause D, Publisher agrees not to publish or disseminate the source code without Developer's written consent.

XVI. GENERAL

A. Publisher shall have full freedom and flexibility in marketing efforts for the Program, including the freedom to decide its method of marketing, terms, conditions, and prices.

ALTERNATIVE CLAUSE A.

A. Publisher shall consult with Developer regarding marketing plan and prices. However, Publisher shall have final say regarding these items.

ALTERNATIVE CLAUSE A.

A. Publisher shall consult with Developer regarding marketing plan and prices. Should a disagreement arise concerning the items mentioned in the preceding sentence, Developer's position shall prevail.

ALTERNATIVE CLAUSE A.

A. Publisher shall submit a proposed price schedule to Developer for the Program. Developer retains the right to approve the price schedule, and Publisher agrees not to release the Program until the price schedule is approved by the Developer.

ALTERNATIVE CLAUSE A.

A. Publisher agrees to submit all proposed advertisements and promotional literature concerning Program to Developer. Developer retains the right to reject any advertisement. Rejection must be made in writing within _____ week(s) of submittal. Developer shall pay actual production costs of any advertisement proposals that are rejected under this clause.

B. Neither party may sell, transfer, assign, delegate, or subcontract any rights or obligations under this agreement without the prior written consent of the other party.

ALTERNATIVE CLAUSE B.

B. Neither party may sell, transfer, assign, delegate, or subcontract any rights or obligations under this agreement without the prior written consent of the other party, which shall not be unreasonably withheld.

ALTERNATIVE CLAUSE B.

B. This agreement is freely assignable by the Publisher.

ALTERNATIVE CLAUSE B.

B. This agreement is assignable by the Publisher providing that the Developer gives written consent.

C. Any notice from one party to the other required by this agreement shall be deemed made on the date of mailing if sent by certified mail and addressed to the address specified below.

[Publisher's Address]

[Developer's Address]

D. This contract shall be construed under the law of the State of _____ .

E. This agreement sets forth the entire understanding between the parties; it may be changed or modified only in writing and must be signed by both parties.

F. This contract is binding upon and shall inure to the benefit of the legal successors and assigns of the parties.

_____ Developer   _____ Publisher
SIGNED   SIGNED

_____   _____
DATE   DATE

THIS SAMPLE LICENSE AGREEMENT MAKES MANY ASSUMPTIONS WHICH YOU MAY OR MAY NOT SHARE. READ IT CAREFULLY AND, IF IT SUITS YOUR NEEDS, USE IT. I RECOMMEND, HOWEVER, THAT YOU CREATE YOUR OWN LICENSE AGREEMENT BASED ON THE SAMPLE CLAUSES WHICH YOU MAY FIND IN THE APPENDIX IMMEDIATELY PRECEDING THIS CONTRACT.

LICENSE AGREEMENT

I. INTRODUCTION

This is a licensing agreement between _____ (Developer) and _____ (Publisher), in which Developer grants Publisher certain rights in the software program _____ (Program).

II. DEFINITIONS

A. "Derivative work" shall mean a work that is based on one or more preexisting works and that, if prepared without permission of the program owner, would constitute a copyright infringement.

B. "Supporting documentation" shall mean information that describes the format, organization, and content of machine-readable diskettes to be supplied to Publisher under the terms of this contract.

C. "Manual" royalty should the Consumer Price Index (CPI) published by the Bureau of Labor Statistics of the U.S. Department of Labor increase. The increased royalty shall be computed as follows: On _____ _____ of each year starting with 198_____ and continuing for the life of this agreement, the royalty amount due to Developer shall be increased by the same percentage as the CPI measured on _____ of that year increased over the CPI of _____ _____ of the previous year. CPI of _____ _____ of the previous year. The royalty section does far more than merely state the amount the developer is to be paid. It provides the structural balance to the license section and, if well drafted, visions of this section, Publisher shall be allowed 50 royalty free copies of the Program for in-house use. A royalty payment of $15 shall be paid for each program after the fiftieth program that is put into in-house use.

III. MAINTENANCE, MODIFICATION, AND TRAINING

A. For a period of _____ months after _____ _____ , 198_____ , if Publisher notifies Developer of program error(s) or Developer has other reason to believe that error(s) exist(s) in the Program, Developer shall use his/her best efforts to verify and fix the error(s) within _____ working days after notification. If a verified error cannot be fixed within _____ days, Developer shall devote five hours per day toward correcting the error until the error has been corrected. Developer shall promptly notify Publisher if an error cannot be verified within a reasonable time. Error corrections shall be machine-readable and shall be such that the Publisher can update the Program immediately.

B. Publisher shall assume financial and legal responsibility for the quality, reliability, and accuracy of the Program and shall pay all expenses associated with any recalls or updates.

C. For a period of _____ months after _____ _____ , 198_____ , Developer shall supply at no charge to Publisher any Program enhancements that improve performance, utility, or existing syntax, and that improve or reduce storage requirements.

C. Publisher shall have the right to make Program enhancements subject to Developer's approval. Publisher may charge the cost of these enhancements against royalties due to Programmer from the sale of the enhanced Program. Before initiating any enhancement, Publisher shall offer Developer the right to do the enhancement at Developer's expense. The Developer retains the right to veto any proposed enhancement.

D. Should Publisher request training in the use of the Program, Developer shall be paid actual travel expenses and $_____ per day for each of Developer's employees who furnish such training.

IV. EXCLUSIVE LICENSE

A. Developer hereby grants to Publisher a worldwide, exclusive license to market copies of the Program for use on all existing or yet-to-be-developed computers. This license shall include the right of Publisher to grant sublicenses to other parties subject to the section of this agreement titled "Royalties" and subject to the limitations of this license.

B. The license granted under clause A of this section shall begin _____ _____ , 198_____ , and expire _____ _____ , 19_____ .

C. Upon termination of this license for any reason all rights granted herein shall immediately revert to the Programmer.

D. Developer hereby reserves all rights in the Program not specifically granted by this license agreement.

V. ACCEPTANCE

A. After Developer delivers Program, Publisher shall have _____ days to test Program. If developer is not notified in writing within _____ days of delivery of the Program that the Program is unacceptable, Publisher shall be deemed to have accepted the Program.

B. Publisher shall also be deemed to have accepted the Program if the Publisher makes Program available for sale.

VI. ROYALTIES

A. In consideration for the rights and license granted herein, and subject to the conditions set forth elsewhere in this agreement, Publisher shall pay Developer a royalty based on a percentage of net sales, as defined in Section II of this Agreement:

_____ % for the first _____ programs sold or sublicensed
_____ % for the next _____ programs sold or sublicensed
_____ % for the next _____ programs sold or sublicensed
_____ % for the next _____ programs sold or sublicensed

Notwithstanding the aforementioned percentage, Publisher shall pay Developer a minimum of $_____ for each program sold or transferred.

B. Royalty payments for the preceding calendar quarter shall be made to Developer within _____ days after the last day of each calendar quarter during the term of this agreement.

C. Notwithstanding the provisions of this section, minimum quarterly royalty payments shall be due as follows:

First quarter — $_____
All quarters thereafter — $_____

Should royalties accrued on actual sales be less than the applicable minimum royalty payment, Publisher shall pay in addition to the accrued royalties the amount necessary to reach the minimum royalty payment. This additional amount, if paid, shall be regarded as nonrefundable compensation in addition to royalties and shall not be considered as an advance on royalties.

D. If Publisher is more than _____ days late on any one payment, Developer may cancel the license granted in Section VI of this contract provided that Developer sends written notice by registered mail to Publisher of his intention to cancel and provided that Publisher does not make full payment within _____ days of receipt of notice.

E. Upon execution of this agreement, Publisher shall pay Programmer a $_____ advance on royalties. No further royalty payments shall be made until the amount of royalties accrued exceeds the amount of the advance made under this clause. The advance on royalties shall be nonrefundable.

F. Notwithstanding the other provisions of this section, Publisher shall be allowed _____ royalty-free copies of the Program for in-house use. A royalty payment of $_____ shall be paid for each program after the fiftieth program that is put into in-house use.

G. Notwithstanding the other clauses of this section, no royalties shall be paid for dealer demonstration programs. However, Publisher shall keep accurate records of the number of demos released, and all demos shall bear a label on the diskette and on the Manual that reads, "Dealer Demo and Not For Resale."

H. No royalties shall be paid to Developer for the sale of any Manuals unless they are sold or transferred independently of the Program. For each copy of the Manual transferred without a simultaneous transfer of a copy of the Program, Publisher shall pay Developer a royalty of $_____ .

VII. ACCOUNTING

A. Publisher shall keep accurate records covering all transactions relating to Program sales and transfers. At the time each royalty payment is due, Publisher shall furnish Developer with a statement setting forth the number of Programs sold or sublicensed, the amount charged, and the net sales received. Developer and/or Developer's agent, upon giving ____ days written notice, shall have the right to inspect these records during business hours at Publisher's place of business. Developer agrees to sign or require agent to sign nondisclosure agreements obligating Developer and agent not to disclose matters that do not pertain to Developer or Program.

B. Publisher's records shall accurately contain the following information.
   1. The number of copies of the Program that have been sold or transferred to third parties or put into internal use by Publisher.
   2. The number of copies of the Manual sold or transferred to third parties without simultaneous transfer of a copy of the Program.
   3. The number of copies of the Program marked "Not for Resale" or "Dealer Demo" and put into use internally or provided to third parties.
   4. The net sales amounts received from sale of the Program.

VIII. WARRANTIES

A. Developer warrants that Developer has the legal right to grant Publisher the license as set out in Section VI of this agreement and that such license does not infringe any third parties' property or personal rights.

B. Developer warrants that there are no pending lawsuits concerning any aspect of the Program and that the Program has not been published in such a way as to lose any of its copyright protection.

IX. INDEMNIFICATION

A. Provided that Publisher promptly notifies Developer of all claims, Developer shall defend Publisher against claims that the Program infringes a patent, copyright, trade secret, or other property right of a third party and shall pay the resultant court costs, legal fees, and any damages finally awarded, up to the amount of royalties received or accrued for the Program as of the date the award or settlement is paid.

B. Publisher shall indemnify and defend Developer against any claim regarding the quality of the Program up to the total dollar amounts received for sale of the program less the amount of royalties actually paid as of the date the claim is settled or the award paid.

X. COPYRIGHTS

A. All copies of the Program or Manual shall contain an appropriate copyright notice in the name of the Developer.

B. If the Program or Manual has not been registered previously in the U.S. Copyright Office, Publisher will register the aforementioned items within _____ days of publication in the name of the Developer. Developer hereby authorizes Publisher to act as Developer's agent for the purpose of registration. Developer shall perform all acts necessary to enable Publisher to register, including signing necessary documents and supplying printouts of the first and last twenty-five pages of the object code of the Program.

C. Developer shall enforce its copyrights against infringers or shall authorize Publisher to do so at Publisher's expense.

XI. TERMINATION

A. Either party shall have the right to terminate this agreement in the event that the other party commits a material breach of its obligations. Intent to terminate shall be made by a written notice, sent by certified mail to the breaching party, that sets forth the details of the breach. Termination shall become effective _____ days from the date that the notification of intent to terminate was mailed, unless the breaching party has corrected the breach prior to that _____ day period.

B. Notwithstanding clause A above, termination shall be effective immediately if one or more of the following events occurs:
  1. A petition of bankruptcy is filed by or against Publisher.
  2. Publisher ceases through no fault of Developer to make Program available to buyers for more than _____ consecutive days.
  3. Publisher announces that it intends to cease publishing Program.

C. Notwithstanding termination of this agreement, the following obligations and rights continue in full force:
  1. All warranties under the section titled "Warranty" and obligations under the sections titled "Indemnification" and "General" shall survive and continue to bind the parties for _____ years after the date of termination.
  2. Persons and companies who obtained the Program prior to termination shall continue to have the right to use the Program.
  3. Publisher shall honor any remaining obligations under the section of this agreement titled "Royalties."
  4. Publisher may continue, under the terms of this agreement, to sell copies of the Program and Manual in existence prior to the mailing of the notice of termination.

XII. ARBITRATION

Any dispute relating to the interpretation or performance of this agreement shall be resolved at the request of either party through binding arbitration. Arbitration shall be conducted in _____ , _____ , in accordance with the then-existing rules of the American Arbitration Association. Judgment upon any award by the arbitrators may be entered by the state or federal court having jurisdiction. The parties intend that this agreement to arbitrate be irrevocable.

XIII. SOURCE CODE

A. Within _____ days of the date of this agreement and for a period of _____ years thereafter, Developer shall keep a current copy of the Program Source Code and Documentation in a safe-deposit box at the _____ located at _____ .

B. Developer shall update the Program Source Code and Documentation within _____ days after supplying updated object code to Publisher.

C. Developer shall provide Publisher with a key to the safe-deposit box mentioned in clause A.

D. Developer hereby grants Publisher a contingent license, which is subject to the conditions in this section, to use the source code for maintenance purposes only. This contingent license shall become effective if Developer, within _____ years of the date of this agreement, refuses or otherwise becomes unable to provide maintenance for Publisher for any reason. This contingent license shall continue for _____ years from the date it becomes effective. Should the parties disagree on whether the Developer has refused or become unable to provide maintenance, the matter shall be decided by binding arbitration as set out in the section titled, "Arbitration."

E. Publisher hereby agrees not to open the safe-deposit box unless the conditions noted in clause D are met.

F. Developer agrees to pay all fees associated with the safe-deposit box.

G. When the period mentioned in clause A expires, Developer's obligations under this section of this agreement shall expire.

H. If the source code is obtained by Publisher under Clause D, Publisher agrees not to publish or disseminate the source code without Developer's written consent.

XIV. GENERAL

A. Publisher shall consult with Developer regarding marketing plan and prices. However, Publisher shall have final say regarding these items.

B. Neither party may sell, transfer, assign, delegate, or subcontract any rights or obligations under this agreement without the prior written consent of the other party, which shall not be unreasonably withheld.

C. Any notice from one party to the other required by this agreement shall be deemed made on the date of mailing if sent by certified mail and addressed to the address specified below.

[Publisher's Address]

[Developer's Address]

D. This contract shall be construed under the law of the State of _____ .

E. This agreement sets forth the entire understanding between the parties; it may be changed or modified only in writing and must be signed by both parties.

F. This contract is binding upon and shall inure to the benefit of the legal successors and assigns of the parties.

_____ Developer   _____ Publisher
SIGNED   SIGNED

_____   _____
DATE   DATE

appendix f
disclaimer of warranty

DISCLAIMER OF WARRANTY

THIS SOFTWARE AND MANUAL ARE SOLD "AS IS" AND WITHOUT WARRANTIES AS TO PERFORMANCE OR MERCHANTABILITY. THE SELLER'S SALESPERSONS MAY HAVE MADE STATEMENTS ABOUT THIS SOFTWARE. ANY SUCH STATEMENTS DO NOT CONSTITUTE WARRANTIES AND SHALL NOT BE RELIED ON BY THE BUYER IN DECIDING WHETHER TO PURCHASE THIS PROGRAM.

THIS PROGRAM IS SOLD WITHOUT ANY EXPRESS OR IMPLIED WARRANTIES WHATSOEVER. BECAUSE OF THE DIVERSITY OF CONDITIONS AND HARDWARE UNDER WHICH THIS PROGRAM MAY BE USED, NO WARRANTY OF FITNESS FOR A PARTICULAR PURPOSE IS OFFERED. THE USER IS ADVISED TO TEST THE PROGRAM THOROUGHLY BEFORE RELYING ON IT. THE USER MUST ASSUME THE ENTIRE RISK OF USING THE PROGRAM. ANY LIABILITY OF SELLER OR MANUFACTURER WILL BE LIMITED EXCLUSIVELY TO PRODUCT REPLACEMENT OR REFUND OF THE PURCHASE PRICE.

USER FEEDBACK CARD TO BE USED WITH ABOVE DISCLAIMER OR WHEN ALL WARRANTIES ARE DISCLAIMED

USER FEEDBACK CARD

We want to keep in touch with our users. Please fill out and mail this card immediately.

Name: _____

Address: _____

City: _____

State: _____ Zip: _____ Phone: (_____) _____

Where did you buy _____ ?
When?
How much did you pay?
How would you rate the user manual?   ☐ excellent   ☐ good   ☐ poor
How would you rate the program?   ☐ excellent   ☐ good   ☐ poor

LIMITED WARRANTY TO BE USED WHEN ALL WARRANTIES ARE NOT DISCLAIMED.

LIMITED WARRANTY

THIS PROGRAM, INSTRUCTION MANUAL, AND REFERENCE MATERIALS ARE SOLD "AS IS," WITHOUT WARRANTY AS TO THEIR PERFORMANCE, MERCHANTABILITY, OR FITNESS FOR ANY PARTICULAR PURPOSE. THE ENTIRE RISK AS TO THE RESULTS AND PERFORMANCE OF THIS PROGRAM IS ASSUMED BY YOU.

HOWEVER, TO THE ORIGINAL PURCHASER ONLY, THE PUBLISHER WARRANTS THE MAGNETIC DISKETTE ON WHICH THE PROGRAM IS RECORDED TO BE FREE FROM DEFECTS IN MATERIALS AND FAULTY WORKMANSHIP UNDER NORMAL USE FOR A PERIOD OF NINETY DAYS FROM THE DATE OF PURCHASE. IF DURING THIS NINETY-DAY PERIOD THE DISKETTE SHOULD BECOME DEFECTIVE, IT MAY BE RETURNED TO THE PUBLISHER FOR A REPLACEMENT WITHOUT CHARGE, PROVIDED YOU HAVE PREVIOUSLY SENT IN YOUR LIMITED WARRANTY REGISTRATION CARD TO THE PUBLISHER OR SEND PROOF OF PURCHASE OF THE PROGRAM.

YOUR SOLE AND EXCLUSIVE REMEDY IN THE EVENT OF A DEFECT IS EXPRESSLY LIMITED TO REPLACEMENT OF THE DISKETTE AS PROVIDED ABOVE. IF FAILURE OF A DISKETTE HAS RESULTED FROM ACCIDENT OR ABUSE THE PUBLISHER SHALL HAVE NO RESPONSIBILITY TO REPLACE THE DISKETTE UNDER THE TERMS OF THIS LIMITED WARRANTY.

ANY IMPLIED WARRANTIES RELATING TO THE DISKETTE, INCLUDING ANY IMPLIED WARRANTIES OF MERCHANTABILITY AND FITNESS FOR A PARTICULAR PURPOSE, ARE LIMITED TO A PERIOD OF NINETY DAYS FROM DATE OF PURCHASE. PUBLISHER SHALL NOT BE LIABLE FOR INDIRECT, SPECIAL, OR CONSEQUENTIAL DAMAGES RESULTING FROM THE USE OF THIS PRODUCT. SOME STATES DO NOT ALLOW THE EXCLUSION OR LIMITATION OF INCIDENTAL OR CONSEQUENTIAL DAMAGES, SO THE ABOVE LIMITATIONS MIGHT NOT APPLY TO YOU. THIS WARRANTY GIVES YOU SPECIFIC LEGAL RIGHTS, AND YOU MAY ALSO HAVE OTHER RIGHTS WHICH VARY FROM STATE TO STATE.

WARRANTY REGISTRATION CARD

NAME: _____

COMPANY: _____

ADDRESS: _____

CITY: _____

STATE AND ZIP: _____

TYPE OF BUSINESS: _____

PROGRAM PURCHASE: _____

SERIAL NUMBER: _____

DATE PURCHASED: _____

COMPUTER BRAND: _____

index

about the author

Daniel Remer is a partner of Remer, Remer & Dunaway, Mountain View, California, a law firm specializing in the fields of law which apply to the computer industry. He graduated from the University of California and received his law degree from the University of San Francisco School of Law. In addition to writing *Legal Care for Your Software*, he has written extensively on software law for major periodicals. He is currently working on a new book, "Computer Power for Law Offices," and is a member of the commercial panel of the American Arbitration Association.

NOLO PRESS Self-Help Law Books

BUSINESS & FINANCE

How To Form Your Own California Corporation

By attorney Anthony Mancuso. Provides you with all the forms, Bylaws, Articles, stock certificates and instructions necessary to file your small profit corporation in California. It includes a thorough discussion of the practical and legal aspects of incorporation, including the tax consequences. California Edition $19.95

The Non-Profit Corporation Handbook

By attorney Anthony Mancuso. Completely updated to reflect all the new law changes effective January 1980. Includes all the forms, Bylaws, Articles and instructions you need to form a non-profit corporation in California. Step-by-step instructions on how to choose a name, draft Articles and Bylaws, attain favorable tax status. Thorough information on federal tax exemptions which groups outside of California will find particularly useful. California Edition $17.95

Bankruptcy: Do-It-Yourself

By attorney Janice Kosel. Tells you exactly what bankruptcy is all about and how it affects your credit rating, your property and debts, with complete details on property you can keep under the state and federal exempt property rules. Shows you step-by-step how to do it yourself and comes with all forms and instructions necessary.
National Edition $12.95

Legal Care for Software

By Dan Remer. Here we show the software programmer how to protect his/her work through the use of trade secret, tradework, copyright, patent and, most especially, contractual laws and agreements. This book is full of forms and instructions that give programmers the hands-on information to do it themselves.
National Edition $19.95

The Partnership Book

By attorneys Denis Clifford and Ralph Warner. When two or more people join to start a small business, one of the most basic needs is to establish a solid, legal partnership agreement. This book supplies a number of sample agreements with the information you will need to use them as is or to modify them to fit your needs. Buy-out clauses, unequal sharing of assets, and limited partnerships are all discussed in detail.
California Edition $15.95
National Edition $15.95

Plan Your Estate: Wills, Probate Avoidance, Trusts & Taxes

By Clifford. Here in one place for the first time people can get information on making their own will, alternatives to probate, planning to limit inheritance and estate taxes, living trusts, and providing for family and friends.
California Edition $15.95
Texas Edition $14.95

Chapter 13: The Federal Plan to Repay Your Debts

By attorney Janice Kosel. This book allows an individual to develop and carry out a feasible plan to pay one's debts in whole over a three-year period. Chapter 13 is an alternative to straight bankruptcy and yet it still means the end of creditor harassment, wage attachments and other collection efforts. Complete with all the forms & worksheets you need. $12.95
National Edition

Billpayers' Rights

By attorneys Honigsberg and Warner. Complete information on bankruptcy, student loans, wage attachments, dealing with bill collectors and collection agencies, credit cards, car repossessions, homesteads, child support and much more.
California Edition $7.95

The California Professional Corporation Handbook

By attorneys Mancuso and Honigsberg. In California there are a number of professions which must fulfill special requirements when filing a corporation. Among them are lawyers, dentists, doctors and other health professionals, accountants, certain social workers. This book contains detailed information on the special requirements of every profession and all the forms and instructions necessary to file a professional corporation.
California Edition $19.95

Small-Time Operator

By Bernard Kamoroff, C.P.A. Shows you how to start and operate your own small business, keep your books, pay your taxes and stay out of trouble. Comes complete with a year's supply of ledgers and worksheets designed especially for small businesses, and contains invaluable information on permits, licenses, financing, loans, insurance, bank accounts, etc. Published by Bell Springs Press. National Edition $8.95

We Own It!

By C.P.A.s Kamoroff and Beatty and attorney Honigsberg. This book provides the legal, tax and management information you need to start and successfully operate all types of co-ops and collectives. $9.00

FAMILY & FRIENDS

How To Do Your Own Divorce

By attorney Charles Sherman. Now in its tenth edition, this is the original "do your own law" book. It contains tear-out copies of all the court forms required for an uncontested dissolution, as well as instructions for certain special forms--military waiver, pauper's oath, lost summons, and publication of summons.
California Edition $9.95
Texas Edition $9.95

The People's Guide to Calif Marriage and Divorce

By attorneys Ihara and Warner. This book contains invaluable information for married couples and those considering marriage on community and separate property, names, debts, children, buying a house, etc. Includes sample marriage contracts, a simple will, probate avoidance information and an explanation of gift and inheritance taxes. Discusses "secret marriage" & "common law marriage."
California Edition $12.95

How To Adopt Your Stepchild

By Frank Zagone. Shows you how to prepare all the legal forms; includes information on how to get the consent of the natural parent and how to conduct an "abandonment" proceeding. Discusses appearing in court, making changes in birth certificates, etc.
California Edition $10.00

After The Divorce: How To Modify Alimony, Child Support and Child Custody

By attorney Joseph Matthews. Detailed information on how to increase alimony or child support, decrease what you pay, change custody and visitation, oppose modifications by your ex. Comes with all the forms and instructions you need. Sections on joint custody, mediation, inflation.
California Edition $12.00

The Living Together Kit

By attorneys Ihara and Warner. A legal guide for unmarried couples with information about buying or sharing property, the Marvin decision, paternity statements, medical emergencies and tax consequences. Contains a sample will and Living Together Contract.
National Edition $8.95

Sourcebook for Older Americans

By attorney Joseph Matthews. The most comprehensive resource tool on the income, rights and benefits of Americans over 55. Includes detailed information on social security, retirement rights, Medicare, Medicaid, supplemental security income, private pensions, age discrimination and much more. $10.95
National Edition

A Legal Guide for Lesbian/Gay Couples

By attorneys Hayden Curry & Clifford. Here is a book that deals specifically with legal matters of lesbian and gay couples. Discusses areas such as raising children (custody, support, living with a lover), buying property together, wills, etc. and comes complete with sample contracts & agreements. National Edition $12.95

Men's Rights: A Handbook for the 80s

Published by Cragmont Publications. This book discusses rights and issues with which men (and women) are concerned: living together, abortion, fatherhood, employment, child custody, support, visitation, etc.
National Edition $6.95

RULES & TOOLS

The People's Law Review

Edited by Ralph Warner. This is the first compendium of people's law resources ever published. It celebrates the coming of age of the self-help law movement and contains a 50-state catalog of self-help law materials; articles on mediation and the new "non-adversary" mediation centers; information on self-help law programs and centers (programs for tenants, artists, battered women, the disabled, etc.); articles and interviews by the leaders of the self-help law movement, and articles dealing with many common legal problems which show people "how to do it themselves" without lawyers. National Edition $8.95

Fight Your Ticket

By attorney Dave Brown. A comprehensive manual on how to fight your traffic ticket. Radar, drunk driving, preparing for court, arguing your case to a judge, cross-examining witnesses are all covered. California Edition $12.95

Legal Research: How To Find and Understand the Law

By attorney Steve Elias. A hands-on guide to unraveling the mysteries of the law library. For paralegals, law students, consumer activists, legal secretaries, business and media people. Shows exactly how to find laws relating to specific cases or legal questions, interpret statutes and regulations, find and research cases, understand case citations and Shepardize them. National Edition $12.95

California Tenants' Handbook

By attorneys Moskovitz, Warner & Sherman. Discusses everything tenants need to know in order to protect themselves: getting deposits returned, breaking a lease, getting repairs made, using Small Claims Court, dealing with an unscupulous landlord, forming a tenants' organization, etc. Completely up-dated to cover new rent control information and law changes for 1981. Sample Fair-to-Tenants lease & rental agreements. California Edition $9.95

Everybody's Guide to Small Claims Court

By attorney Ralph Warner. Guides you step-by-step through the Small Claims procedure, providing practical information on how to evaluate your case, file and serve papers, prepare and present your case, and, most important, how to collect when you win. Separate chapters focus on common situations (landlord-tenant, automobile sales and repair, etc.).
California Edition $8.95
National Edition $8.95

How To Change Your Name

By David Loeb. Changing one's name is a very simple procedure. Using this book, people can file the necessary papers themselves, saving $200-$300 in attorney's fees. Comes complete with all the forms and instructions necessary for the court petition method or the simpler usage method. California Edition $10.95

Protect Your Home With A Declaration of Homestead

Under the California Homestead Act, you can file a Declaration of Homestead and thus protect your home from being sold to satisfy most debts. This book explains this simple and inexpensive procedure and includes all the forms and instructions. Contains information on exemptions for mobile homes and houseboats. California Edition $6.95

Marijuana: Your Legal Rights

By attorney Richard Moller. Here is the legal information all marijuana users and growers need to guarantee their constitutional rights and protect their privacy and property. Discusses what the laws are, how they differ from state to state, and how legal loopholes can be used against smokers and growers. National Edition $9.95

Landlording

Written for the conscientious landlord or landlady, this comprehensive guide discusses maintenance and repairs, getting good tenants, how to avoid evictions, recordkeeping, and taxes. Published by Express Press. National Edition $15.00

IN A LIGHTER VEIN . . .

29 Reasons Not To Go To Law School

A humorous and irreverent look at the dubious pleasures of going to law school. By attorneys Ihara and Warner with contributions by fellow lawyers and illustrations by Mari Stein. $4.95

The Unemployment Benefits Handbook

By attorney Peter Jan Honigsberg. Comprehensive information on how to find out if you are eligible for benefits, how the amount of those benefits will be determined. It shows how to file and handle an appeal if benefits are denied and gives important advice on how to deal with the bureaucracy and the people at the unemployment office. National Edition $5.95

Don't Sit in The Draft

By Charles Johnson. A draft counseling guide with information on how the system works, classifications, deferments, exemptions, medical standards, appeals and alternatives. National Edition $6.95

Computer Programming for The Complete Idiot

By Donald McCunn. An excellent introduction to computers. Hardware and software are explained in everyday language and the last chapter gives information on creating original programs. $6.95

Write, Edit and Print

By Donald McCunn. Word processing with personal computers. A complete how-to-manual including: evaluation of equipment, 4-fully annotated programs, operating instructions, sample application. 525 pages $24.95

PACIFIC RIM SERIES

California Dreaming: The Political Odyssey of Pat and Jerry Brown

By Roger Rapoport. Here for the first time is the story of the First Family of California Politics from the Gold Rush to the 1980s. Based on more than 200 interviews, access to papers previously unavailable to scholars, lengthy talks and travels with Pat and Jerry Brown and their family. $9.95

Order Form _____

QUANTITY	TITLE	UNIT PRICE	TOTAL

Prices subject to change

☐ Please send me a
  catalogue of your books

Tax: (California only) 6½% for Bart,
  Los Angeles, San Mateo & Santa
  Clara counties; 6% for all others

Name_____

Address_____

_____

SUBTOTAL _____

Tax _____

Postage & Handling ____ $1.00 ____

TOTAL _____

Send to:

NOLO PRESS
950 Parker St.
Berkeley, CA 94710

or

NOLO DISTRIBUTING
Box 544
Occidental, CA 95465

Order Form _____

QUANTITY	TITLE	UNIT PRICE	TOTAL

Prices subject to change

☐ Please send me a
catalogue of your books

Tax: (California only) 6½% for Bart,
Los Angeles, San Mateo & Santa
Clara counties; 6% for all others

Name_____

Address_____

_____

SUBTOTAL _____

Tax _____

Postage & Handling _____ $1.00 _____

TOTAL _____

Send to:

NOLO PRESS
950 Parker St.
Berkeley, CA 94710

or

NOLO DISTRIBUTING
Box 544
Occidental, CA 95465